Beyond Reflection

Li Hongwei is a contemporary artist. He currently works and lives in Beijing and New York. He is recognized as one of China's most accomplished and innovative artists. He was first known by his early series "Weight of Meditation"; his recent work combining porcelain and stainless steel has given him widespread attention and praise. His works have been collected by: The British Museum, the Museum of Fine Arts in Boston, the Art Institute of Chicago, the Israel Museum, Harvard Art Museums and the Philadelphia Museum of Art, among others. His works have been exhibited in the National Art Museum of China, the Louvre, the New Mexico Museum of Art, the Fox Art Gallery of the University of Pennsylvania, and the Dublin Castle in Ireland, among others. In 2013, he was awarded the Taylor Prize by the 2013 France International Salon.

He is a member of the International Academy of Ceramics (Geneva), the Chinese Sculpture Institute (Beijing), as well as the Taylor Foundation (established in Paris, 1844). In 2015, he was invited to lecture as a visiting artist at Harvard University. Hongwei holds a bachelor's degree in sculpture from the Central Academy of Fine Arts, Beijing, and a master's in ceramic art from the New York State College of Ceramics at Alfred University at Alfred, NY.

www.lihongwei.com

BEYOND REFLECTION

THE ART OF **LI HONGWEI**

ESSAYS BY

Tao Wang

Wayne Higby

Mary Drach McInnes

Michaël Amy

Andrew L. Maske

Published by
Pucker Art Publications

Distributed by
Syracuse University Press

Beyond Reflection:
The Art of Li Hongwei

Copyright ©2018 by Pucker Art Publications and Li Hongwei

All rights reserved. No part of this work may be reproduced or used in any forms or by any means (graphic, electronic or mechanical, including photocopying or information storage and retrieval systems) without written permission from the copyright holder Pucker Art Publications.

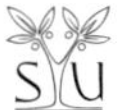

PUCKER ART
PUBLICATIONS

Published by Pucker Art Publications
240 Newbury Street, 3rd Floor
Boston, MA 02116
www.puckergallery.com

Distributed by Syracuse University Press
Syracuse, NY 13244-5160
www.syracuseuniversitypress.syr.edu

EDITOR
Jeanne V. Koles

AUTHORS
Tao Wang
Wayne Higby
Mary Drach McInnes
Michaël Amy
Andrew L. Maske

GRAPHIC DESIGN
Yihong Liu

PRINTED BY
Shanghai Artron Art Printing Co., Ltd , China

PAPER
200gsm Oji paper
157gsm Orienta beauty
130gsm Cosmos Silver

COVER
Pilgerflasche (detail)
2017
Reduction fired porcelain
4.5×4.5×12.2 inches
Collection of the artist

152 pages, 116 color illustrations

ISBN: 978-1-879985-37-7

Library of Congress Cataloging-in-Publication Data

Names: Wang, Tao, 1979- writer of added commentary.
Title: Beyond reflection : the art of Li Hongwei / essays by Tao Wang [and 4 others].
Description: Boston, MA : Pucker Art Publications, [2018]
Identifiers: LCCN 2019000140 | ISBN 9781879985377
Subjects: LCSH: Li, Hongwei, 1980--Criticism and interpretation. | Mixed media (Art)
Classification: LCC NK4210.L3657 B49 2018 | DDC 702.81--dc23
LC record available at https://lccn.loc.gov/2019000140

PHOTO CREDITS
Boyuan Zhao: p.26, p.27, p.142, p.143, p.144
Luqing Li: p.41, p.55, p.57, p.63
Patrick Power: p.21
Raymond: p.54, p.60
Wang Xiang: p.140, p.141

Courtesy of The British Museum, London, UK: p.127
Courtesy of The Museum of Fine Arts, Boston, MA: p.133
Courtesy of The Art Institute of Chicago, Chicago, IL: p.90, p.91
Courtesy of Asian Art Council of AIC, Chicago, IL: p.51
Courtesy of The Israel Museum, Jerusalem, Israel: p.129
Courtesy of The Philadelphia Museum of Art, Philadelphia, PA: p.95
Courtesy of Harvard Art Museums, Cambridge, MA: p.25
Courtesy of Vassar College Art Museum, Poughkeepsie, NY: p.138
Courtesy of San Angelo Museum of Fine Arts, San Angelo, TX: p.37
Courtesy of Alfred University Ceramic Art Museum, Alfred, NY: p.23, p.34, p.35

All other photos: Li Hongwei Studio

CONTENTS

Materiality and Thing:

A Comment on Li Hongwei's Ceramic Sculptures

—— Tao Wang
Pritzker Chair of Asian Art & Curator of Chinese Art
The Art Institute of Chicago

Modern art is perceived to a large degree as conceptual art. For many contemporary artists, idea is more important than artworks and making art is more or less a game of installation, word-play, or performance. On the other side, going against the trend of de-materialization, the discussion and experimentation of materiality in art has increasingly become the focus of a number of artists and critics.

The contemporary art scene in China is hugely diversified and multifaceted, but one of the pressing questions is always: "what is the difference between Chinese contemporary art and contemporary art in the West?" If we compare these arts from a historical perspective, we see that the materials used for creating art in fact laid out different paths from the very beginning. Chinese art has a unique range of materials with which artists have developed special techniques and ideas, for example shuimo or water-ink paintings. Porcelain was invented in China, playing a significant role in the history of Chinese art. An artist, whether in the past or today, inevitably faces the question of the material he employs. The material is an agent that brings new challenges and changes; an exploration of materiality opens up new possibilities. In William C. Williams' words: "No idea but in things." Here, the "thing" is no longer merely a physical object. It implies shape, color, distinction (as it was first used in Chinese language), as well as the metaphor for the basic categorization. It has a mysterious power over people, combining the past and present. Ceramic is a perfect example of such a "thing," and artists in China are gifted with this heavenly material.

Dr. Tao Wang is the Executive Director of Initiatives in Asia, Pritzker Chair of Asian Art and Curator of Chinese Art of the Art Institute of Chicago. Dr. Tao Wang was the former Senior Vice President and Head of Chinese Works at Sotheby's New York.

As one of China's most accomplished and innovative young artists, Li Hongwei is intelligent, hard-working, and resourceful. His outlook on the world is shaped by his study of both Chinese and western art. And he is a master of the material he uses. In contrast to his early sculptures, his recent works are made of porcelain and stainless steel. Inspired by crystal-glazed ceramics of China's old dynasties, the artist has experimented with glazed ceramics for years. The two crystal-glaze recipes he created, and with which he has made this porcelain work, bear unreproducible colors and patterns. Because of this uniqueness, he obtained China National Invention Patents in 2015. By comparing and connecting the crystal-glazed porcelain to the stainless steel, the artist explores the aesthetic of porcelain within the contemporary art context. The abstract form of the sculptures frees porcelain from being merely a functional object and allows it to exist as a non-functional work of art. The ovoid bodies of the sculptures echo the Chinese ideas of beauty, harmony, subtlety, and simplicity. The artist expresses modern concepts and seeks a connection between historical, hand-made porcelain and contemporary, industrial stainless steel. The smooth shaped porcelain bodies are reminiscent of Chinese classic porcelain vessels. Their reflection on the surface of stainless steel creates a dynamic dialogue between traditional and contemporary abstract art. Through the combination of Chinese traditional aesthetic and contemporary art form, Li Hongwei's work revives and empowers porcelain within the cultural context of our age.

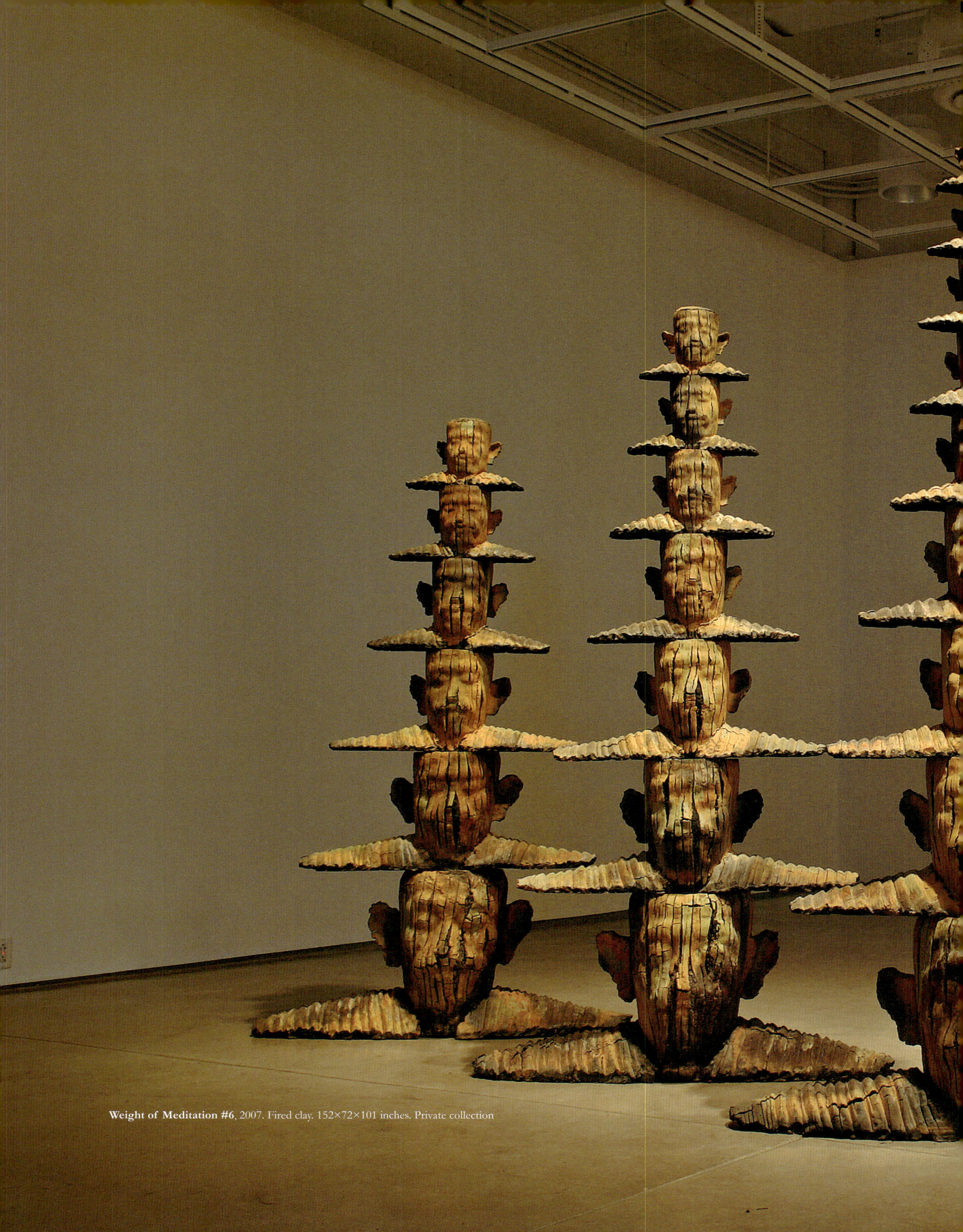

Weight of **Meditation #6**, 2007. Fired clay. 152×72×101 inches. Private collection

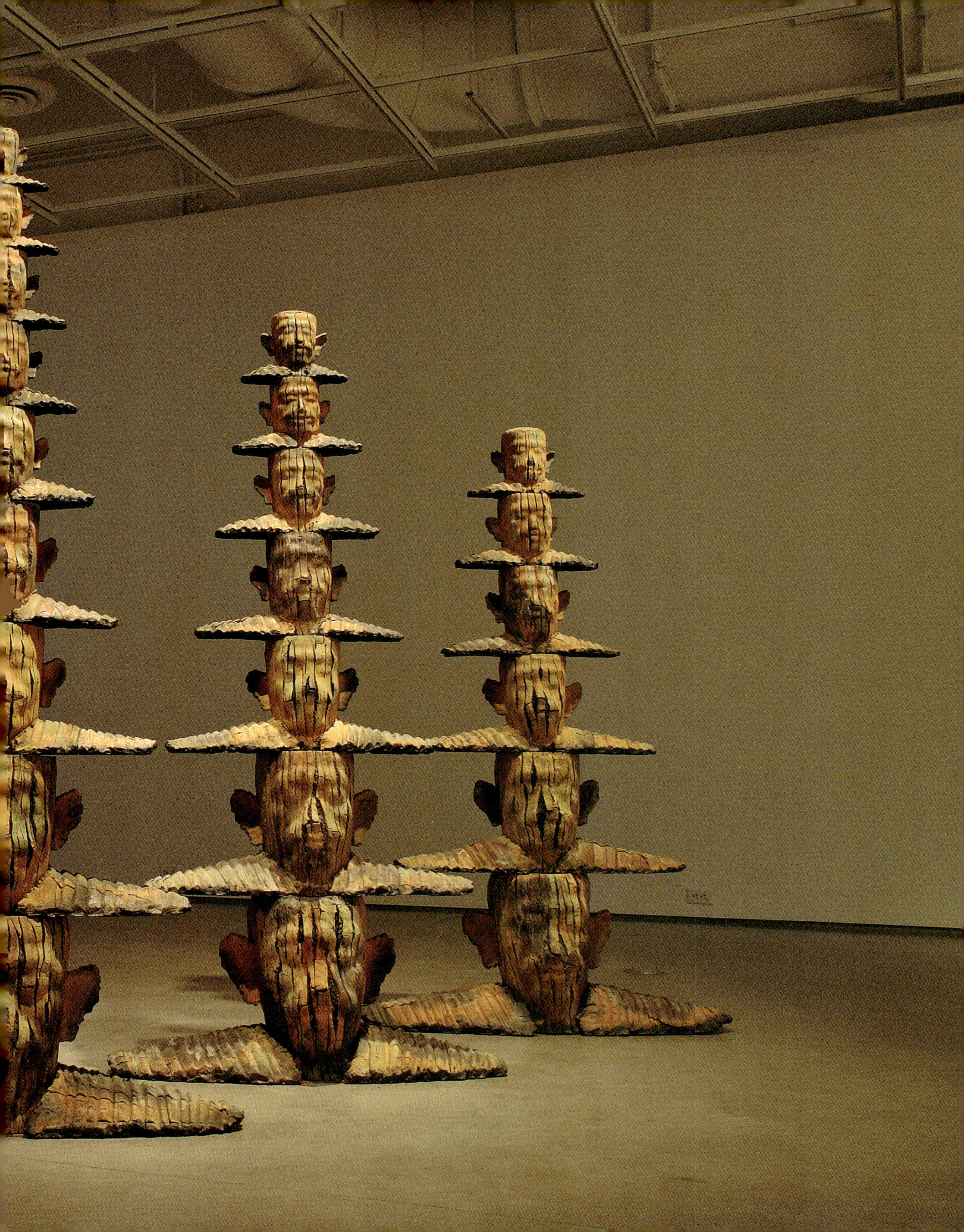

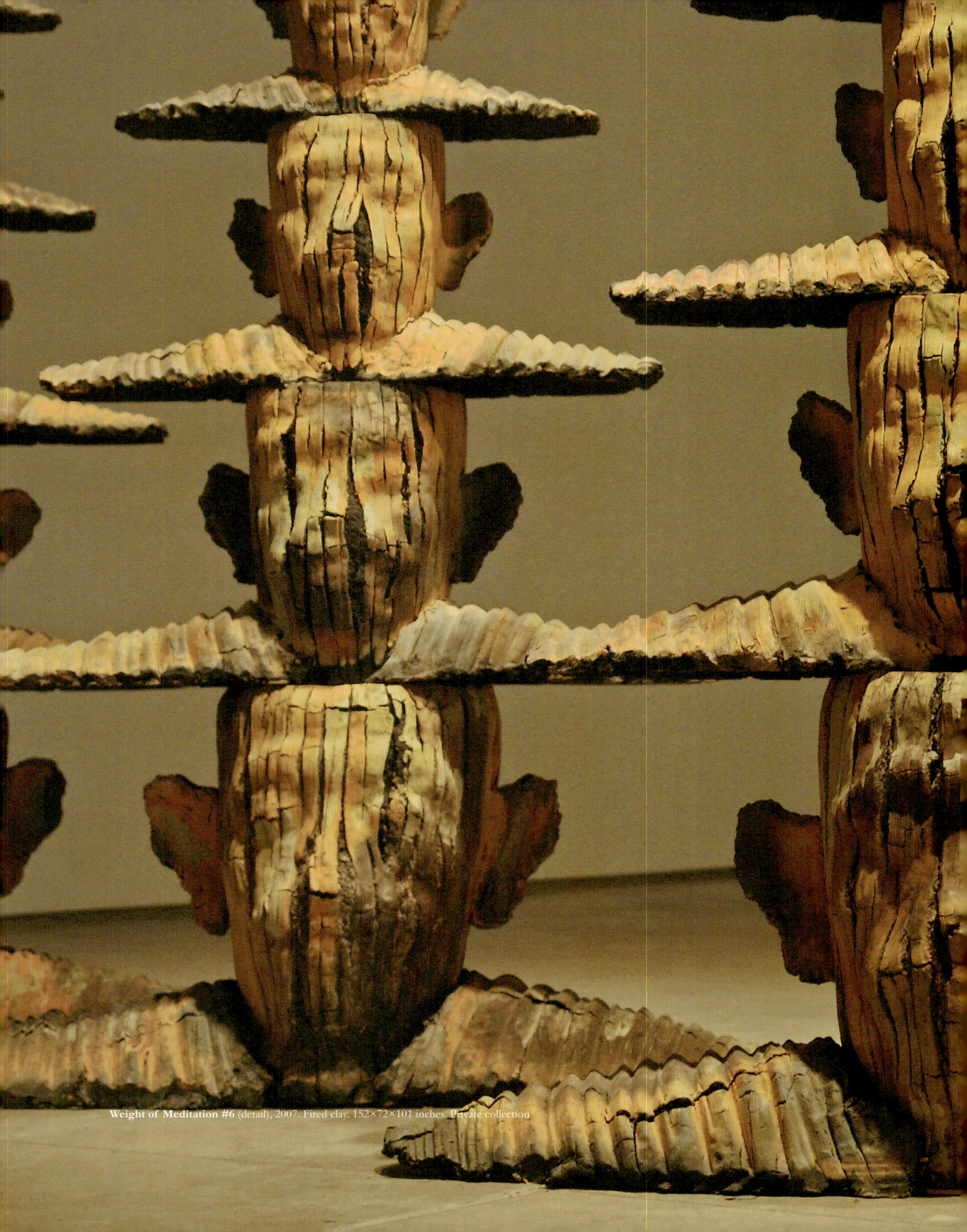

Weight of Meditation #6 (detail), 2007. Fired clay. 152×72×101 inches. Private collection

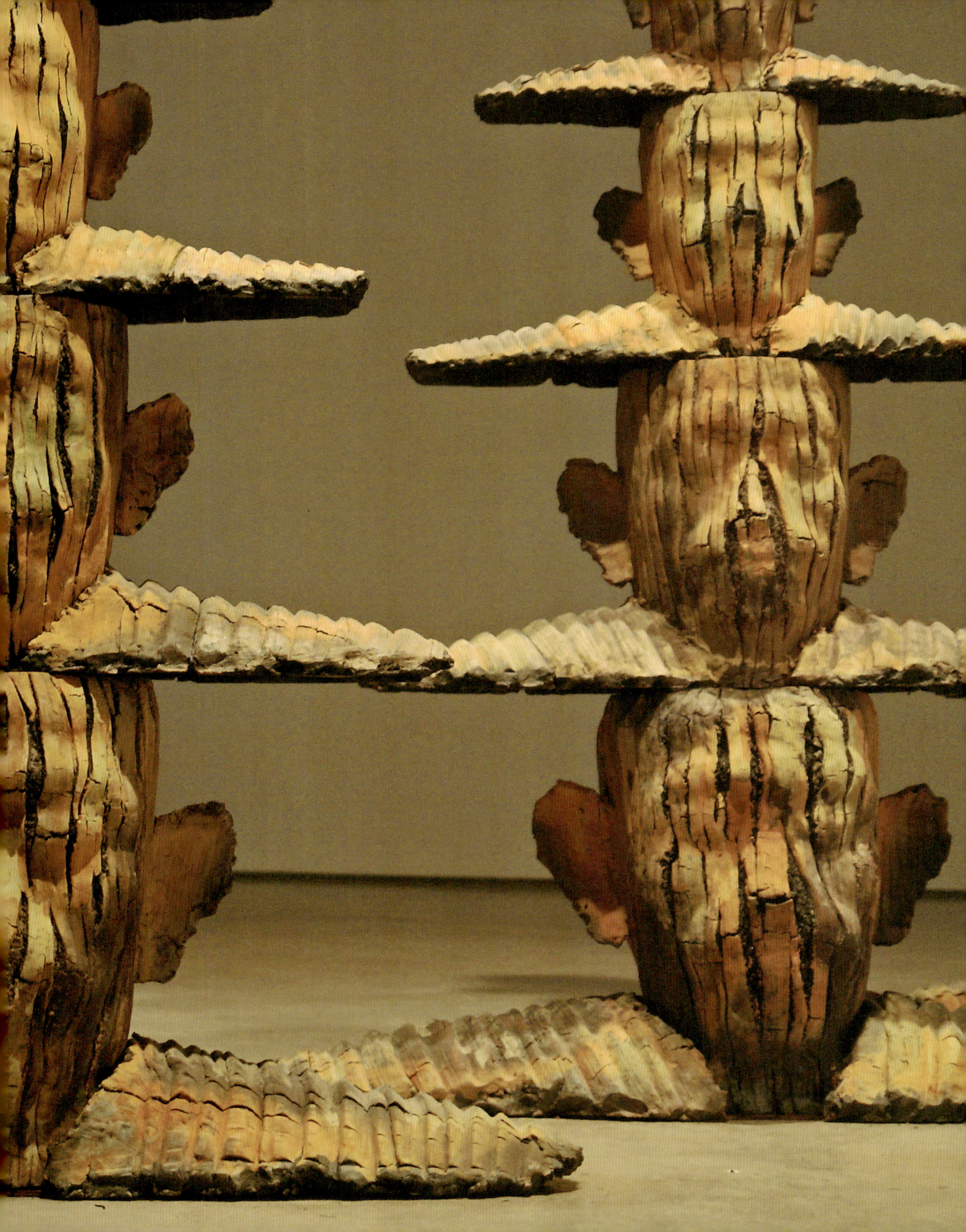

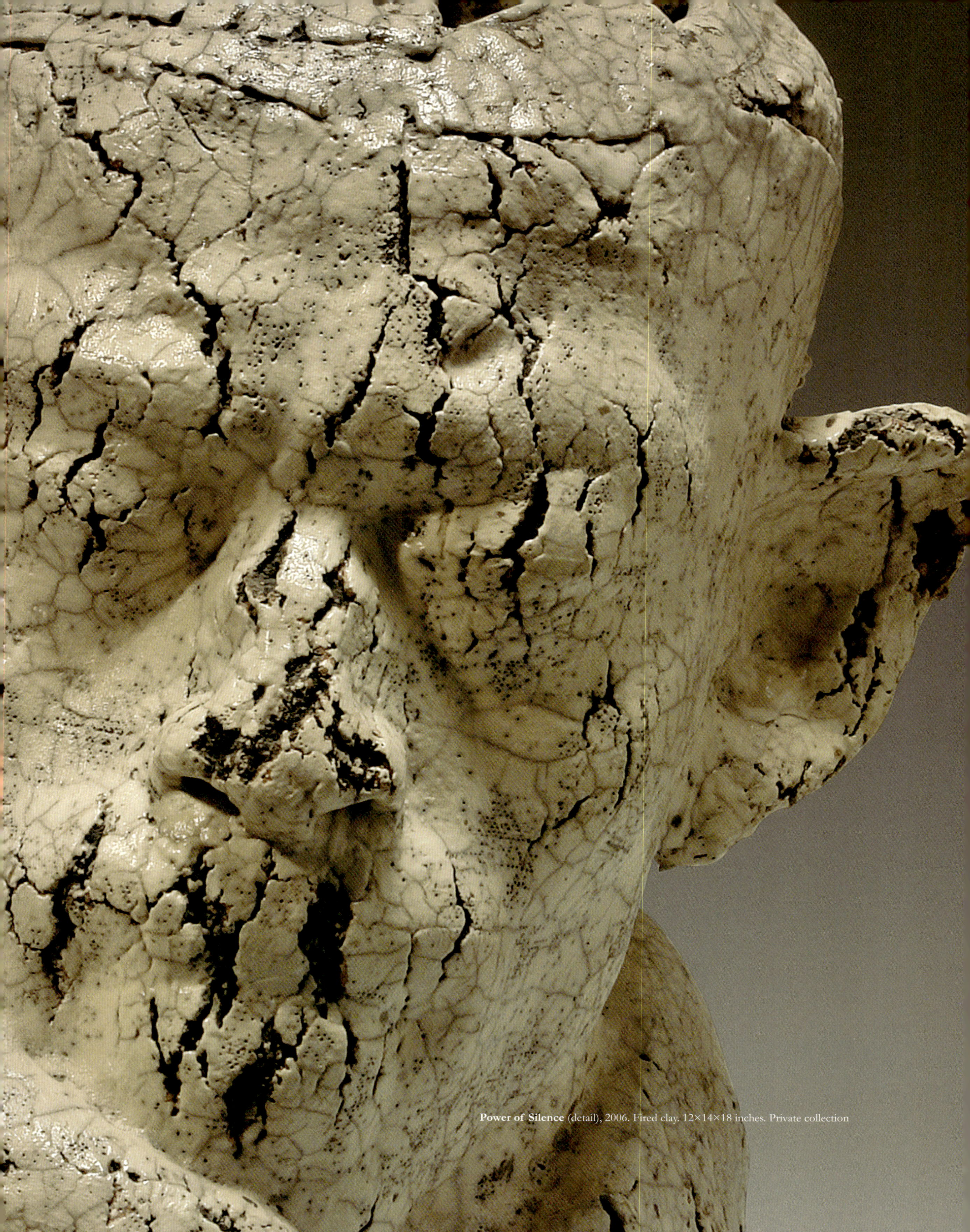

Power of Silence (detail), 2006. Fired clay. 12×14×18 inches. Private collection

Self-Portrait: The Art of Li Hongwei

—— Wayne Higby
Director and Chief Curator of Alfred Ceramic Art Museum
Alfred University

"The self-portrait has become the defining visual genre of our confessional age … One of the wonders of self-portraits is their capacity to induce levels of uncertainty in the viewer. Is the artist looking at us with a view to portraying or judging us? Is the artist looking at a mirror, with the view to portraying or judging themselves? Is the artist creating a persona to serve specific ends? Or have they delved into the book of memory, myth, imagination to create a work personal in its meaning?" [i]

Li Hongwei is among the new generation of artists who have taken a deeply rooted, Chinese national identity and revolutionized it via individual perspectives. His achievement in ceramic art is especially significant. Li Hongwei's acceptance into the renowned Masters of Fine Arts program in Ceramic Art at Alfred University marked a significant step in his development as an artist and a significant step in the arc of his life. For Li Hongwei, studying in America brought his personal life story into deep scrutiny. The cultural diversity between China and America offered a comparative analysis that focused the challenging question: *Who am I?* In an attempt to answer that question, the artist began a series of self-portraits in fired ceramic.

Li Hongwei's exploration of the self-portrait finds a powerful rationale in the material matters of his work. His concentration on the individual artist as subject is also rooted in the intellectual framework of modernist art theory and the idea of autonomy. The idea of autonomy is part of the modernist mythology regarding the social history of art. As European society's structural systems began to change during the mid- to late-19th century, due to the important influence of the industrial revolution, an independence

[i] James Hall, *The Self-Portrait: A Cultural History* (London: Thames and Hudson Ltd, 2014).

"

of individual thought and practice began to assert itself conceptually among the artist of early modernism. Artists in all media began to focus on their own experiences and emotions. The commonplace became a forum for investigation. No longer tied to the patronage of the church or court, artists found a new audience in the rise of a middle class. Although still dependent on the support of the consumer-collector, a sense of freedom from service to a specific patronage liberated art from political, mythical, and religious constraint. [ii]

This idea of autonomy has had far reaching impact. Throughout the full length of the 20th century in Europe and America the central phenomena has been the rise and strengthening of the individual artist as hero and visionary. Integral to the globalization of art in the 21st century is the fixed idea of individualism and art. The autobiography of the artist has become an important backdrop to critical discourse.

Although the artistic practice of self-portraiture is certainly not unique to the modern era, it has been one avenue of individualism that is of special interest. Gustave Courbet's self-portrait, *The Desperate Man*, painted in 1845, is a magnificent example of an artist's intimate, personal investigation of physiological pathways. Vincent van Gogh's self-portraits are legendary examples of an artist's search for the particular in the self-image. Egon Schiele, Edvard Munch, Pierre Bonnard, and Pablo Picasso are especially notable modernists who produced numerous self-portraits. More recently, self-portraits of Frida Kahlo, Andy Warhol, David Hockney, and Cindy Sherman have brought intensity to investigations of individual identity, of race, ethnicity, and gender. America, as a nurturing home for the cult of individualism, has had a profound influence on art and artists globally. The influence of the United States has infiltrated much of what we view as the global mainstream of art making. It must be acknowledged, however, that artists from many cultures around the world have brought their considerable gifts and national perspectives to American contemporary art. American art has been greatly influenced by artists representing a vast array of nationalities living, working, exhibiting, and studying in America. The investigation of self has been reflected in a multiplicity of cultural dimensions as artists from around the world have found their way to the US for short or extended periods of time.

[ii] Hal Foster, Rosalind Krauss, Yve-Alain Bois, and Benjamin H. D. Buchloh,
The Social History of Art: Models and Concepts, Art Since 1900 (New York, NY: Thames and Hudson, 2004).

The celebration of the individual artist as a singular autonomous being working outside traditionally sanctioned artistic programs has not been part of Chinese art history. The practice of landscape painting and calligraphy has celebrated the individual energy or spirit of the artist, but it is nonetheless tied to the specificity of canonized principles imbedded in a discipline of tempering originality. Although self-portraiture is not unknown in the history of Chinese art, the subject of the artist himself or herself in self-portraiture has been by in large avoided—until recently.

Li Hongwei's investigation of the self-portrait in ceramic material as a manifestation of contemporary art and life is a bridge between East and West, as well as a bridge between tradition and the urgency of the present moment. His study in America certainly brought the self-portrait to the center of his practice, but his investigations in ceramic art reach back into the thousand-year-old history of Chinese ceramics. For China is, in fact, the taproot of ceramic art. Chinese ceramic art must be studied and appreciated both for its technical story and the brilliance of its aesthetic achievement.

The traditions of Chinese painting and calligraphy are also clearly evidenced in Li Hongwei's work. He brings to the individualist's program of the self-portrait a sensitivity to Chinese aesthetics exemplified, for example, by literati painting of the Song Dynasty, which was aligned with poetry in a focus on the emotional state of the artist. The subject of Chinese scholar painting was, in large part, the artist's inner feelings.[iii] Li Hongwei refers in his work to a mindscape of ideas and feelings reveled not so much in a rendering of image, but in an engagement of process. His self-portrait image is deeply connected to the phenomology of the ceramic medium as a carrier of the content in the work. This approach rejects form-likeness in favor of sprit-resonance. The self is the subject, but similar to Chinese ink painting the subject is also the flow and dynamic interaction of the hand-body-

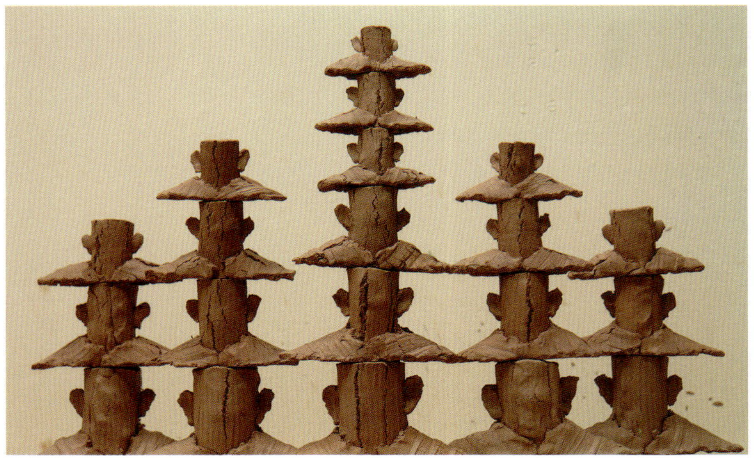

Study of Weight of Meditation #6, 2006. Earthenware. 15×7×10 inches

iii James Cahill, *Three Thousand Years of Chinese Painting* (New Haven: Yale University Press, 1997).

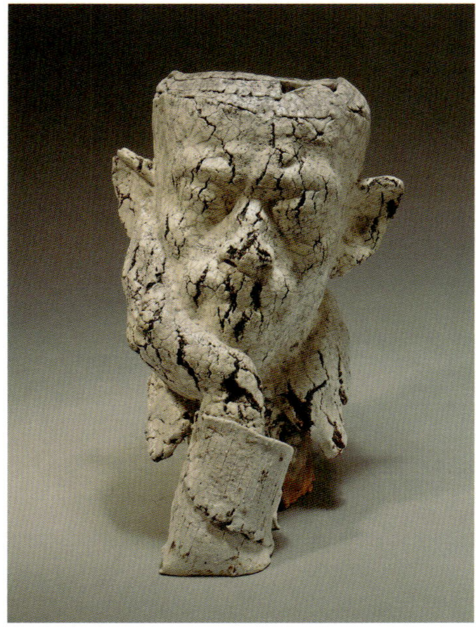

Power of Silence, 2006. Fired clay. 12×14×18 inches. Private collection

material interface in the moment of creation. This aspect of body labor is continually in evidence in Li Hongwei's work and gives profound meaning to the portrait of the self with which he is engaged.

Li Hongwei's large-scale sculpture, *Weight of Meditation #6*, is a manifestation of extensive body labor and self-reflective engagement. This piece consists of 35 handmade self-portrait heads of various sizes stacked in a series of 5 columns or towers. The layered meaning encoded in this work is reflective of Li Hongwei's deep connection to his Chinese ethnicity and his sensitive introspective nature. The compositional arrangement of *Weight of Meditation #6* is reminiscent of Brancusi's *Column of the Infinite*, which is part of his tri-part monument to the Rumanian heroes of the First World War. This reference is a reading of modernist art history as well as an insightful formal, sculptural device that allows the sculpture to imaginatively multiply in scale as it refers to an infinite human population in which the individual is but one singular entity, an entity that, nevertheless, has special meaning as a singular poetic, spiritual reflection of the whole. The faces of the individual heads are rendered with eyes closed as if in some introspective meditation. This condition engenders a quiet reflectiveness to the entire work which otherwise speaks of a systematic ordering of chaos. Li Hongwei's structure of stacking seems to allude to the regimentation of society, which has the potential to empower and restrain the life of the individual. In a beautiful stylistic gesture, Li Hongwei connects his towers with the traditional architecture of the Chinese pagoda, which has its origins in Buddhism, but has become a universal, secular symbol associated with Chinese cultural history.

Li Hongwei's manipulations of material speak of his individual body and touch as mentioned, but also focus on earth as material and place. Li Hongwei incorporates, via his use of clay, the metaphors associated with the Earth as the essential home of human kind and, in Western, Christian mythology, the origin of the very, physical body of man. Li Hongwei's compositional arrangement of columns or towers is further arranged in a horizontal installation clearly suggesting landscape. We see in his sculpture the trinity that houses the fundamentals of human experience— figure, architecture, and landscape. In addition, we witness in Li Hongwei's sculpture the metaphor of transformation as the wet earth or clay is transformed by fire into stone. This metamorphosis, in concert with the self-portrait, alludes to the internal and external struggle of the individual to resolve the questions of life and thereby gain enlightenment or transcendence. Trial by fire is a real aspect of ceramic art that suggests struggle, which leads to renewed purpose. The sculpture becomes a transmitter of the collective human consciousness regarding the immortality of the spirit. Li Hongwei's autobiography achieves universal resonance.

Weight of Meditation #6 is clearly a major sculpture. *Power of Silence*, although a far less dramatic piece, is nevertheless a very significant one. Its palpable state of quiet introspection is especially compelling. There is weight, mass, gravity clearly engaged; yet it is the tilt of the head with chin resting in the hand, eyes slightly closed, that captures an intangible moment of thought. The manipulations of material give to the work a sense of living energy. The work seems to breathe gently. Fissures in its ceramic surface, as well as the crazed network of its glaze, suggest trials and tensions creating an overall rendering that speaks of the forces of time and stress. Present moment and history are encapsulated physically and graphically. *Power of Silence* has the fluidity and intimacy of a drawing suspended in volumetric space. One is reminded of the work of the late 19th century Italian sculptor Medardo Rosso, whose work in wax and plaster bridge the space between painting and sculpture. One can find hints of Auguste Rodin here as well, in particular with regard to the figurative fragment as sculpture replete with the residue of the

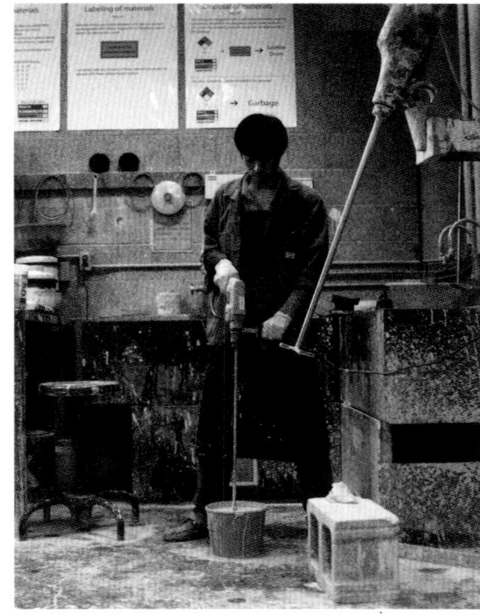

Making glaze, Alfred, NY, 2005

making. Li Hongwei's connections to the classics of late-19th and early-20th century art are perhaps no surprise given his educational background. At the Central Academy of Fine Arts, he was exposed to a tradition of academic figure drawing and modeling largely imported from the West. However, unlike traditional figure modeling, a unique and fascinating aspect of Li Hongwei's self-portrait is the fact that it is formed largely from the inside. In other words, the sculpture is hollow and expands into space around an interior volume. This gives the effect of the form asserting itself into space from somewhere inside the image. This offers up an uncanny quality of becoming or coming into being that challenges the sculpture's factual condition of material opacity and weight.

Li Hongwei is on the threshold of a major career as a ceramic sculptor. His masterful skills, as well as his attentiveness to the traditions of ceramics and figurative sculpture, combined with his sensitivity to the poetry of human vulnerability, situate his work both in the canon of historical masterworks and at the forefront of contemporary Chinese ceramic art. His work reveals a depth of seriousness and commitment to goals other than the trivial exercise of self-indulgence so ubiquitous in surveys of current ceramic work in China. Although the self-portrait could be considered to be a form of artistic narcissism, Li Hongwei manages to deliver a powerful and poignant reading of the self far beyond the superficial desire for attention.

The early 21st century is a dynamic, unruly time for art in China: wonderful for creativity, but almost impossible to sort out. Art that is taken seriously seems to require an element of cultural

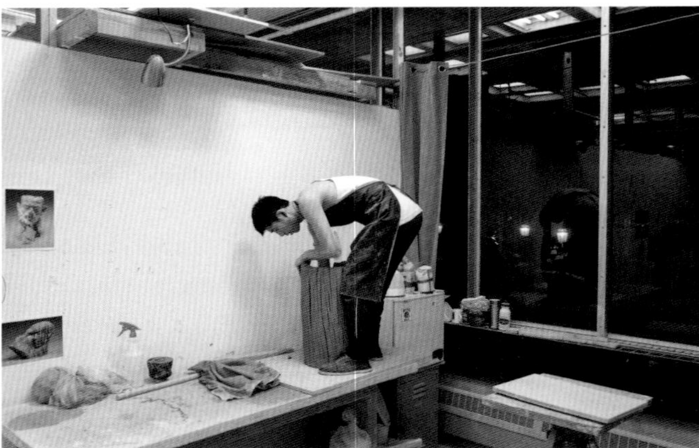

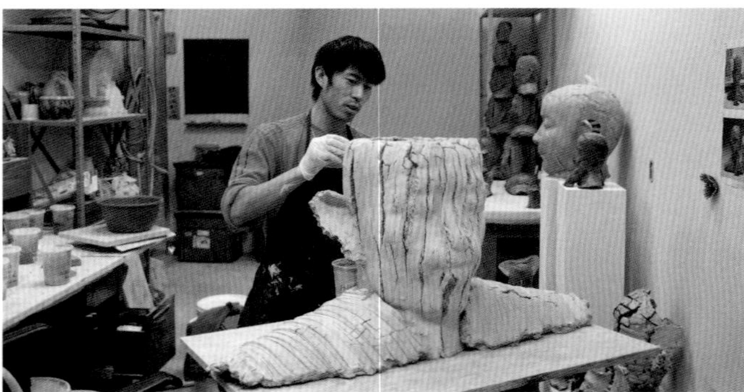

Working in the studio, Alfred, NY, 2006
Working in the studio, Alfred, NY, 2007

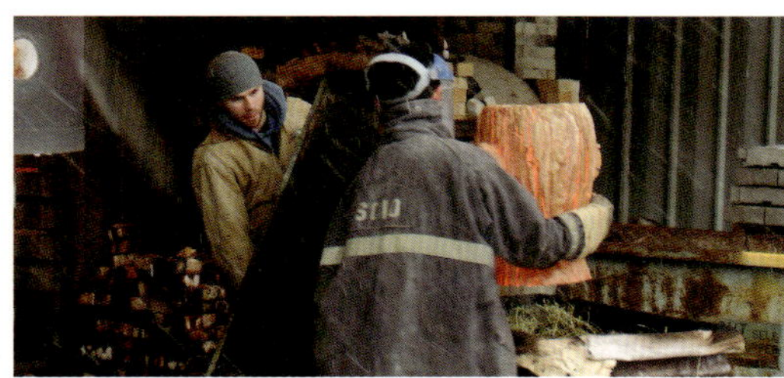

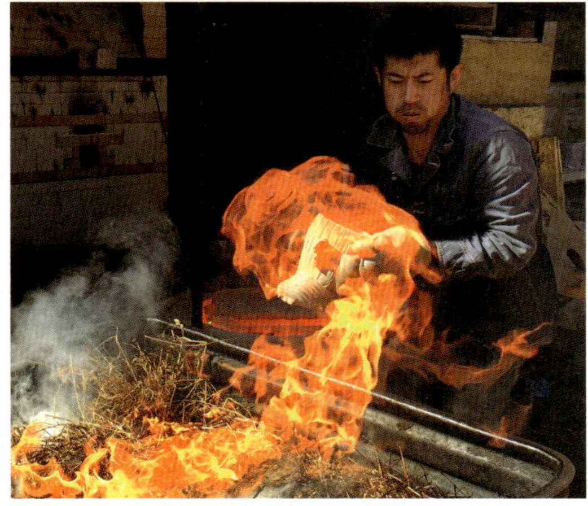

critique imbedded in it, most often a superficial, edgy punch line that seems geared to sympathies of Western-international consumption. Refreshingly, some work stands out simply based on knowledgeable, powerful assertions of material savvy, and artistic intuition that avoids cliché.

Li Hongwei's work is a strong encapsulation of the concept of a new individualism. He offers us his self-portrait expanded or expanding against the backdrop of old China: the classics of traditional painting and calligraphy as well as the traditions of Western academic modernism. Ceramics plays the role of history and tradition, but also of body and landscape giving the individualism encapsulated a place—the place it has always had in the larger perspective of the human being and earth. The work is respectful, sensitively considered, deeply felt, and audaciously centered in the assured commitment of a personal vision impervious to commonplace trends.

Wayne Higby is the Director and Chief Curator of Alfred Ceramic Art Museum at Alfred University. He is a professor and the Robert C. Turner Chair of Ceramic Art at the New York State College of Ceramics, School of Art and Design, Alfred University. Higby is a published authority on ceramic art, acknowledged for his articulate lectures, essays and critical evaluations. Higby is a Member of Honor of the United States National Council on Education for the Ceramic Arts (NCECA), Honorary Board Member of the Haystack Mountain School of Crafts, and Vice President of the International Academy of Ceramics, Geneva, Switzerland.

Raku firing, Alfred, NY, 2007
Raku firing, Alfred, NY, 2012

WEIGHT OF MEDITATION

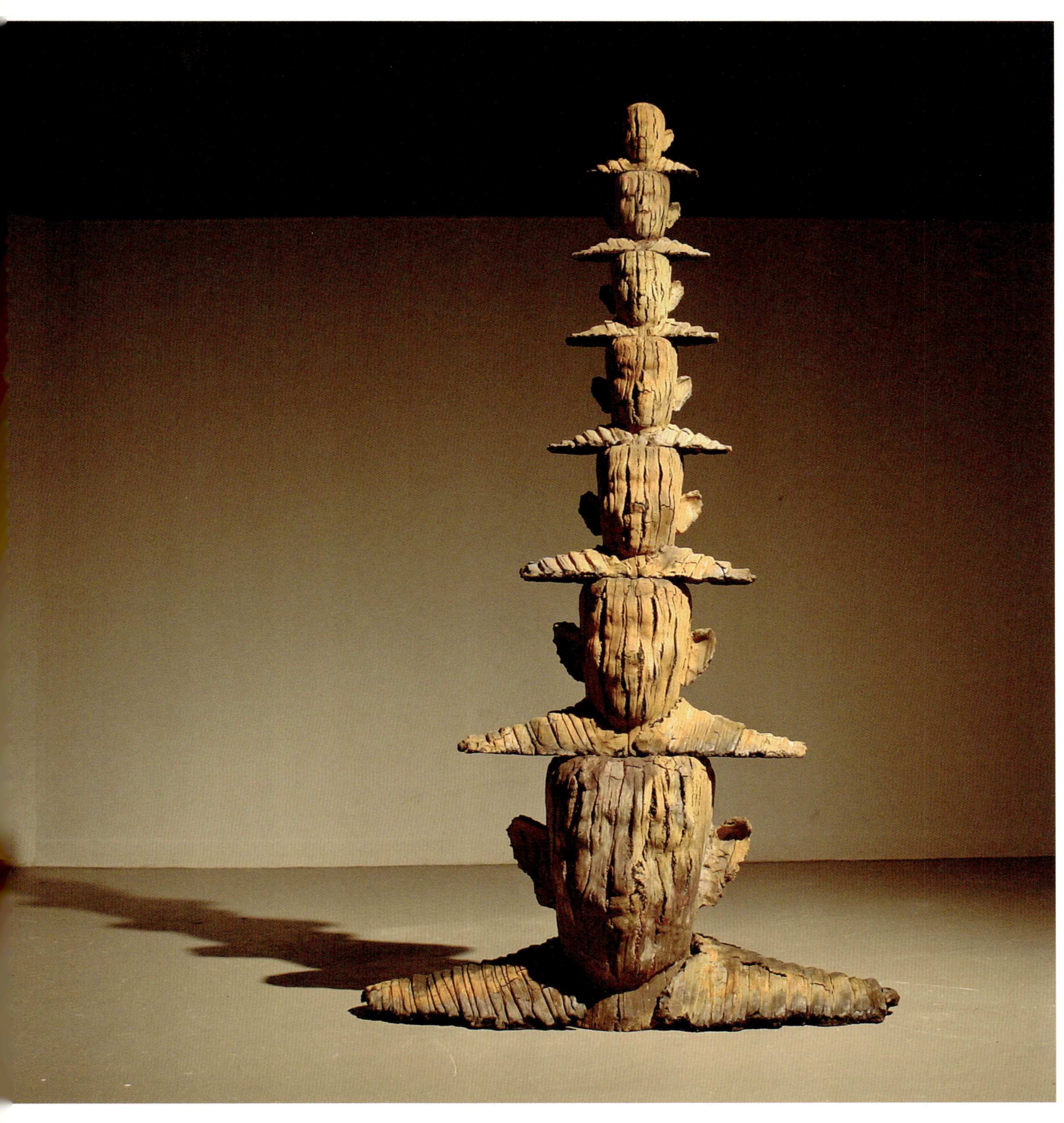

Weight of Meditation #2, 2006. Fired clay. 43×18×65 inches. Collection: Alfred University Ceramic Art Museum, Alfred, NY

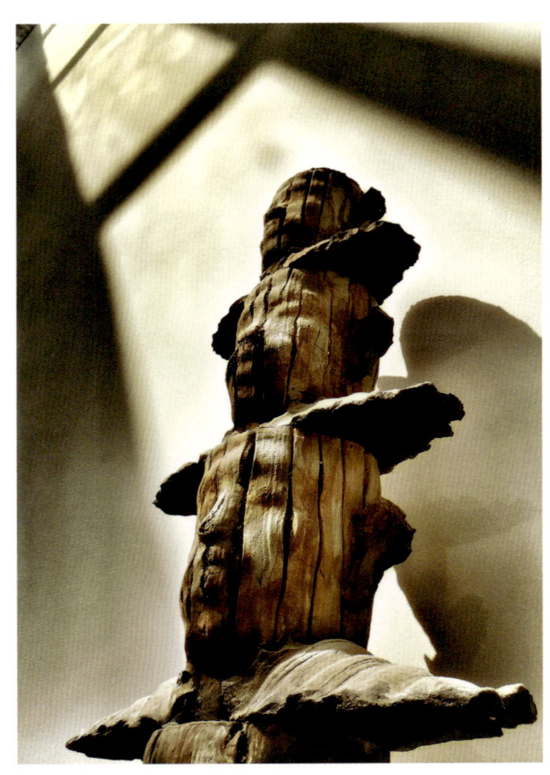

Weight of Meditation #4
2008. Fired clay. 16×9×27 inches. Collection of the artist

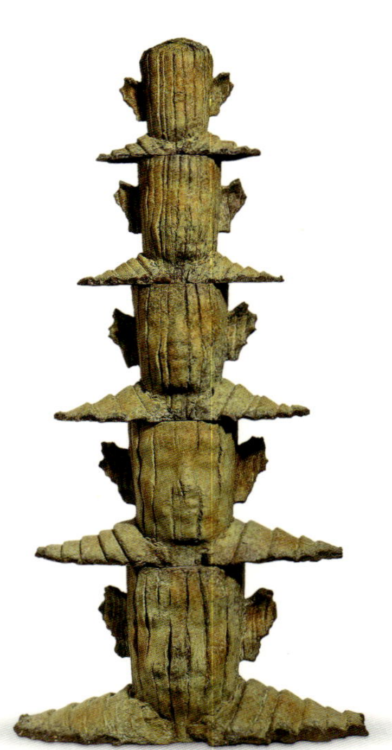

Weight of Meditation #5
2012. Bronze. 17.3×9×28.5 inches. Collection of the artist

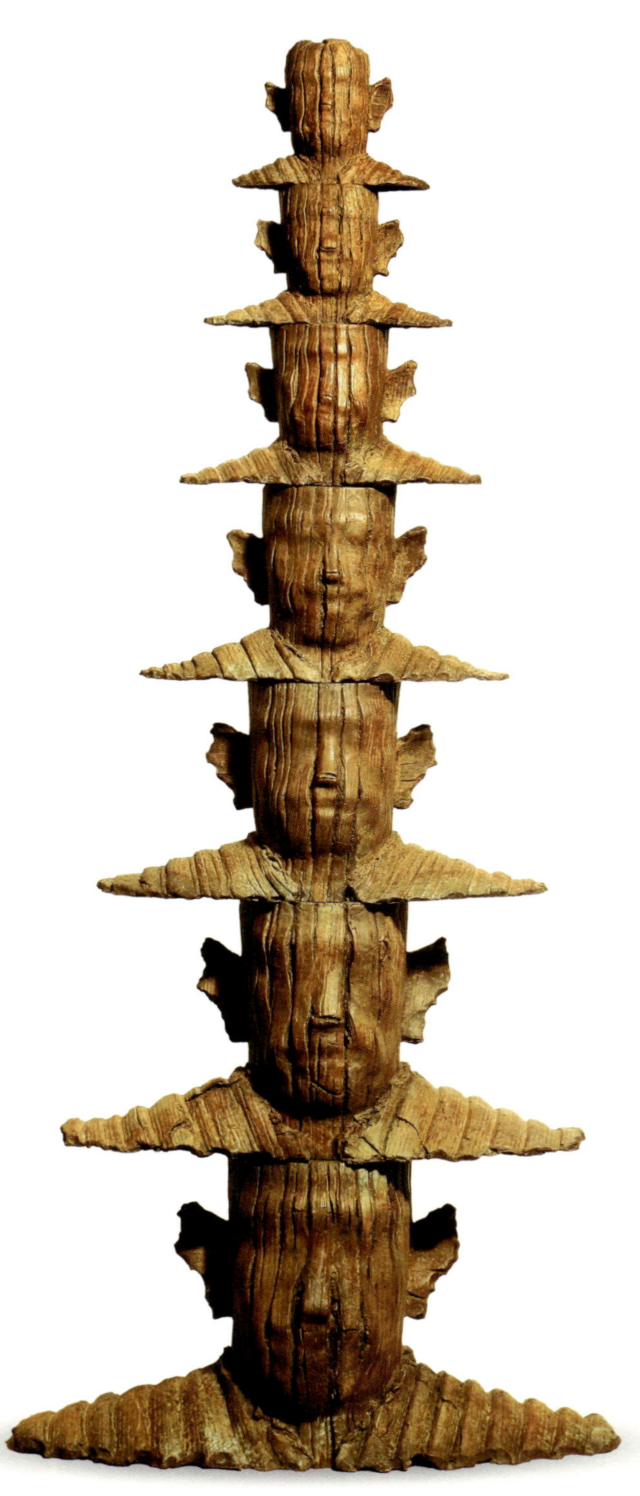

Weight of Meditation, 2012. Bronze. 39.5×16×71 inches. Collection: Museum of Fine Arts, Boston, MA

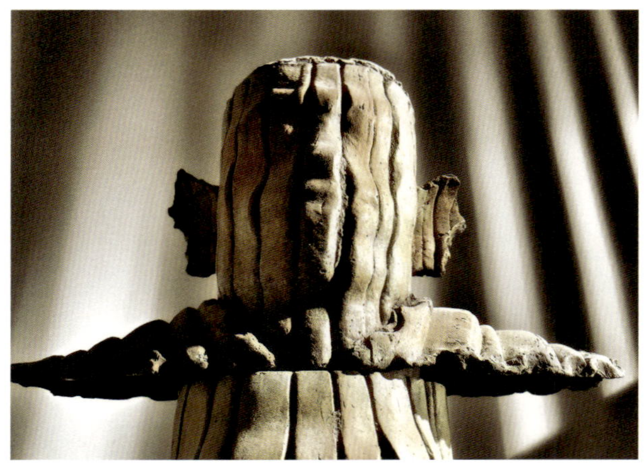

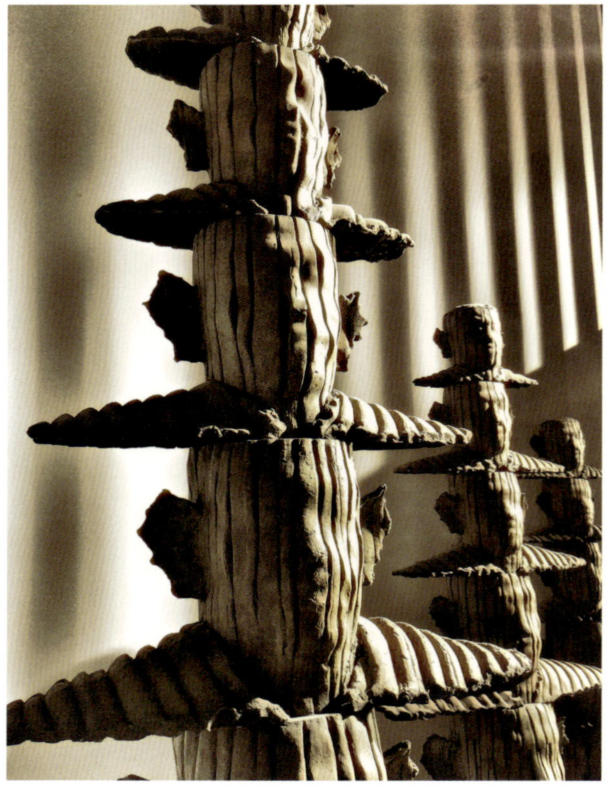

Weight of Meditation #7 (detail 1), 2012. Bronze. 180×85×118 inches. Collection of the artist

Weight of Meditation #7 (detail 2), 2012. Bronze. 180×85×118 inches. Collection of the artist

Weight of Meditation #7, 2012. Bronze. 180×85×118 inches. Collection of the artist

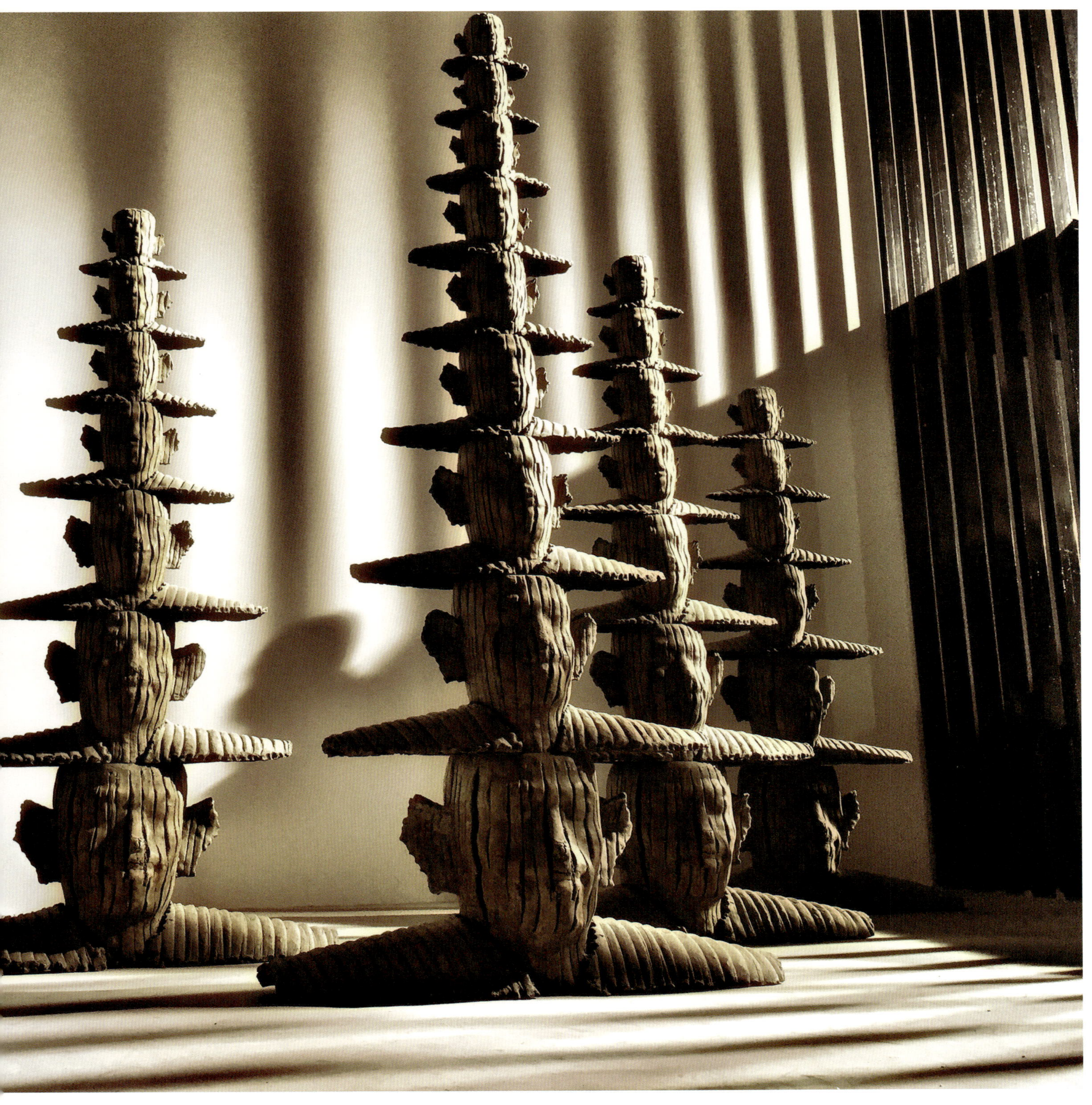

SELF-PORTRAIT

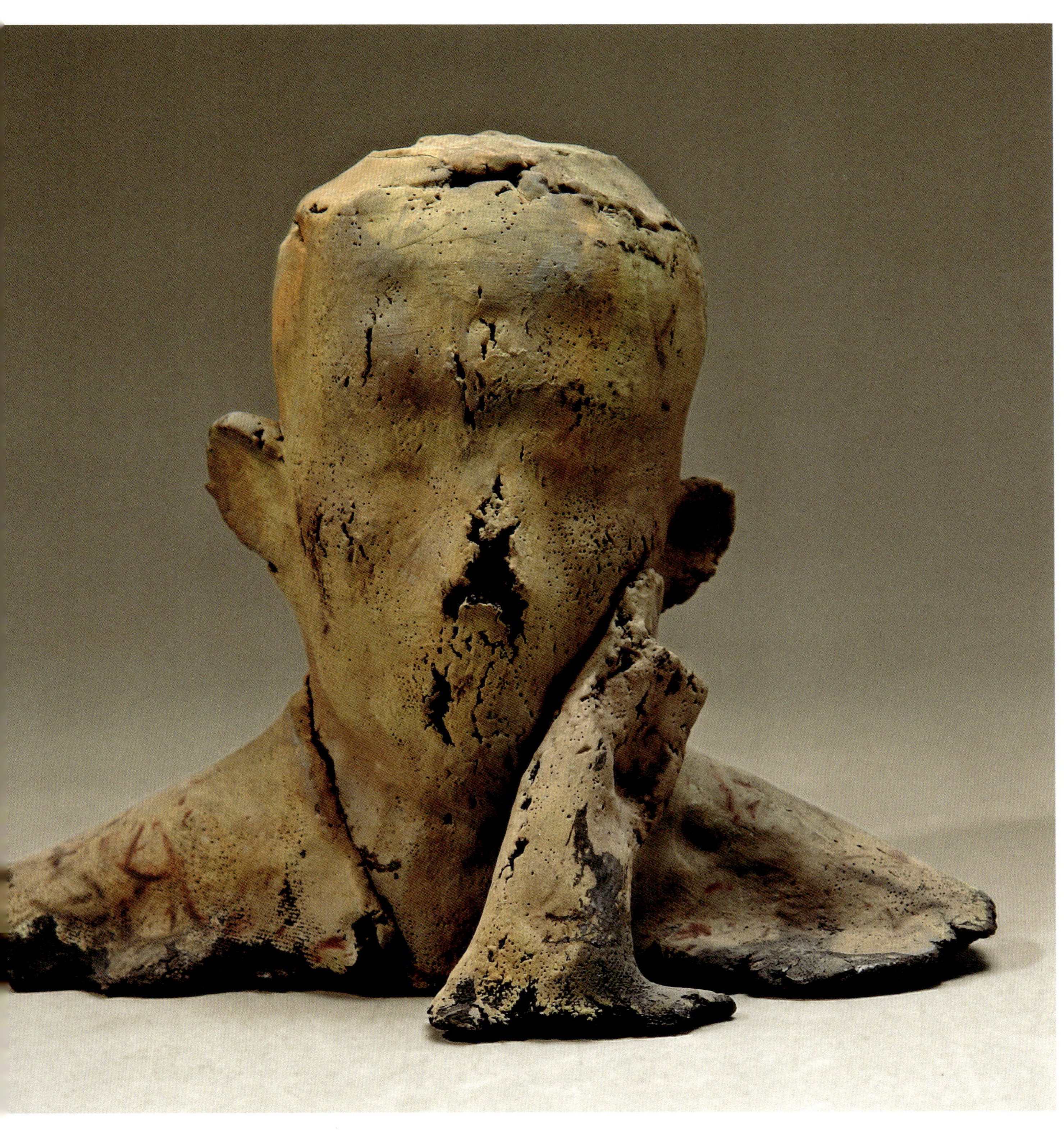

Meditation #2, 2006. Fired clay. 14×6×18 inches. Private collection

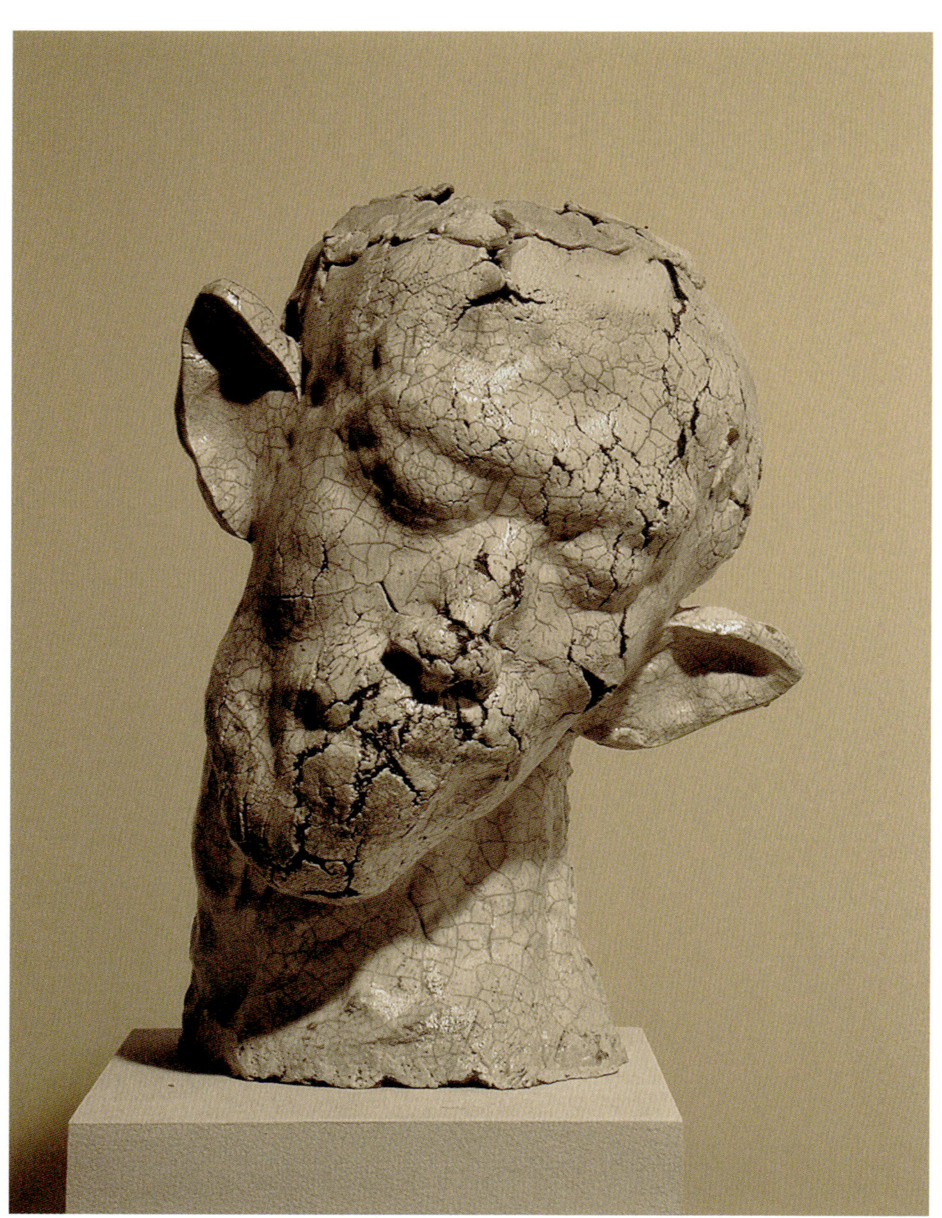

Day Dreaming, 2006. Fired clay. 11×12×17 inches. Private collection

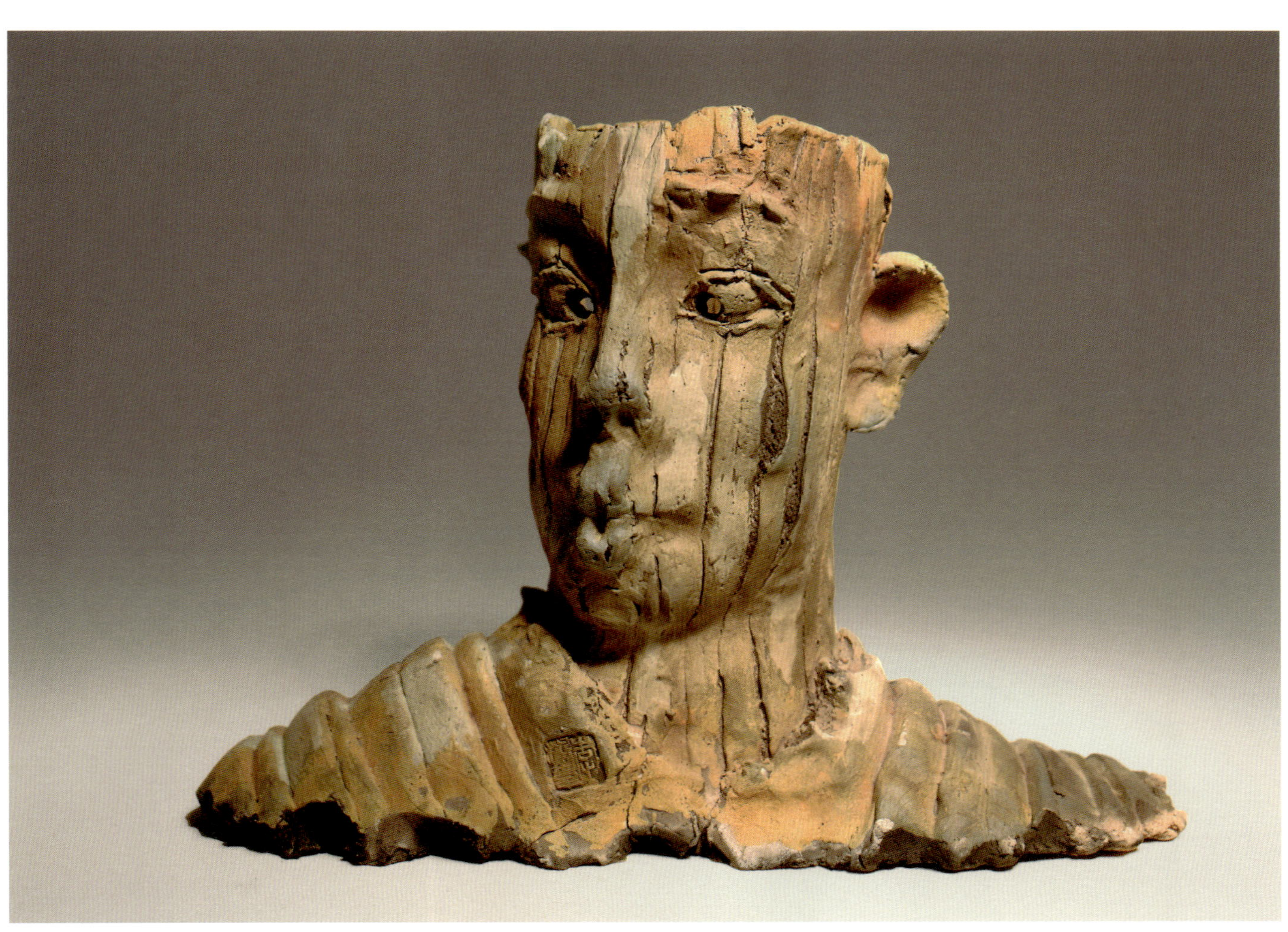

Between Conscious and Subconscious, 2012. Fired clay. 18×9×18 inches. Collection of the artist

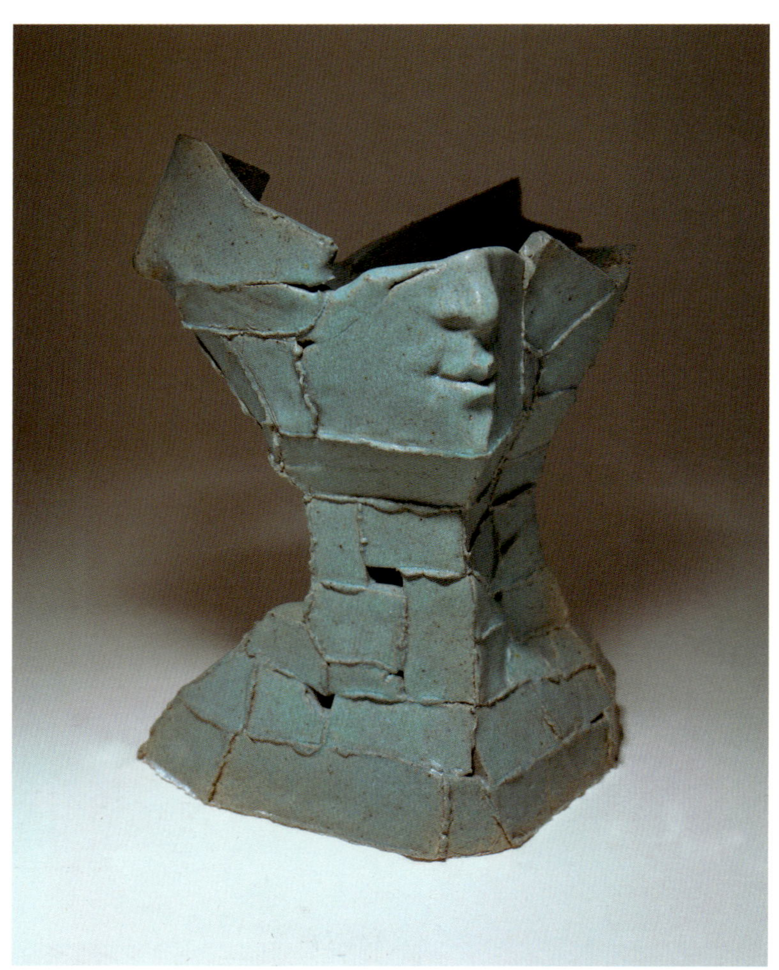

When Logic Is Sleeping #3, 2012. Fired clay. 10×7×12.5 inches. Collection of the artist

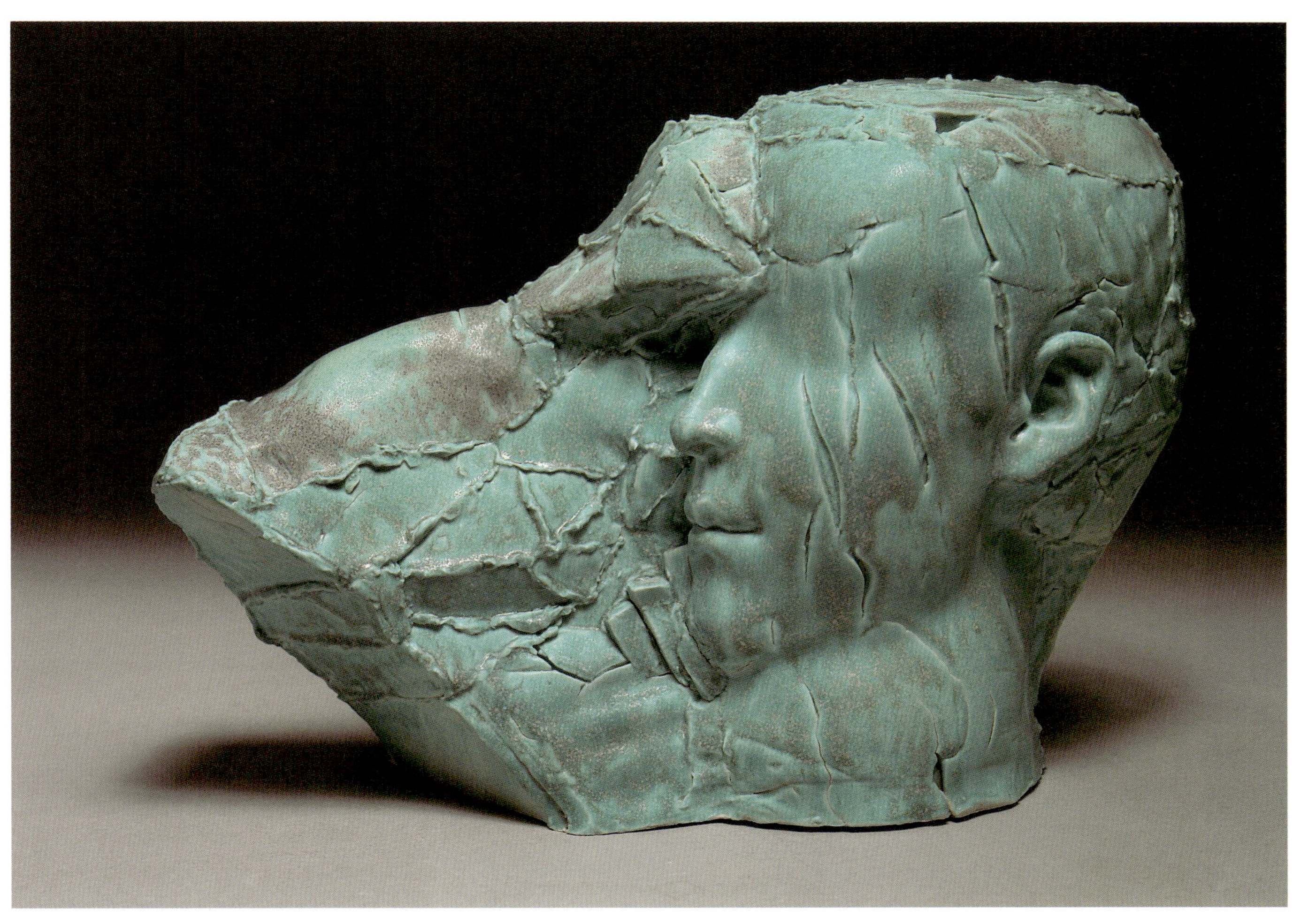

When Logic Is Sleeping #2, 2012. Fired porcelain. 19×8×15 inches.
Collection: Herrick Memorial Library, Alfred University, Alfred, NY

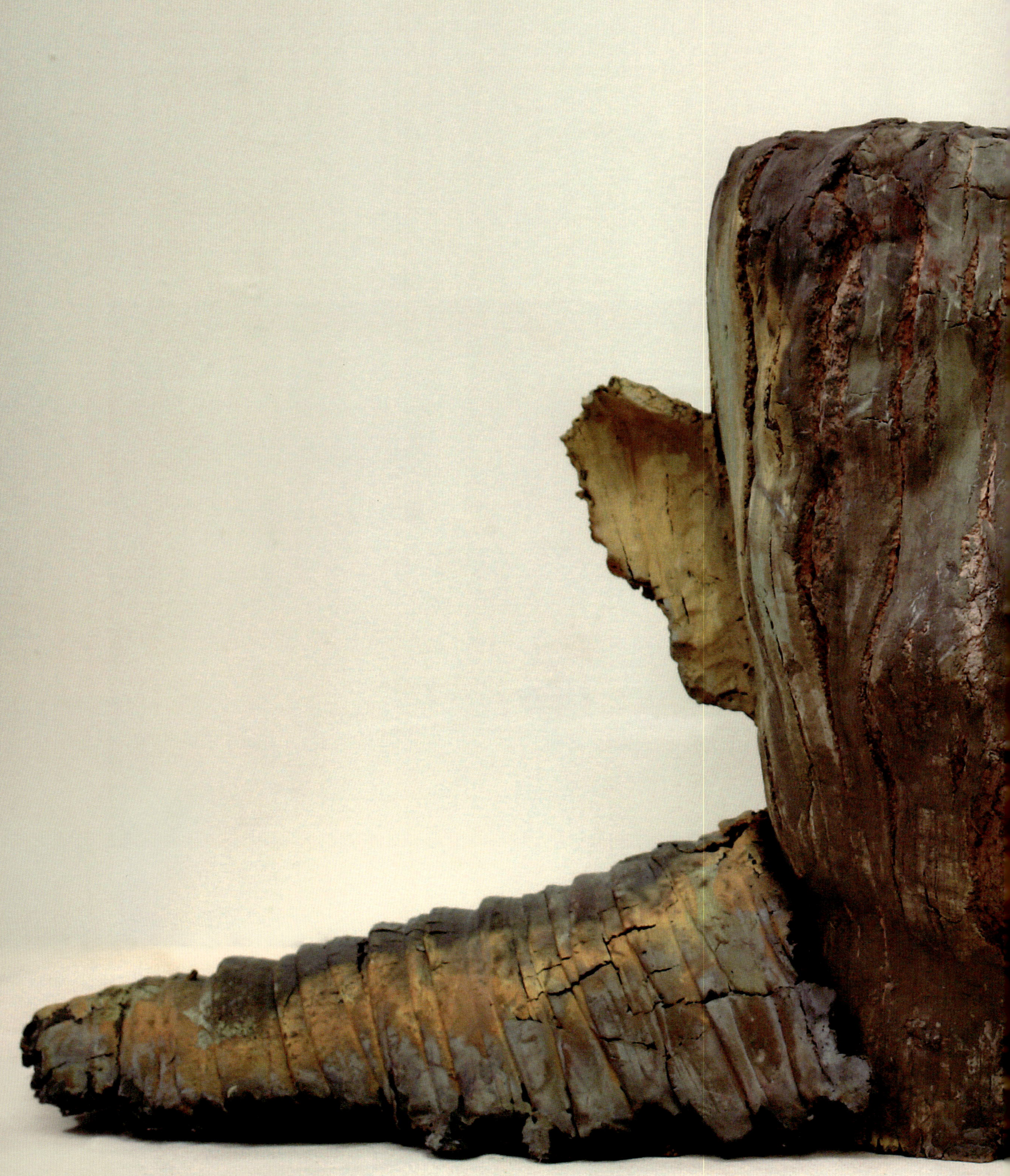

Dialogue with Medardo Rosso, 2006. Fired clay. 43×18×20 inches. Collection: Alfred University Ceramic Art Museum, Alfred, NY

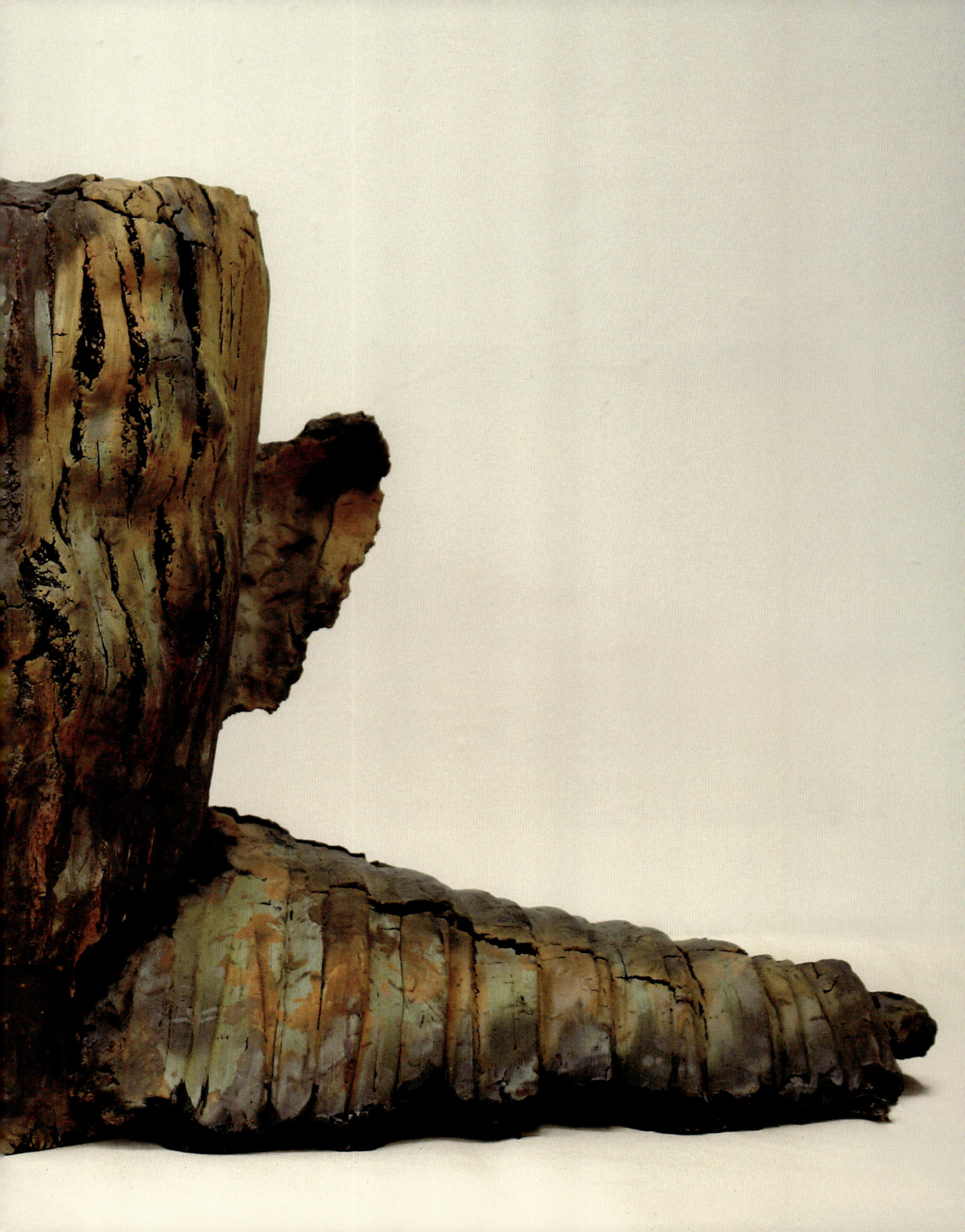

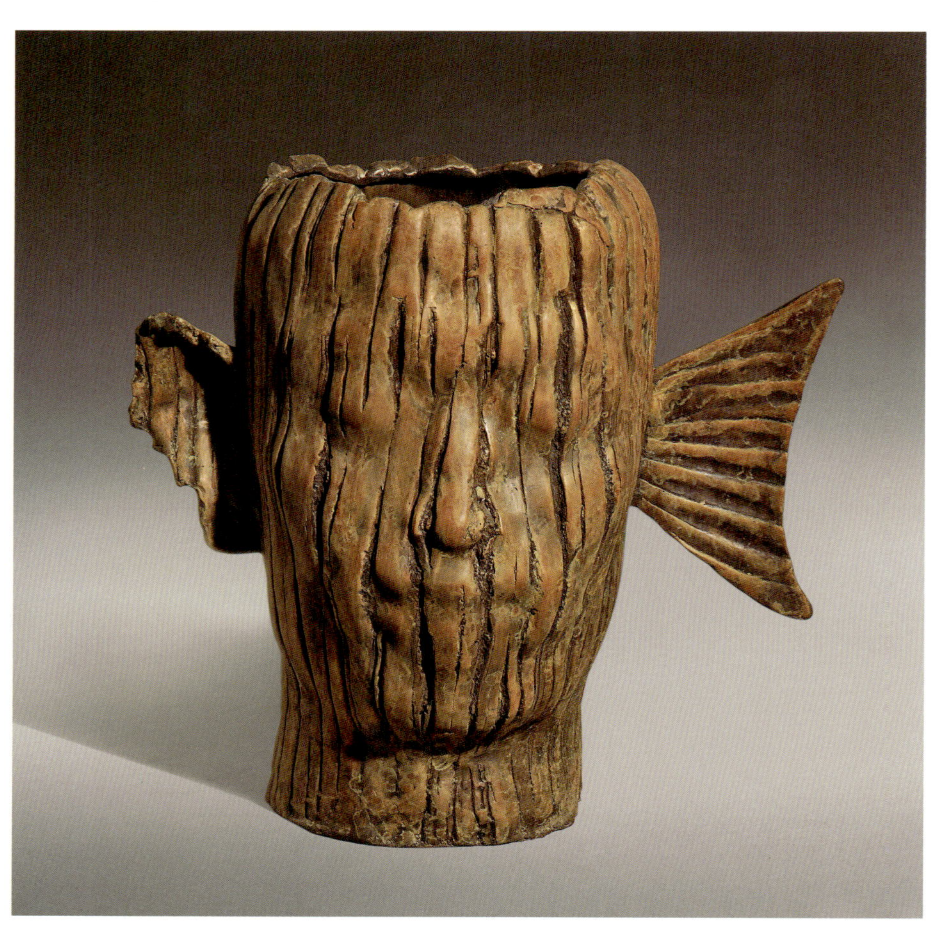

When Logic Is Sleeping, 2014. Bronze. 20×14×18 inches. Collection of the artist

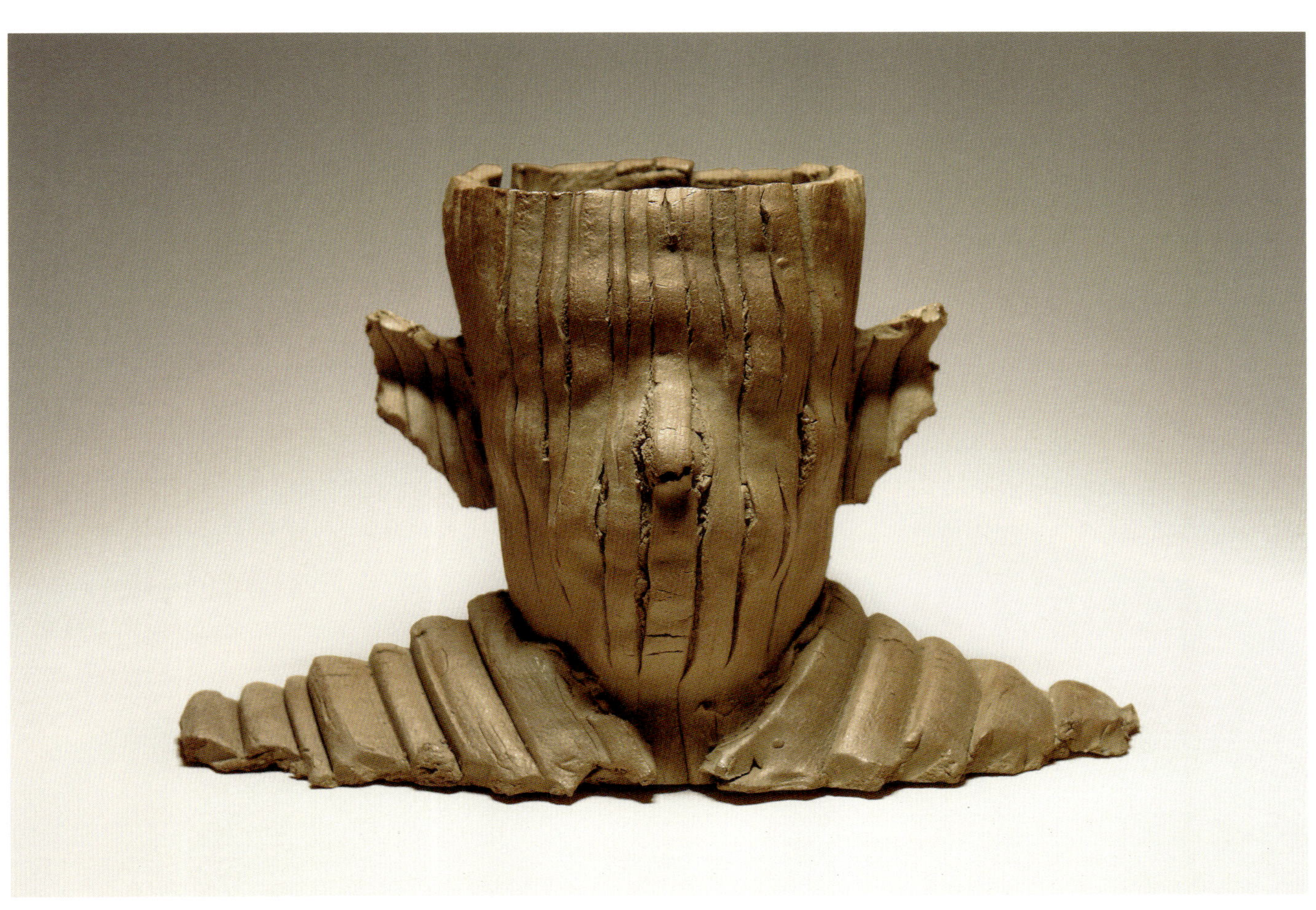

Self-Portrait #11, 2009. Fired clay. 8×12×8 inches. Collection: San Angelo Museum of Fine Arts, San Angelo, TX

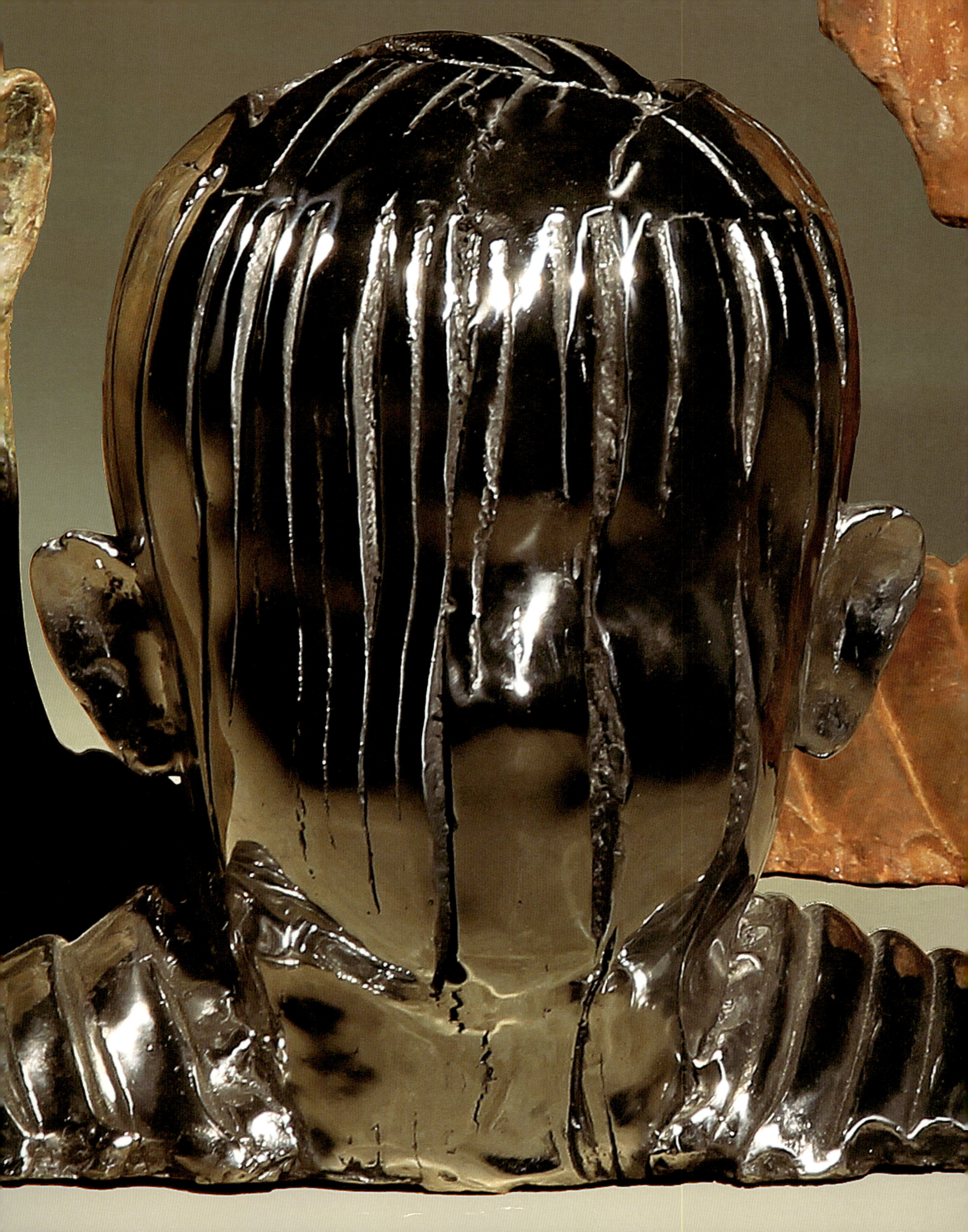

Summoning Eternal Life

—— Mary Drach McInnes
Professor & Division Head of Art History
Alfred University

The bust … demonstrates above all a search for truth that is not limited to mere appearance of phenomena … nor is it outside it: the psychological dynamic and the life energy are captured in a specific situation. The image is not formed from an idea, but from a revelation that permits the correlation between the visible and the invisible.

Medardo Rosso[i]

Three modestly sized heads, cast in various scales and materials, are gathered into a familial portrait. This view marks the beginning of our apprehending of *Eternal Life #1*. Almost immediately, we organize this sculptural cluster into "father," "mother," and "son." And they share genetic likenesses. We follow the lines of their common features—square chin, soft mouth, slight nose, shut eyes, and smooth brow—across the ancestral field. Stepping back, we work across the sculptural grouping, carefully surveying their scales and materials. All are metallic hollow casts with cracks in the cranial area and long, linear scars running the length of the face. While intimately connected, each head offers an individual presence.

Li Hongwei provides us a work that we survey as a whole, traversing laterally across each element, then moving in a zigzag course to compare one form against another. Their primary divergence lies in the material realm; each head is cast in its own medium—bronze, stainless steel, iron. Their three identities are pronounced and further separated by three surface treatments. On the far left is a bronze head made flesh-like in both its matte patina and its mottled, tan coloring and plum

[i] Museo Reina Sofía last modified 5 September 2015, http://www.museoreinasofia.es. This quote is by the artist speaking of his 1895 Bambino malato (Sick Child). For a fuller discussion of this 1895 work, see: Sharon Hecker, *Medardo Rosso* (NY: Peter Freeman, Inc., 2008).

Eternal Life (detail 1), 2014. Bronze, iron, stainless steel. 41×20×17 inches. Collection of the artist

undertones. The vertical scarring is also purplish in hue, offering a bruised appearance. This face is more obscured than the others—one side concealed as if a cloth has been drawn over the face. We strive to discern the particular features under this veil. The middle figure in the center is smaller than the rest and is made of stainless steel. Thrust into the foreground, the bust has a polished sheen that is marred by the long striations running vertically down the face. Some of these scars open up, revealing a course and gritty surface that commands our compassion. On the right is the patriarch, the largest head. Rusted oranges veined with strands of burnished flesh tones define this head of iron. His features are more pronounced than the others. This "family"—in actuality, three casts of the artist's own features—offers rich material and metaphorical content.

Its physicality is matched by its narrative possibility. In their material composition, the trio evokes historical epochs that span from ancient times to modern culture. In viewing the larger pair, we dive backwards in time to Bronze Age monuments and Iron Age spears. Moving our gaze to their smaller offspring, we speed forward to contemporary manufactured goods. These heads—at once so quickly defined and visually digested, repeatedly lure us back through their varied surfaces.

Their materiality insists on a solid presence, but their surfaces are in a state of transition. Each head has its own persona. The bronze, steel, and iron heads are easily identified; we name them according to scale: mother, son, father. Though their shared features confirm this familial identity, the artist himself unhinges this stable reading. Li Hongwei does not provide us with a conventional portrait. Facial description is veiled by design and patina. Identity is compromised by pitted and pockmarked abrasions. Fragility is conveyed viscerally in the extraordinary cracks atop their skulls and in the deep scarifications that fall vertically down the length of their faces, over eyes, nose, mouth, and

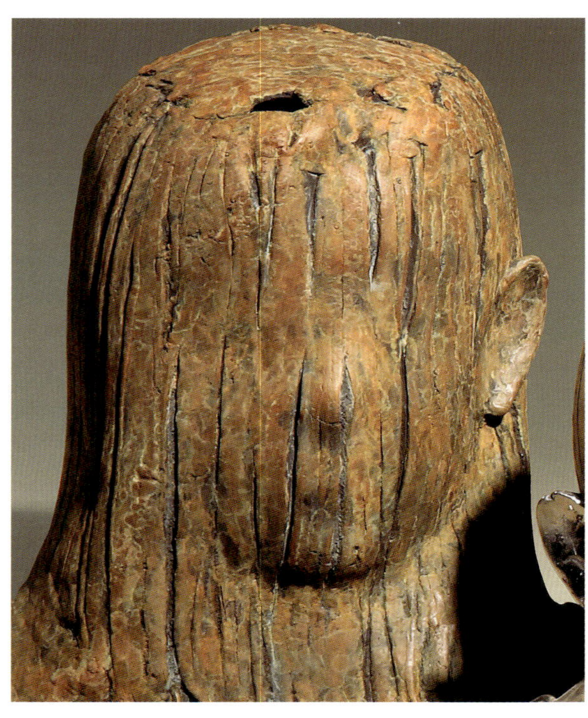

Eternal Life (detail 2), 2014. Bronze, iron, stainless steel. 41×20×17 inches. Collection of the artist

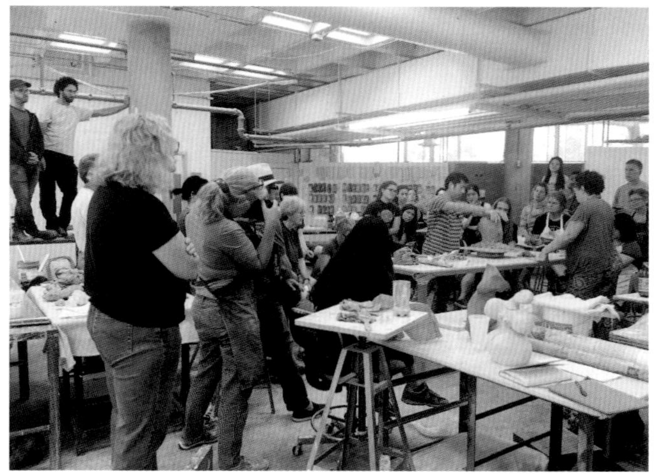

chin. These marks—scars, blemishes, wounds, mutilations—disfigure the heads, suggesting both an undoing of the head's integrity and allowing for a state of becoming. Li Hongwei's portraits exist resolutely in the here-and-now and are equally situated in the fluid temporal space of our imagination. In apprehending *Eternal Life*, we are put on the threshold—both in the profane world of the already formed and the sacred world of becoming.

The act of creation is witnessed on the surface of these figures, as their surfaces bear the evidence of their making. Li Hongwei purposefully eschews verisimilitude as he fractures and abrades these skulls. In doing so, he opens them up to a more engaged and imaginative reading. We focus on skin and skull. In our mind's eye, we try to complete each figure; we imaginatively mend the cracks and tend to the scabs. Like the great works of Auguste Rodin or his Italian contemporary Medardo Rosso, Li Hongwei's heads are both materially actualized and appear to be still in the process of being made.

The lack of finish is indebted to late 19th-century aesthetics. At this time, avant-garde artists moved away from a finished veneer to achieve an unfinished surface. This change, seen in both painting and sculpture, coincided with a shift away from narrative clarity to an emphasis on mark-making and the general process of creation. Rodin, for example, forces us to look past the persona being depicted and at the artist's own manual manipulation. In his fragmented figures, we take in the edges of his sculpting knife, the pressure of his handprint, and the accidents of the foundry. Deviations in surface became the norm in his bronzes. The unfinished nature of his work encourages our own attention to surface anomalies, leading us to repeat and complete the making process as part of our own viewing. Rodin's attention to the surface is readily apparent in viewing his sculpture; it is where meaning itself is lodged.

In *Eternal Life*, the identities of the three figures are partially masked. In all of them, but most especially the bronze head, the sculptor veils individual features to provide an enticing barrier between the viewer and the sculpted heads. We strive to discern their actual appearance, our action akin to being handed a blurred photograph that we are asked to identity. While we may experience frustration, we are also given a space to complete the portrait ourselves. Our recognition is short-circuited, yet our imagination is engaged. As viewers, we move from an initial visual apprehending to a metaphorical encountering. And, finally, in *Eternal Life*, we are led to a summoning.

We have in Li Hongwei's *Eternal Life* a sense of declaration. These heads hail us—we look at them and we attend to them. We touch their surfaces, fill in their cracks, and finish their forms. Li Hongwei's self-portraits make visible the duality between the finality of form and the incomplete task of art. Poet and critic Susan Stewart in her essay "On the Art of the Future" describes our intervention in experiencing art:

> *To say that art-making is a practice indicates from the outset that the task of art is unfinished. Individual works will necessarily exhibit finality of form, but the task of art in general is incomplete. Something continues to call for art, something in the experience of those who make it and something in the experience of those to seek to apprehend it. Nature produces beauty without human intervention, but not artworks, and no artwork can be completed without reception. Our metaphors for those recurring openings to art as a summons to apprehension—to call, to speak, to hear, to touch—reveal the etymology of aesthetics in sense experience that draws on inter subjective apprehension and the continuity between such experiences and face-to-face encounters with other persons.[ii]*

In apprehending and ultimately summoning *Eternal Life*, we encounter both art and our own humanity.

Li Hongwei is a contemporary artist who is deeply learned in the traditions and crafts of sculpture and of ceramics. After receiving his BFA in China at Beijing's Central

[ii] Susan Stewart, "On the Art of the Future," *Chicago Review*, 50, No. 2/3/4 (2004-5): 301.

Academy of Fine Art, he came to the United States to study ceramics at the top-ranked New York State College of Ceramics at Alfred University, where he received his MFA. This intense period studying ceramics in the West was an important interlude for the artist. Even when the artist returned to metal casting, his indebtedness to the field of ceramics was clear. Ceramics is a field that merges three-dimensional form (the traditional realm of sculpture) and two-dimensional surface (the traditional domain of painting). Glaze techniques and applications paint the surface, their cracked and scored skulls alluding to the fissures that often result in terracotta firings. Indeed, Li Hongwei 's primary course of study during his graduate work was the art of Japanese raku, a process that celebrates the accidents of the fire.

This artist negotiates several realms—geographic and aesthetic—in a way reminiscent of sculptor Isamu Noguchi, who also balanced these same spheres. Noguchi, born in Los Angeles of an American mother and a Japanese father, went back to his paternal homeland to absorb and reinterpret that great ceramic tradition. In the 1950s, he created audacious work that inspired the emerging Sodeisha group to create an entirely new category of pottery, that of the nonfunctional vessel. Li Hongwei—whose recent stacked work in his series *Allegory of Balance* remind me of Noguchi's postwar sculptures—has the potential to be equally daring and inspiring.

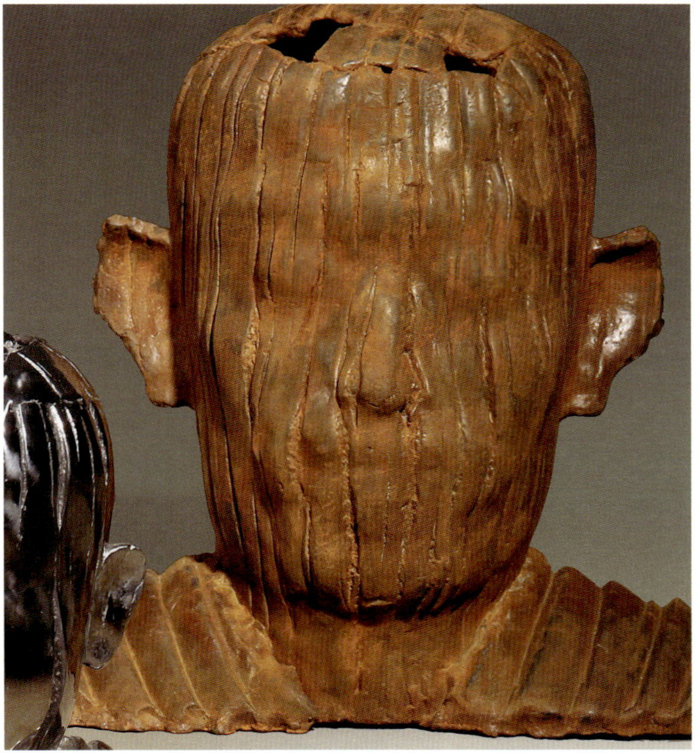

Dr. Mary Drach McInnes is a Professor of Art History at the School of Art and Design at Alfred University. Her research focus is on modern and contemporary sculpture. In addition to academic publications, Dr. McInnes is also a curator and has written several internationally distributed exhibition catalogs.

Eternal Life (detail 3), 2014. Bronze, iron, stainless steel. 41×20×17 inches. Collection of the artist

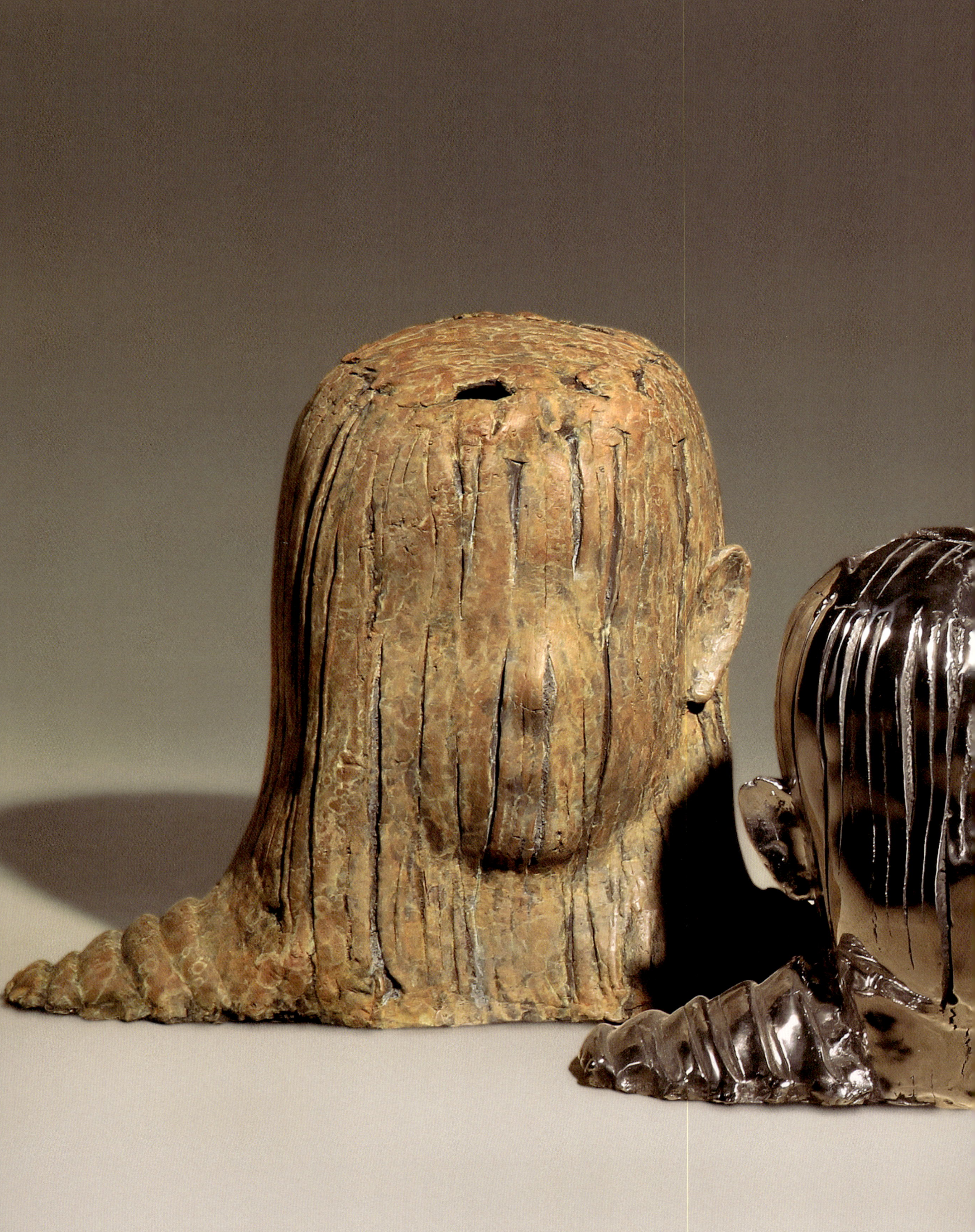

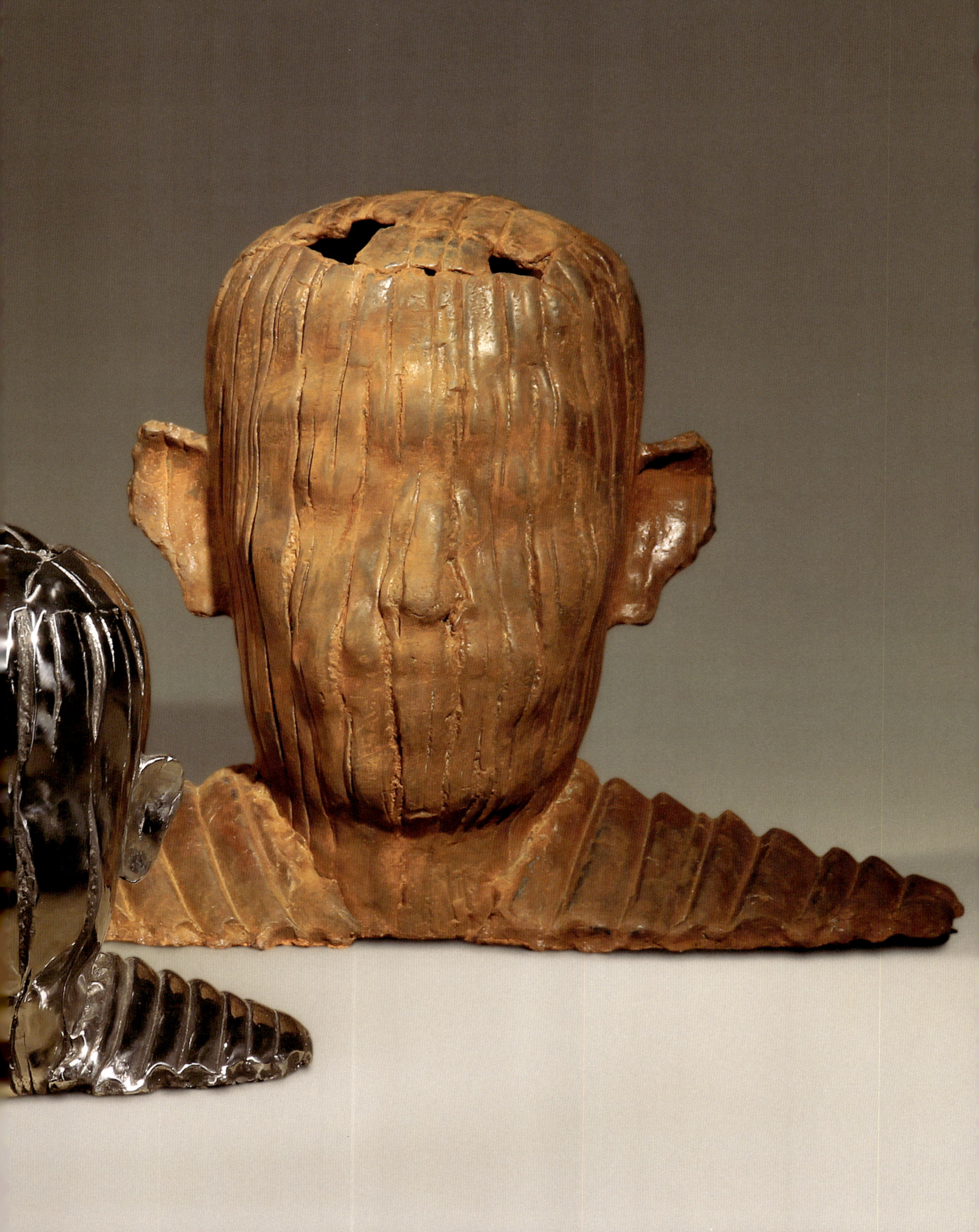

Li Hongwei: Tradition and Change

—— Michaël Amy
Professor of Art History
Rochester Institute of Technology

Working at the intersection of tradition and innovation as he juxtaposes Eastern and Western aesthetics, Li Hongwei expands the parameters of sculpture by introducing the vessels he makes, as a superlatively gifted master of an ancient form of glazed pottery, into the realm of abstraction. By combining baked clay with stainless steel in his sculptures, Li Hongwei joins fragility to solidity. The former medium transformed civilizations around the world before the beginning of history, while the latter medium has ties to industry, construction, and modernism.

When glazes containing crystals are applied by Li Hongwei onto his vases before firing, and then the temperature in the oven is suddenly dropped by opening the hatch, effloresces appear on the surface of the pots, adding immense visual richness to these. In three bodies of Hongwei's work, the vessels are carefully sawn into, at one or both ends of the pot with either a straight or wavy, curvilinear cut. The removed parts are then restored—as it were—with new, stainless steel pieces fashioned by hand, sealing off the hollow body, which was originally open at the top.

The act of removing and replacing could hardly be made more explicit, as not only is there an abrupt, collage-like transition between materials (one brittle, the other hard) and processes (modeling, glazing, and firing versus hammering, soldering, and polishing), but there is also a sudden shift from polychromy and pattern to silvery monochromy. The latter is broken as we, the viewers, approach the metal, see ourselves and our environment reflected in the shiny surface, and witness something even beyond the object's skin that dissolves its integrity.

Xuan #2, 2018. Fired porcelain, stainless steel. 25.5×7.75×7.75 inches. Collection of the artist

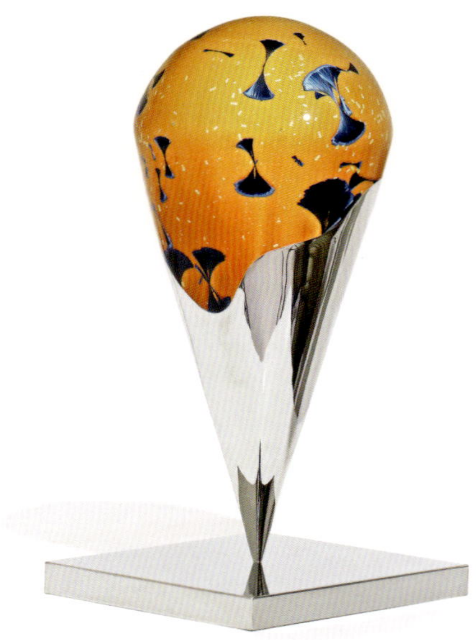

Constantin Brancusi—one of the founding fathers of an entirely autonomous form of abstract sculpture (independent, that is, from the architecture to which it was traditionally attached), and an artist who exploited the tensions obtained by juxtaposing materials and processes—introduced shininess and mirroring effects in many of his works. Jeff Koons brought porcelain and luster back to Western sculpture, and Wim Delvoye embraced both the patterns of Delftware and the gleam of stainless-steel in several of his series of sculptures. Li Hongwei inscribes himself within this fascinating line of avant-garde practice, as he breaks new ground and—by doing so—expands the field of sculpture.

Despite the efforts in the West of the likes of Pablo Picasso, Robert Arneson, Betty Woodman, Anthony Caro, and Peter Voulkos, and despite its deep impact upon generations of sculptors, clay—with its ties to craft and the so-called minor arts— remains marginalized within the world of modernist sculpture. Li Hongwei's work offers a strong argument in favor of clay, ornament, color, and the morphology of vases, as both visually and conceptually enriching forces with the realm of sculpture.

An impression of liquidity, of melting, of a kind of regimented transformation is obtained in *Upwelling of Gravity*, as here—as elsewhere in Li Hongwei's work—a sharp,

Upwelling of Gravity #17, 2018. Fired porcelain, stainless steel. 8×8×15.5 inches. Private collection

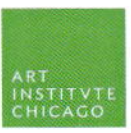
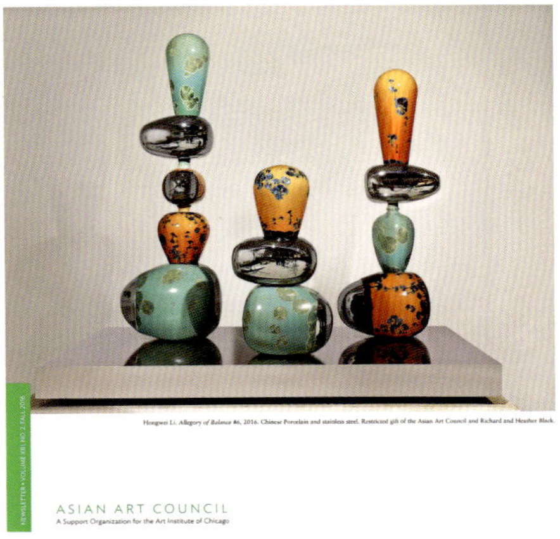

Cover of Asian Art Council Newsletter of AIC
Fall 2016
First acquisition of contemporary Chinese ceramics
and contemporary Chinese sculpture of AIC

hard-edged, curvilinear line separates the porcelain from the stainless steel. The sculptures in this series resemble stylized cones topped by one ball of ice cream, with the flavor running sheet-wise down the biscuit, instead of dripping in rivulets. The porcelain top is perfectly hemi-spherical, and what lies below it gradually and methodically thins down to a stainless steel point situated right beneath the center of the hemisphere. Where the inverted cone suddenly turns into stainless steel, space is reflected and warped, as are we, the nearby onlookers.

But while there is visual equivalence to a scoop of ice cream and its cone, which has associations with popular culture, the implications of Li Hongwei's art are different. Li Hongwei, who works with slow deliberation, attaches the utmost importance to outstanding craftsmanship. Unlike some of his contemporaries, he does not aim for mass appeal and he does not delegate, preferring to make everything himself by hand.

The works belonging to the *Allegory of Balance* series are surprising, playful, and exhilarating. Here, different bodies of porcelain covered with variously colored glazes are forced to "cohabit" (a term deliberately borrowed from the political landscape of 1980's France). Both there and here, the resulting tensions, compromises, balancing acts, deceptions, pyrotechnics, and tricks can be highly entertaining. The combinations of abstract biomorphic forms in this series have more than a little in common with certain works produced by Surrealist artists (card-carrying members of the group, or not) including Joan Miró, Yves Tanguy, and Isamu Noguchi. Unlike Miró however, Li Hongwei does not use chance procedures to arrive at his compositions. Instead, he embraces the rigorous self-discipline of the Chinese calligrapher, or potter, who repeats the same actions over and over again and in so doing arrives at a meditative state.

Allegory of Balance #1 evokes the type of unexpected formations that water, wind, and particles are able to carve out of rock or wood. Here, as elsewhere in this series, bodies are built up of distinct parts stacked one on top of the other. The verticality of these bodies evokes two standing figures, with a person seated in between them. The engineering behind this type of composition heightens our sense of wonder, as the supporting structure is hidden within the hollow forms.

An impression of floating occurs in the *Xuan* series, which is inspired by a Chinese character (玄). In these works, a variation upon the *Upwelling of Gravity* series, bulbous bodies turn into elongated points at the top, from which the forms are suspended in mid-air by means of a wire. Li Hongwei works on as many as five series of abstract

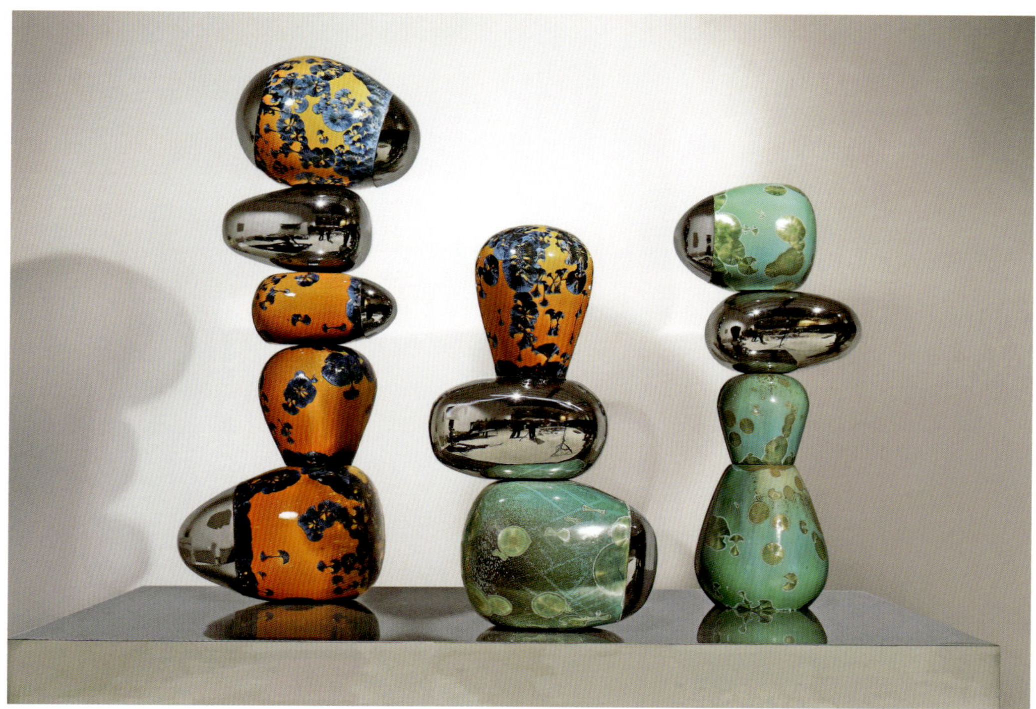

Allegory of Balance #1, 2014. Fired porcelain, stainless steel. 59×35.5×53 inches. Private collection

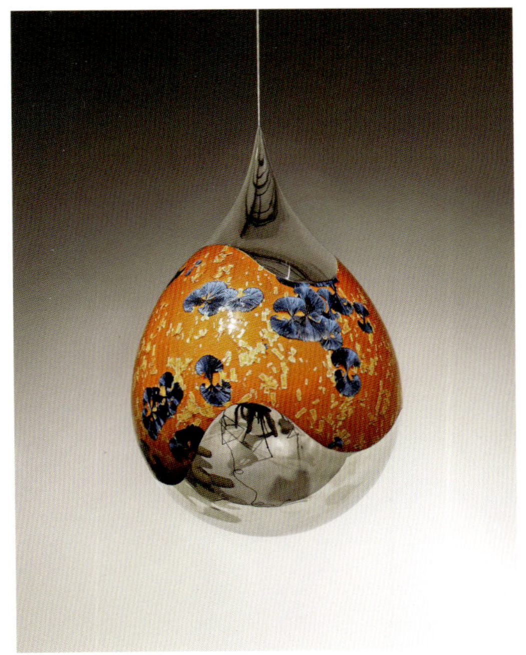

sculptures concurrently, allowing images and ideas to migrate from one body of work to another in an act of cross-pollination.

The forms in the *Xuan* series seemingly melt, gradually and evenly, to become long sharp points at the bottom. There are a couple of exceptions to this rule, as in *Xuan #1* (2018), which resembles a large drop of dew, or a tear a split second before falling and splashing onto the ground. But while tears denote the theme of sadness, this body of work is not sorrowful. Reminiscent of Christmas ornaments, there is a hint of danger in the *Xuan* series, the points in the majority of the pieces facing down seemingly waiting to pin us like butterflies and put us on display. In *Xuan #2* (2018), danger also lurks within visual opulence.

The sense of falling increases in the *Illusion* series, each consisting of a tall vase sliced lengthwise in half and turned upside down to magnify the impression of dropping. Half of the vase is attached along its main axis to the center of a rectangular, mid-sized, vertical sheet of stainless steel. As the metal surface is highly polished, the projecting half of the vase is completed by its own reflection, which seems to appear behind it. In other words, the vase appears to be intact. The sense of falling through the silvery air of the polished steel leads us to imagine the end result, the sound of crashing pottery and shards spreading across the floor. But a vase twists and turns as it tumbles instead of falling perfectly straight. Li Hongwei's gravity-defying performance piece belongs to a world of illusions.

Do the rounded vessels in the *Illusion* series allude to our own bodies? After all, we too are containers—of all manner of things. Are the vases, profiled against a field of silver, metaphors for the fragility of life and the spin of the wheel of fortune? It is well known that it can all come tumbling down, quicker than the flick of a wrist. Li Hongwei's

Xuan #1, 2018. Fired porcelain, stainless steel. 9.5×9.5×19 inches. Collection of the artist

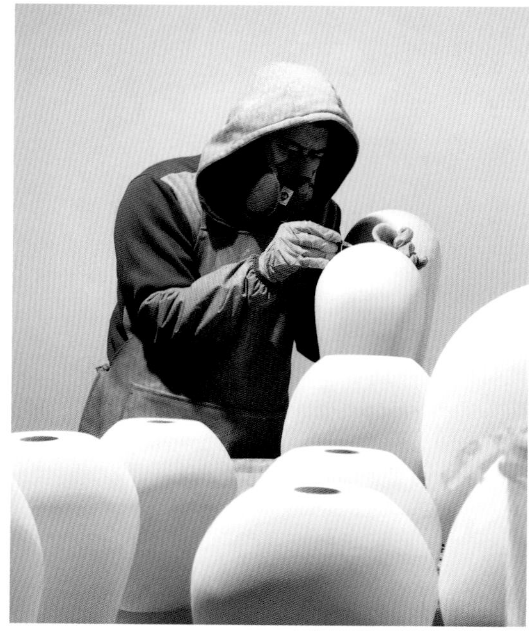

centralized vessels—almost as deadpan in compositional terms as Jasper Johns *Green Target* of 1955, or his gray *Canvas* of the following year—make us wonder whether we dare long for alternatives, we who have been taught the virtues of the golden section and all that jazz. What would a much vaster field of silver, with pots in asymmetrical configurations, look like? What about a single vase off to one side, to disrupt the careful equilibrium? Then, we suddenly realize that discrete asymmetries are present, introduced through chance processes at the level of the glazing, with in one example splendid, silent explosions of varying blues and a few dark grays appearing randomly against a burnt yellow-orange ground.

These wall-bound works belong to the family of relief-sculpture, although they contain important pictorial components, as the flat stainless steel mirrors us and the surrounding space in reverse—as in a painting on polished stainless-steel by Michelangelo Pistoletto. Additionally, the vase—magically completed by its reflection—has a colorful two-dimensional pattern wrapped around it.

Li Hongwei has such exacting standards that he rejects approximately four out of every five vases he makes, whether they are intended as autonomous vessels (he produces such works as well) or as objects to be incorporated in his sculptures. Those pots that did not emerge from the oven just right are eventually smashed to pieces, then deployed in a novel type of sculpture consisting of an open structure, its skeleton exposed to view, which is composed of shards of varying shapes and sizes along with

Working in the studio, Beijing, 2015

intact vases placed on their side or upside down. The resulting totality—a first response to the zany sculptural installations of Judy Pfaff and the crockery paintings of Julian Schnabel—approximates a raft, built by the survivor of a shipwreck or airplane crash, in his or her attempt to escape a desert island. We all need to escape, at the very least from time to time. Art is so very crucial to the quality of our lives, in large measure because it offers us with a means of escaping the dreariness, or ugliness, of everyday reality.

Demolition, and what can arise from the ruin, are the theme of *Rebirth in Breakage*, a new series which comprises only a single large work to date—Li Hongwei's largest, in fact. This sculpture has powerful, classicizing, horizontal and vertical accents, with all of the forms arranged in a tight relationship to the imaginary front plane of the

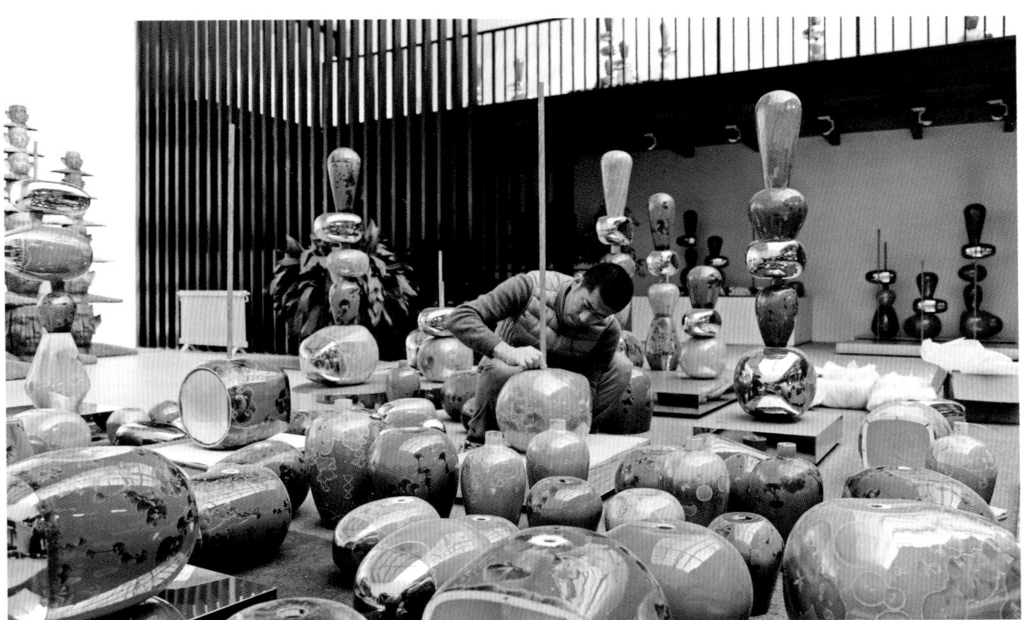

Working in the studio, Beijing, 2017

composition. I suspect that Li Hongwei will soon break away from these vectors and go even further in exploring the third dimension—perhaps with floating sculpture, or in work that is anchored to the wall, floor, or ceiling. The *Allegory of Balance* series gives us an inkling of the amount of quirkiness this artist is willing to explore. *Rebirth in Breakage* reminds us that all creation emerges from destruction, symbolic or not. Perhaps the breakage displayed here—draped across, or pierced by stainless steel bars like ravaged body parts that cannot be pieced back together again—is a commentary on our present plight, when basic freedoms and rights are being trampled in ways that seem impossibly anachronistic? If so, what is being reborn?

In only a short number of years, Li Hongwei has developed an idioyncratic body of sculpture, unmistakeably his own. Its recurring feature is the extraordinary glazed pottery he makes, with its superb crystalline imagery. Moving with steady determination, and thinking in terms of series (as did, many artists including Claude Monet, Alberto Burri, Andy Warhol, Frank Stella, and Gerhard Richter), Li Hongwei expands the language of abstract sculpture.

Michaël Amy is a critic and art historian with a Ph.D. from New York University's Institute of Fine Arts. He is a Professor of the History of Art in the College of Art and Design at the Rochester Institute of Technology, working in Renaissance, Baroque, modern and contemporary art. His articles, interviews with artists, and exhibition reviews have appeared in a wide variety of publications, including *The New York Times, Burlington Magazine, Apollo, Art in America, Sculpture, tema celeste, Viator: Medieval and Renaissance Studies, the Mitteilungen des Kunsthistorischen Institutes in Florenz,* and *CAA Reviews*. Additionally, he has published over fifty essays for books, exhibition catalogues or brochures, on contemporary art. He is the author of One to One: Conversation avec Tony Oursler (Brussels, Facteur Humain, 2006), Michaël Borremans: Whistling a Happy Tune (Ghent, Ludion, 2008), and Hiroshi Senju (with Rachel Baum as co-author, Milan, Skira, 2009), and is a Contributing Editor for the magazine Sculpture.

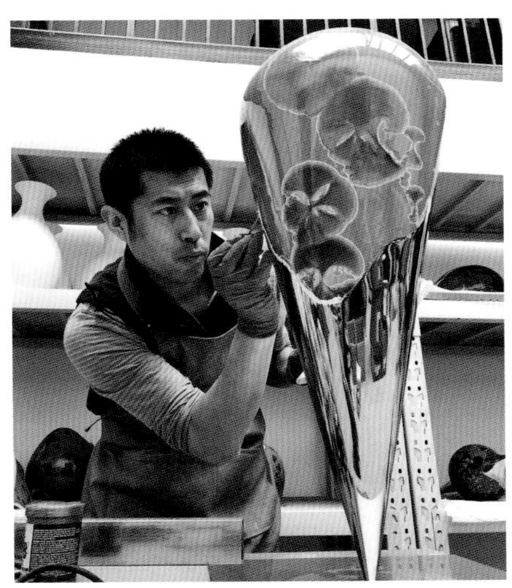

Working in the studio, BeiJing, 2018

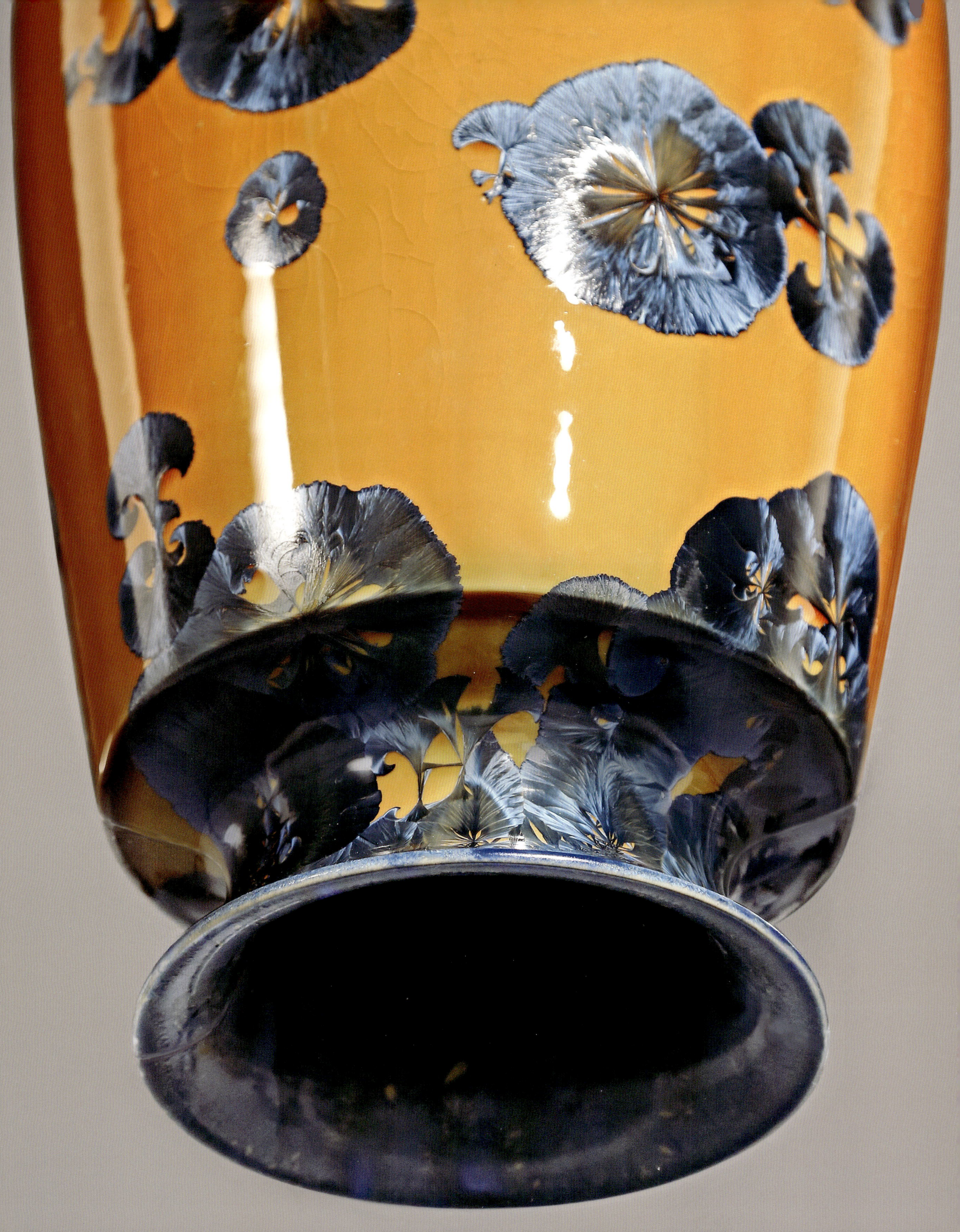

Inner Reflection, Outward Transformation:
The Art of Li Hongwei

—— Andrew L. Maske
Associate Professor
University of Kentucky

For a Chinese ceramic artist, the weight of tradition is a heavy load to bear. As an heir to the world's most highly esteemed body of ceramic culture, the creative Chinese ceramist must continually face the conundrum of how to meet the challenge presented by works of the past without simply copying or imitating them. Li Hongwei appears to have met this challenge in part by distancing himself from China and seeing his own culture from a different perspective.

Hongwei left China in 2005 to pursue a Master of Fine Arts degree in Ceramic Art at the New York State College of Ceramics at Alfred University, one of the world's few institutions of higher education to specialize in the ceramic arts (among the others is Jingdezhen Ceramics Institute in China). Building on his undergraduate degree in Sculpture at the Central Academy of Fine Arts in Beijing, Hongwei's early New York works were a form of figural busts done in the low-fired raku format. He had a difficult time connecting with others at first, so spent much of his time observing the landscape around him and pondering the human relationship to nature.

As he became acquainted with his fellow students and more comfortable in his surroundings, Hongwei's focus gradually changed, and he moved away from the human figure. His interest turned to crystalline glazes and their unpredictable nature. In a sense, this was a logical step forward from the so-called American raku firing process, which often uses various materials in post-firing reduction to create subtle yet largely uncontrollable surface effects on the pieces.

Illusion #4 (detail 1), 2017. Fired porcelain, stainless steel. 25.6×17.7×9 inches. Collection of the artist

At the same time, he found himself able to look back at his own country's ceramic culture with new eyes. He began to appreciate the elegant shapes and refined proportions of the vases created in the Song, Ming, and Qing dynasties. Instead of the perfect celadon glazes and underglaze cobalt blue decoration of the past, Hongwei decided that he would use some of those classic shapes as palettes for new glaze types, ones that combined intense colors with startling effects that occurred spontaneously in the course of firing.

In fact, the appreciation of spontaneous glaze effects has a long, if somewhat marginalized, past in the history of Chinese ceramics. In the Song dynasty, the random glaze crackle that occurred in the celadon types known as Ge and Guan were not only appreciated, but even cultivated and emphasized. Although from a technical point of view, glaze crackle represents a defect in a ceramic piece (since it results from a mismatch of the clay body and glaze in terms of expansion and contraction), Chinese connoisseurs loved the pattern that it created, with later collectors equating it to ice cracking on a pond. Celadon wares with crackled glazes continued to be made and prized throughout the centuries and are still admired today.

Other unpredictable glaze effects were found on pieces made at the Jian kilns of Fujian province. Bowls from these kilns were shipped to Japan in large quantities and were avidly collected and treasured there as tenmoku tea bowls. Their glaze effects were evaluated and named, ranging from "hare's fur" to "oil spot" and "tortoise shell." Most famous of all were the "bright change" tenmoku bowls, of which only a handful exist. This last type displays bright blue iridescent effects that have proven virtually impossible to reproduce, even with modern scientific techniques.

The crystalline blooms that emerge on Hongwei's classic Chinese ceramic forms endow them with a vibrancy unlike that of historical pieces. His works have an energy that transcends

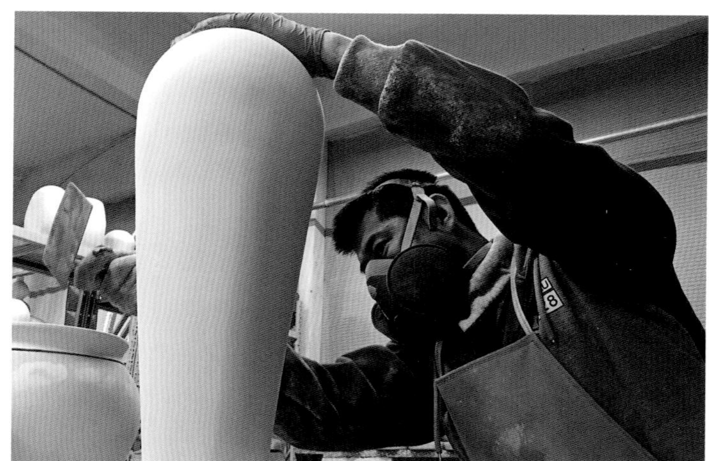

Working in the studio, Beijing, 2014

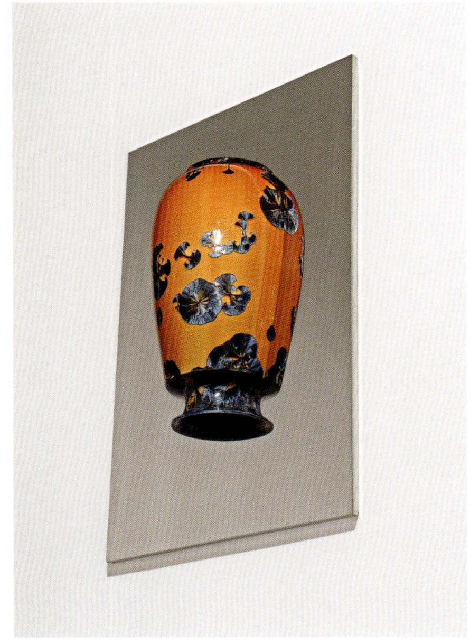

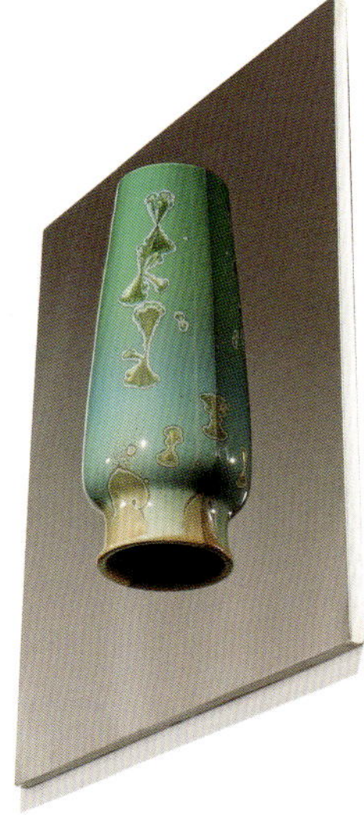

the monochrome examples of the Song dynasty, yet is more organic and mysterious than the Qing dynasty examples decorated with underglaze cobalt blue or copper red. Moreover, the nature of crystalline glazes is such that each glaze develops in a distinctive manner during the firing, making every piece unique.

In addition to his efforts to extend and elaborate on Chinese ceramic vessel tradition, Hongwei explores several fundamental sculptural aspects through his work, namely light, volume, balance, and flow. Although refracted light clearly plays an intrinsic role in his crystalline glazes, Hongwei uses reflected light to make an even more emphatic statement through the incorporation of polished steel in his sculptural works. Certain pieces, like those in his Illusion series (*Illusion#1* and *Illusion#4*) use a mirror to give the sense that what is actually only half of a vase is in fact complete. In his *Upwelling of Gravity* series, a ceramic/steel composite form appears to flow upward, defying the pull of gravity. In *Xuan*, the fluid forms seem to be pulled to the center from both top and bottom, reminding one of suspended mercury or, perhaps, a lava lamp.

Hongwei's most monumental works are those of his *Allegory of Balance* series, in which rounded forms resembling polished stones are stacked one upon the other. This approach hearkens back to his days of raku sculpture, in which he frequently stacked inverted humanoid heads and shoulders to create pagoda-like constructions. Although a number of artists have stacked multiples of ordinary objects to create striking installations, Hongwei creates his own objects and does not require that they be actually balanced in terms of weight distribution. Indeed, what is balanced is the visual effect, not the literal weight.

A conspicuous feature of this series is the mirrored steel sections that create a stark contrast with the colorful ceramic forms. The steel adds another layer of tension to the already rather uncomfortable feel of the

Illusion #4, 2017. Fired porcelain, stainless steel. 25.6×17.7×9 inches. Collection of the artist

Illusion #1, 2017. Fired porcelain, stainless steel. 19.7×15.7×5.1 inches. Collection of the artist

stacked configurations, reflecting the ambient light, the other sculptural components, and even the viewer. The pod-like forms feel both organic and otherworldly, almost as if growing life-forms had robot components added to them. The impression given by these elements differs depending upon the level of ambient or directed light.

Like so many artforms that appear refined yet simple on the surface, the composite steel and porcelain forms are incredibly difficult to create. The marriage of clay and metal requires tedious and seemingly never-ending adjustments to produce the effect that the resulting shape is all of a piece. Hongwei's work emphasizes the truth that the natural and the man-made, the organic and the constructed, must live side by side in our present-day world.

The Daoist philosophy of Hongwei's natal country teaches that balance between Yin and Yang must be maintained in order to preserve health and well-being. While breaking new ground in technique and approach, Li Hongwei's work also hints at profound philosophical concepts that have existed for centuries in the land of his birth.

Andrew L. Maske is Associate Professor Art History & Visual Studies, Arts of Asia at the University of Kentucky. He received his doctorate in Japanese Art History from Oxford University. He teaches courses concentrating on the art of East Asia (China, Korea, and Japan). As a curator of Japanese art between 1999 and 2005, he developed the exhibition *Geisha: Beyond the Painted Smile*, and served as editor and primary author of the critically-acclaimed volume by the same name. Dr. Maske also played a major role in the Metropolitan Museum of Art's 2003 catalogue, *Turning Point: Oribe and the Arts of Sixteenth Century Japan*, which examined the revolution in Japanese aesthetics that began in the late sixteenth century. He has published articles and reviews in *Archaeometry, Journal of Japanese Studies, Orientations*, and *Transactions of the Asiatic Society of Japan*. In 2006-2007 he held a Fulbright research fellowship in China to study the development of contemporary ceramic art there.

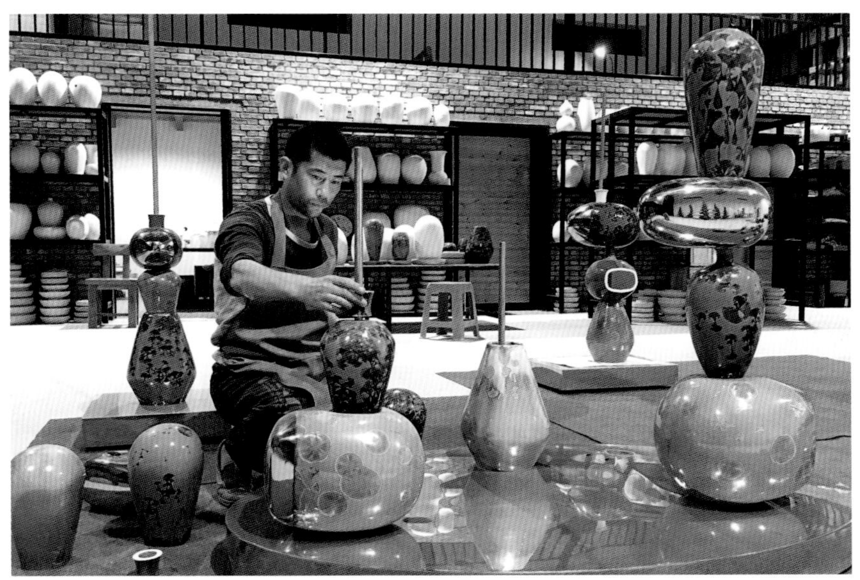

Working in the studio, Beijing, 2016

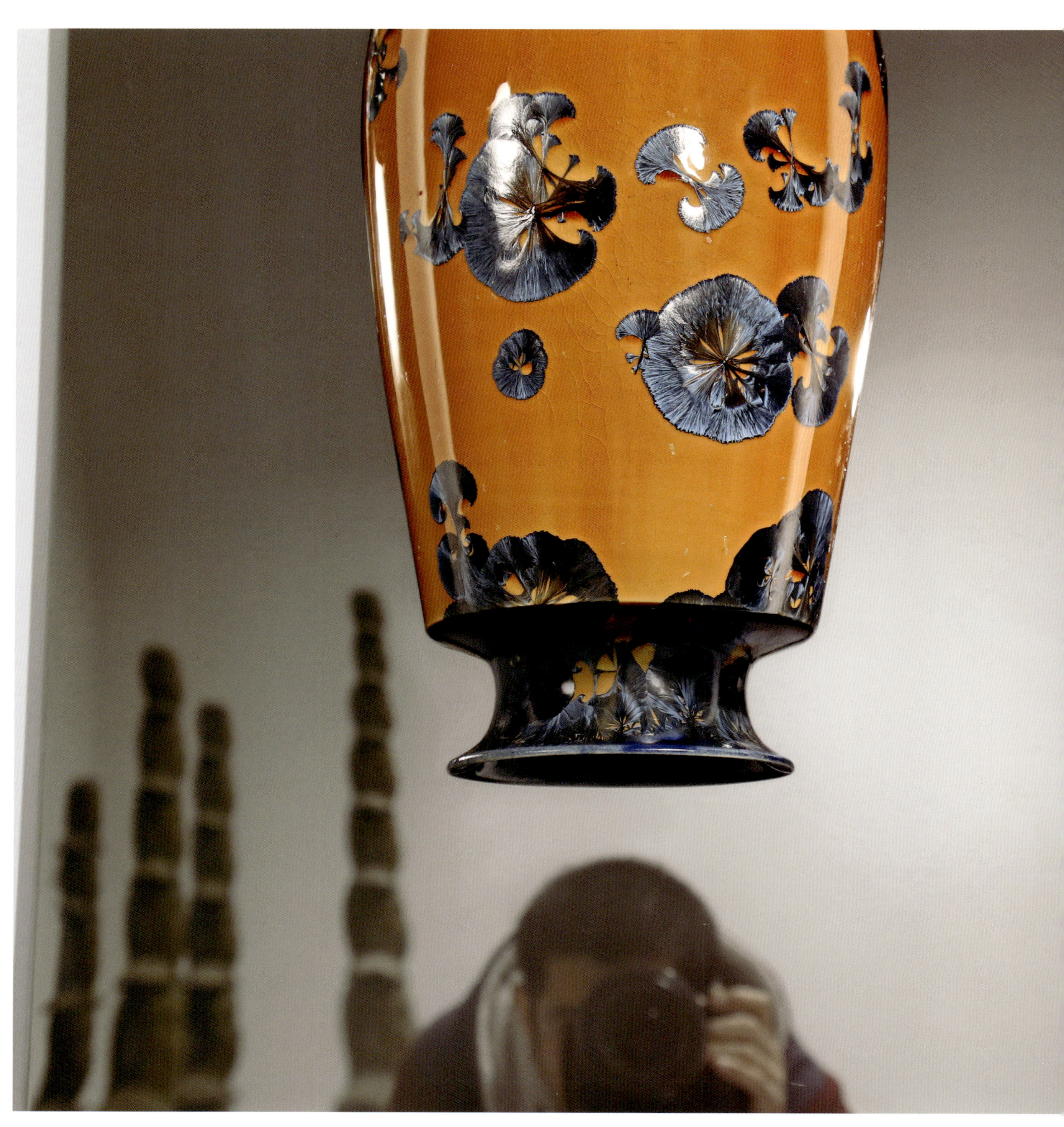

Illusion #4 (detail 2), 2017. Fired porcelain, stainless steel. 25.6×17.7×9 inches. Collection of the artist

ILLUSION

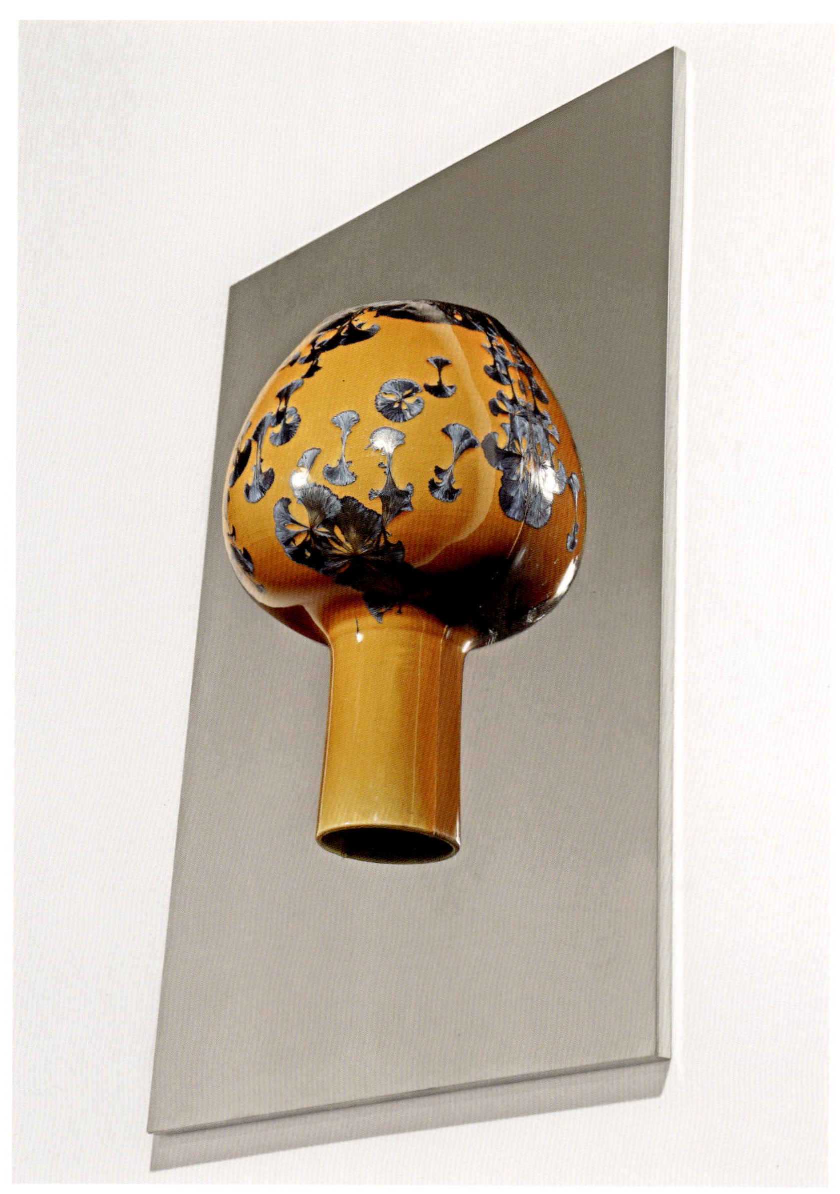

Illusion #3, 2017. Fired porcelain, stainless steel. 25.6×17.7×9.6 inches. Collection of the artist

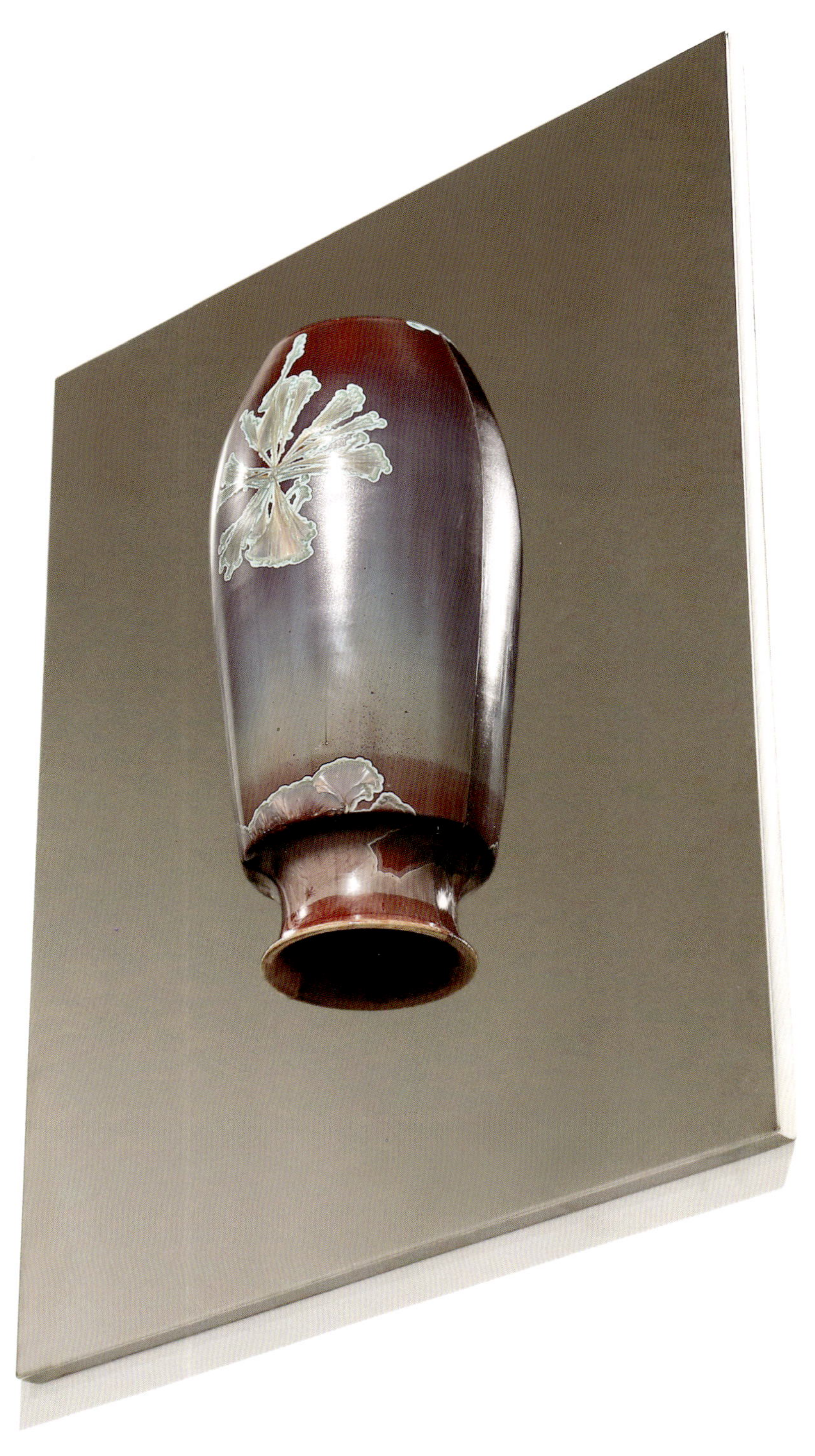

Illusion #6, 2018. Fired porcelain, stainless steel. 19.7×15.7×5.5 inches. Private collection

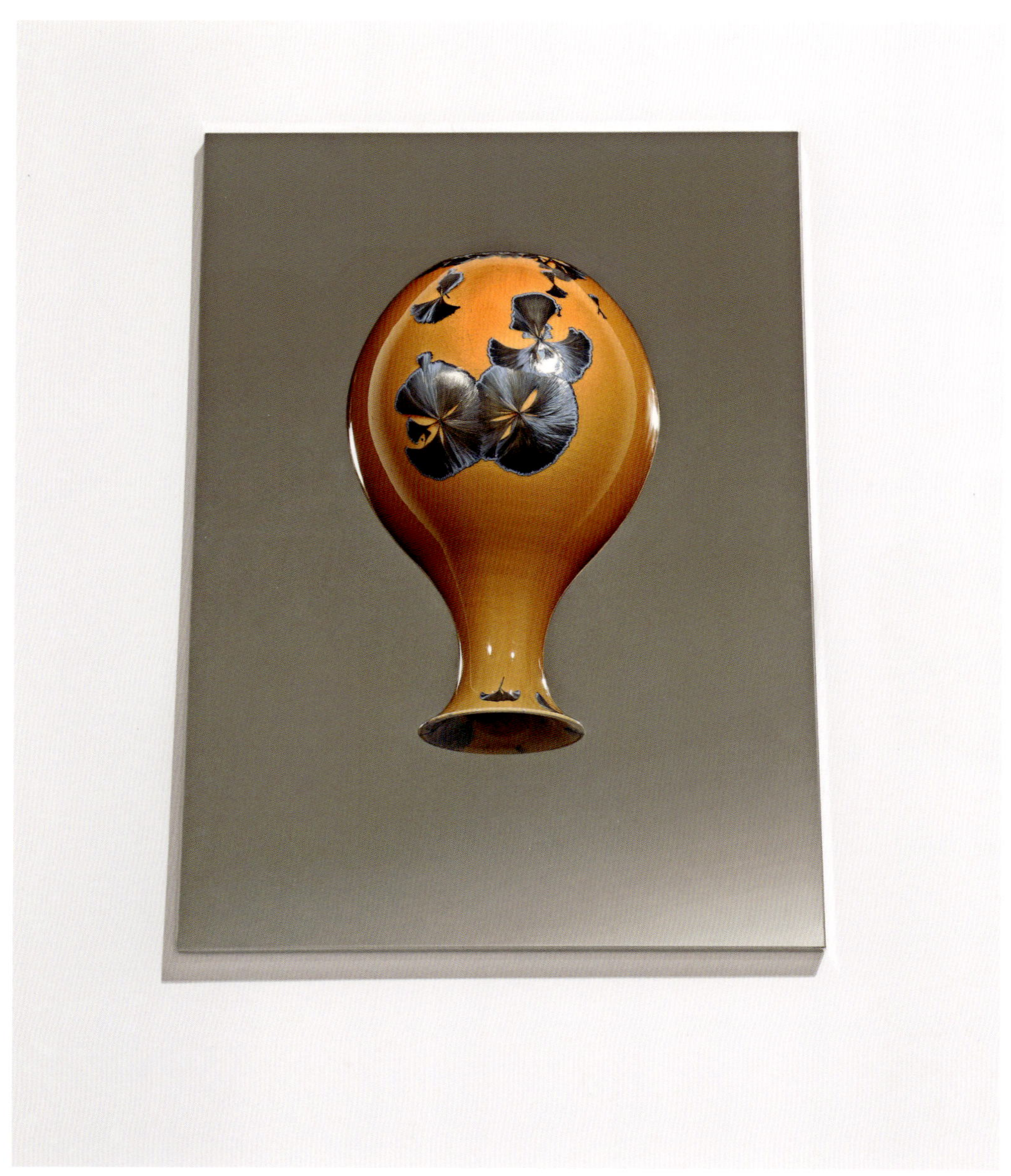

Illusion #2, 2017. Fired porcelain, stainless steel. 25.6×17.7×9 inches. Collection of the artist

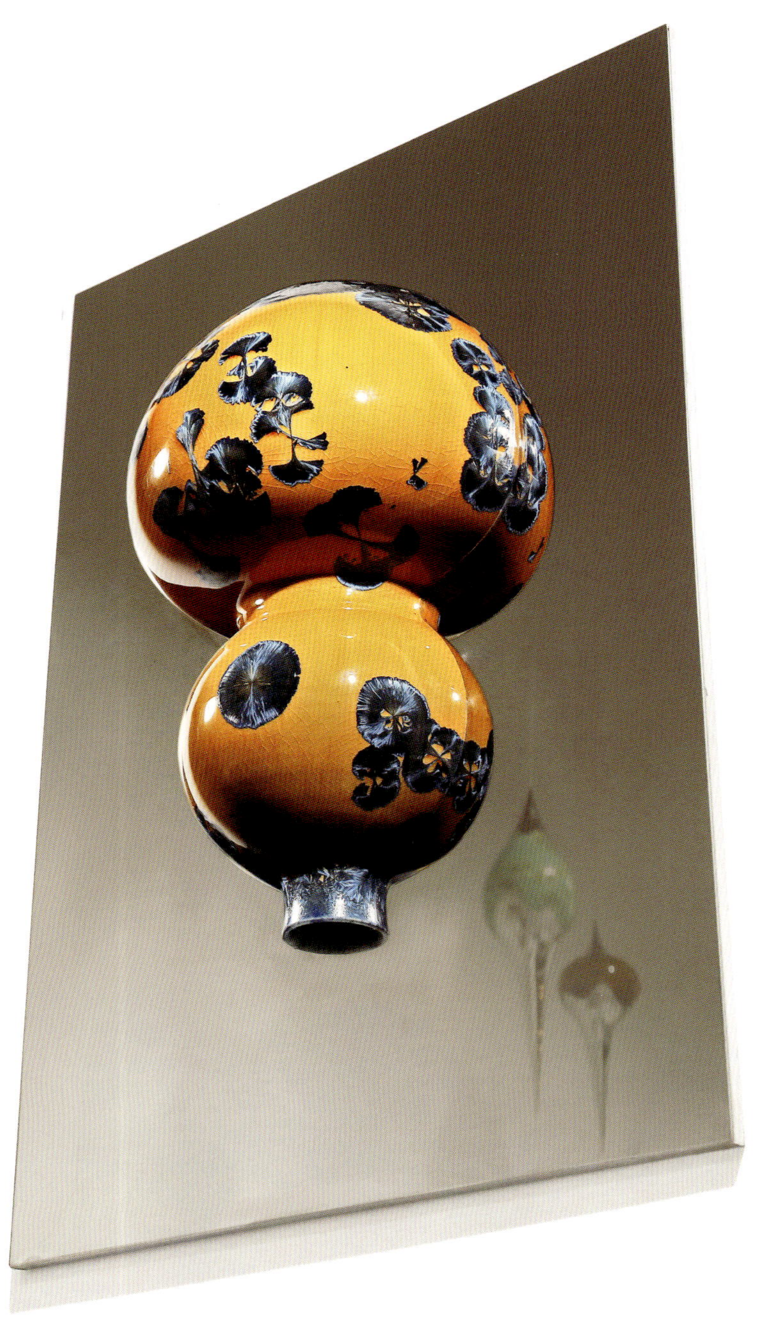

Illusion #7, 2018. Fired porcelain, stainless steel. 25.6×17.7×9.8 inches. Collection of the artist

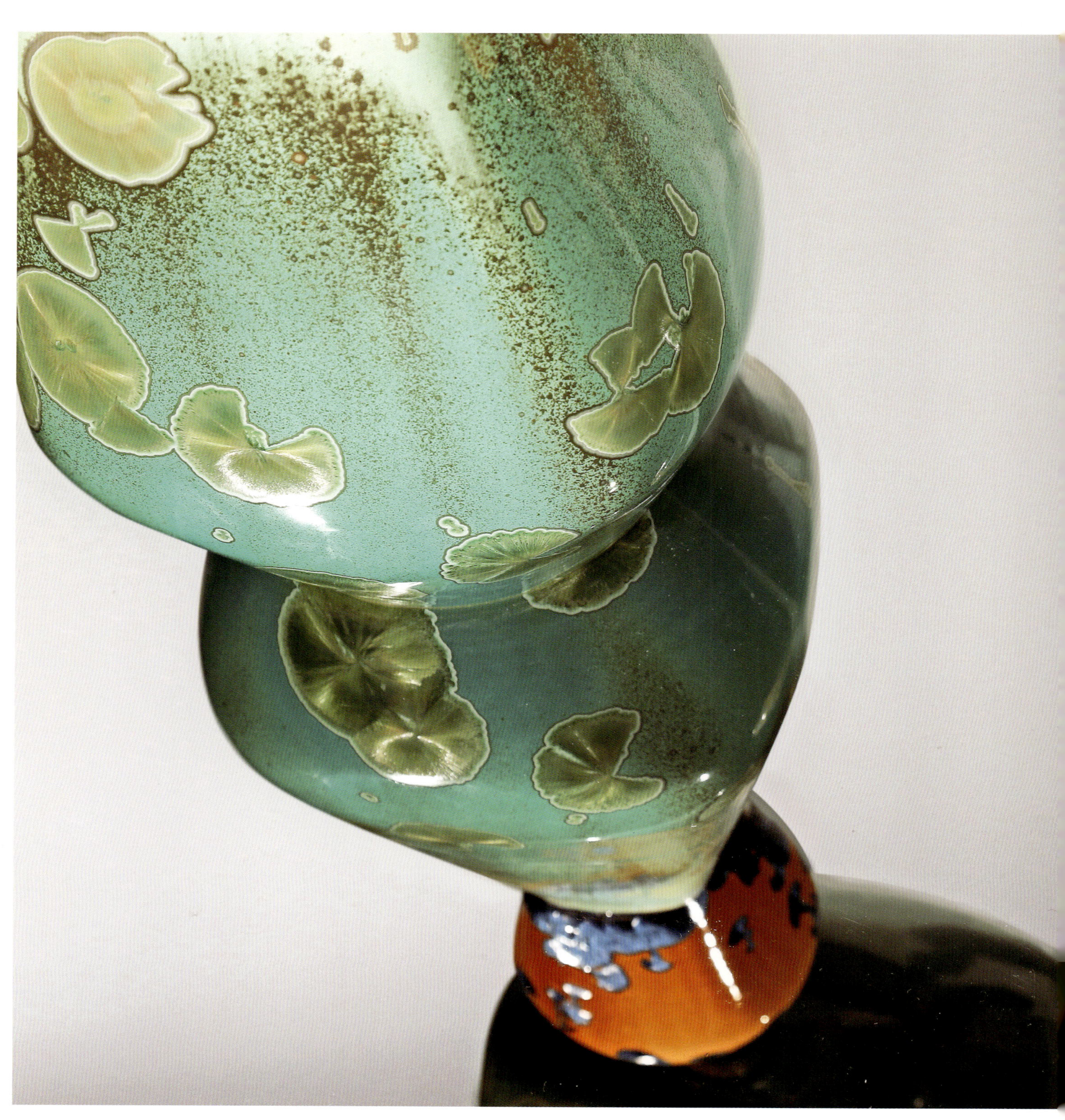

Allegory of Balance #18 (detail), 2017. Fired porcelain, stainless steel. 28×22×62 inches. Collection of the artist

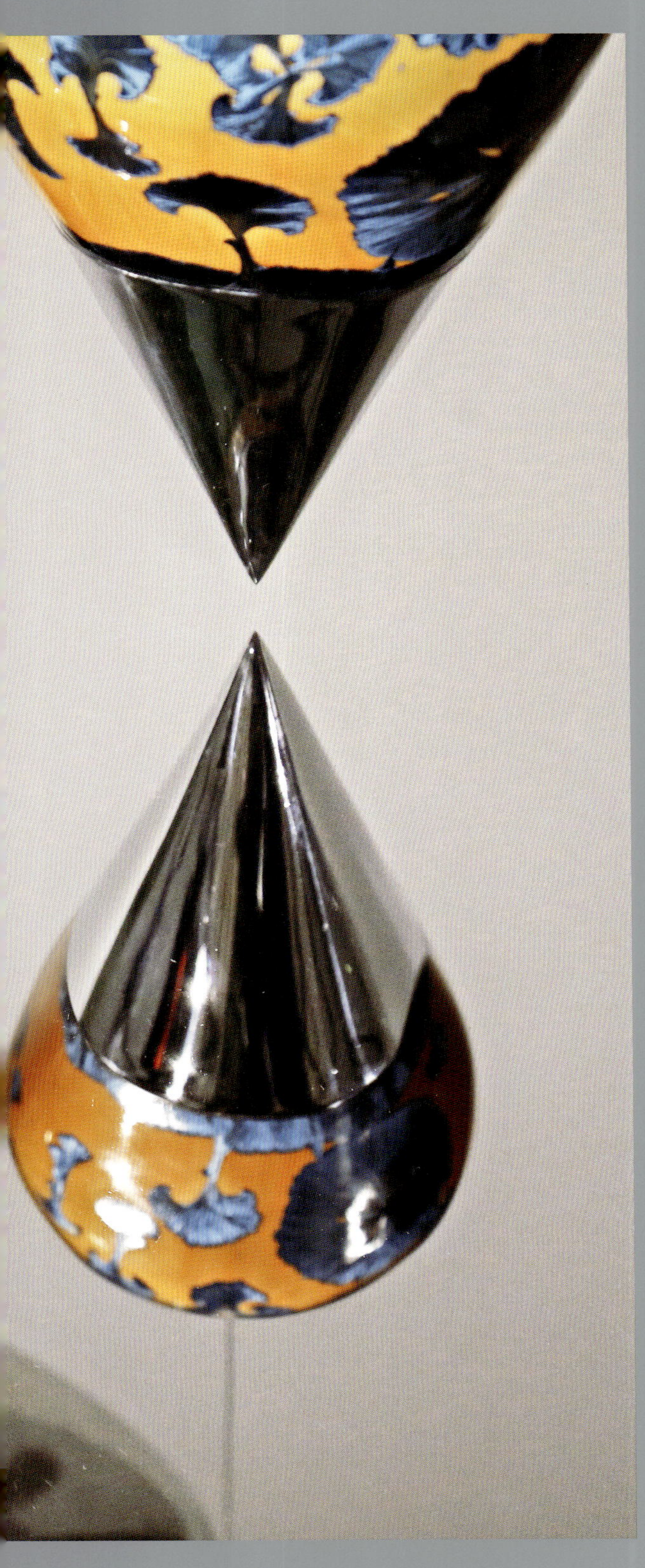

ALLEGORY OF BALANCE

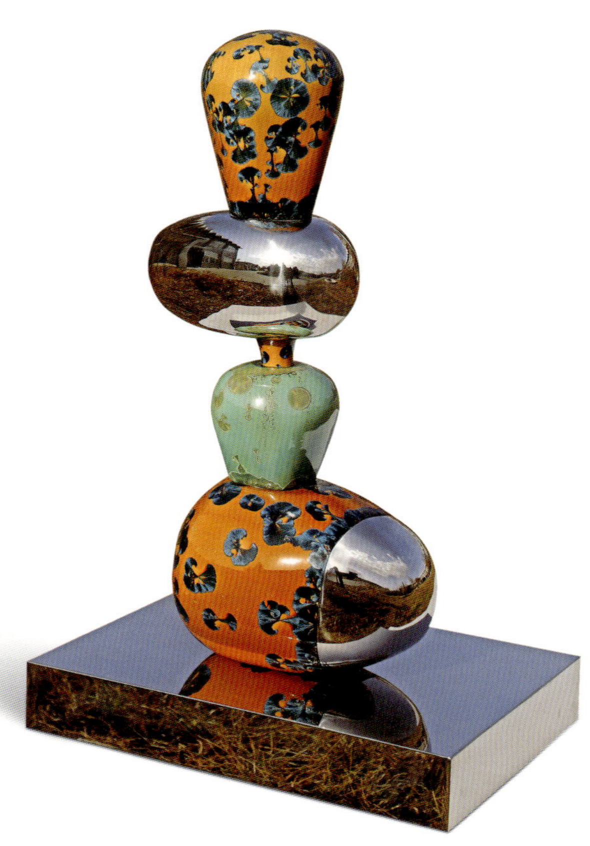

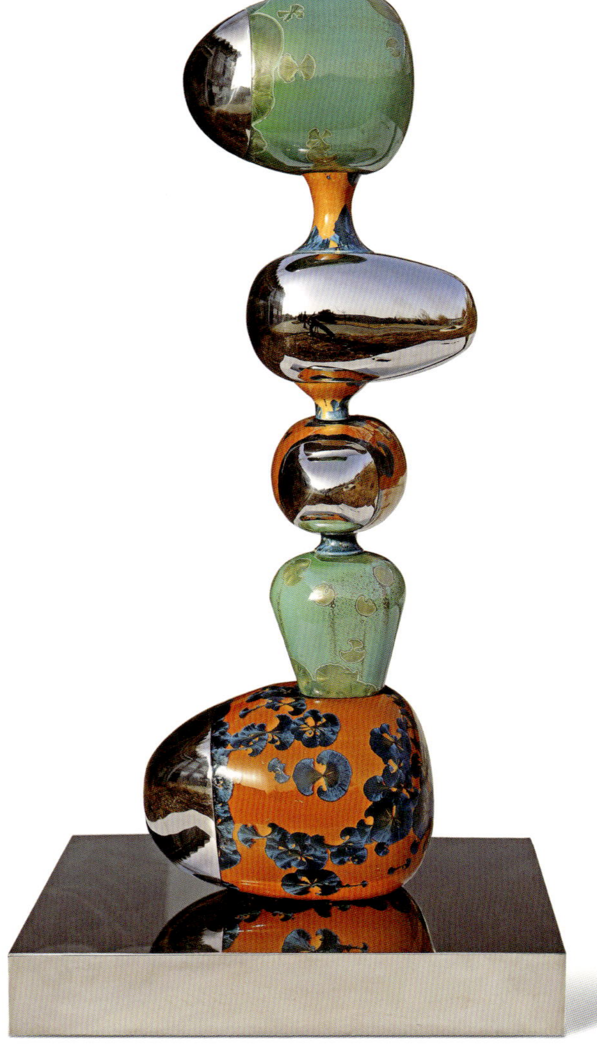

Allegory of Balance #2, 2014. Fired porcelain, stainless steel. 26×18×43 inches. Collection of the artist

Allegory of Balance #3, 2015. Fired porcelain, stainless steel. 26×18×57 inches. Collection: Zhu Zhong Art Museum, Beijing, China

Allegory of Balance #18, 2017. Fired porcelain, stainless steel. 28×22×62 inches. Collection of the artist

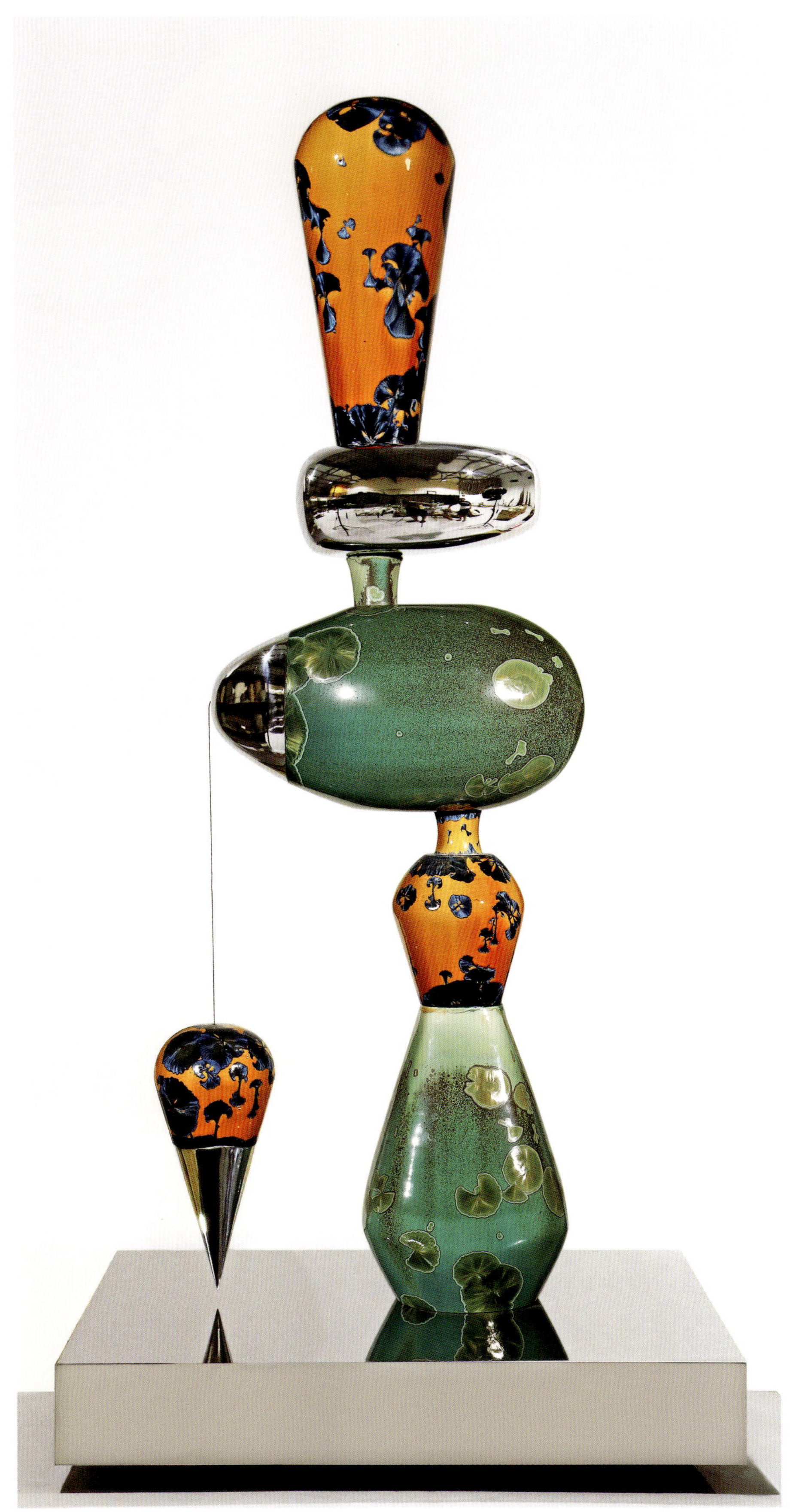

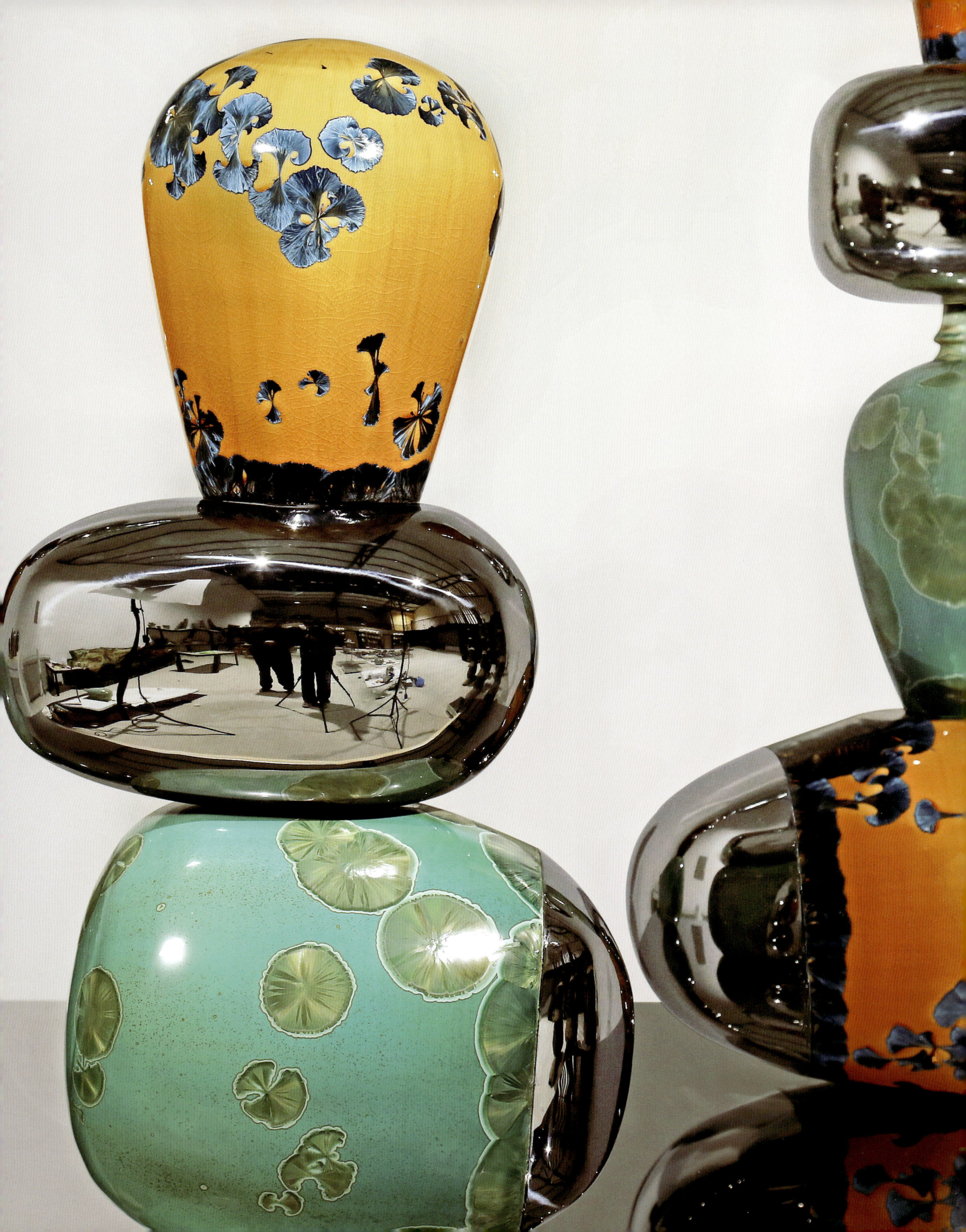

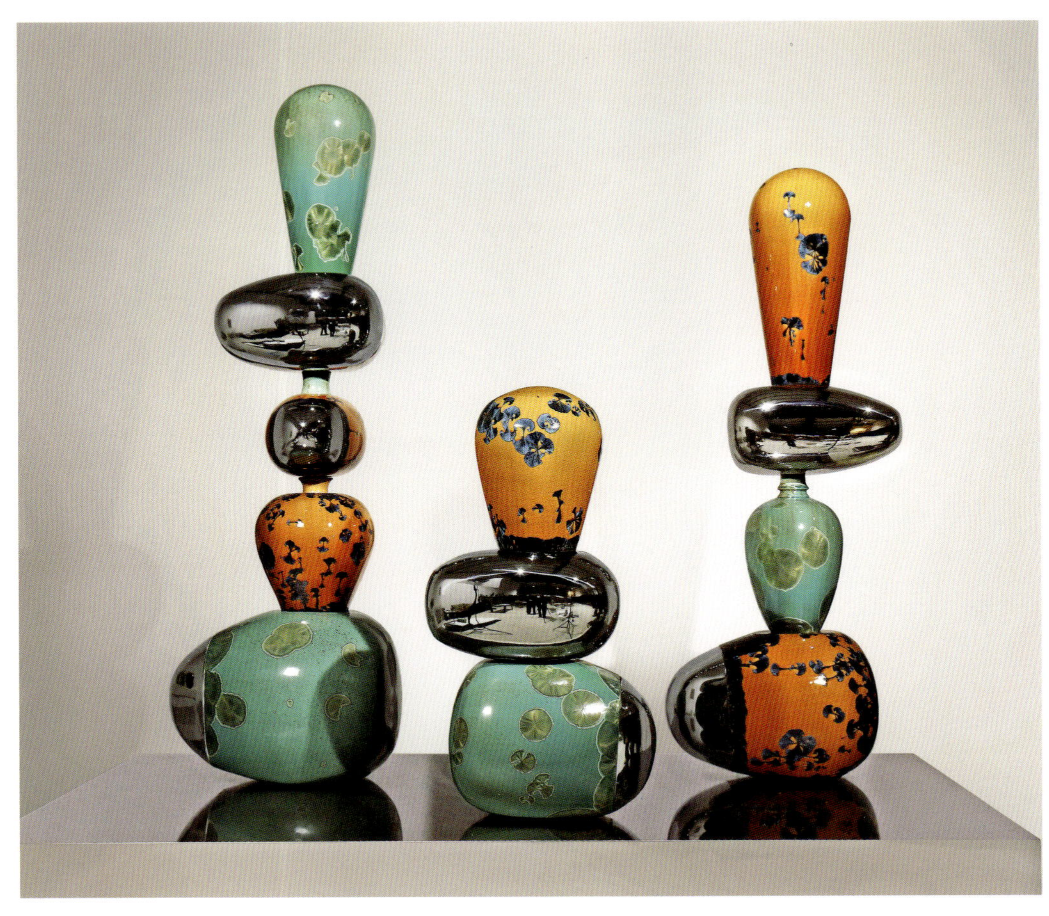

Allegory of Balance #6, 2016. Fired porcelain, stainless steel. 59×35.5×57 inches. Collection: Art Institute of Chicago, Chicago, IL
On view in The Art Institute of Chicago from March 2019 to March 2021
Allegory of Balance #6 (detail), 2016. Fired porcelain, stainless steel. 59×35.5×57 inches. Collection: Art Institute of Chicago, IL

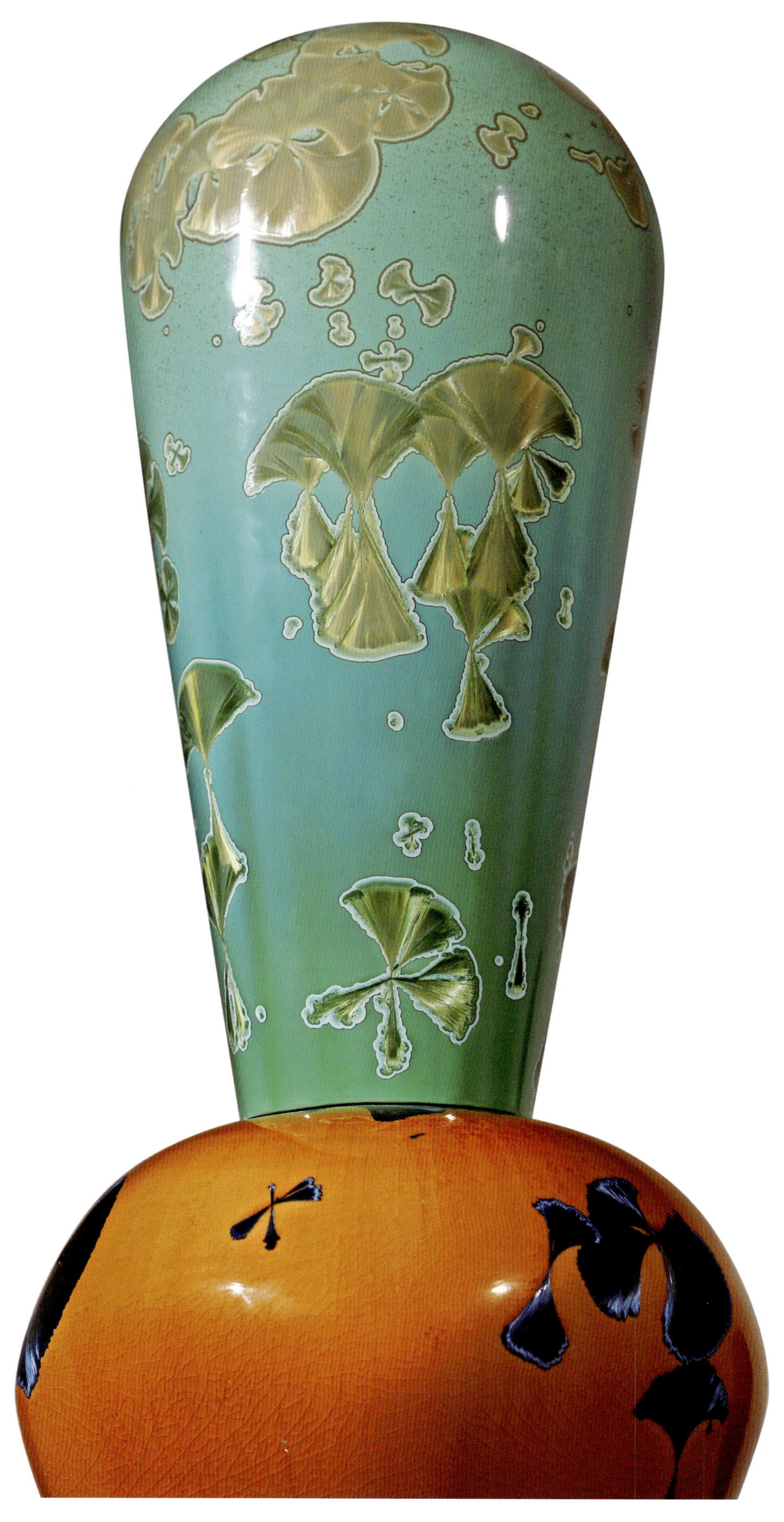

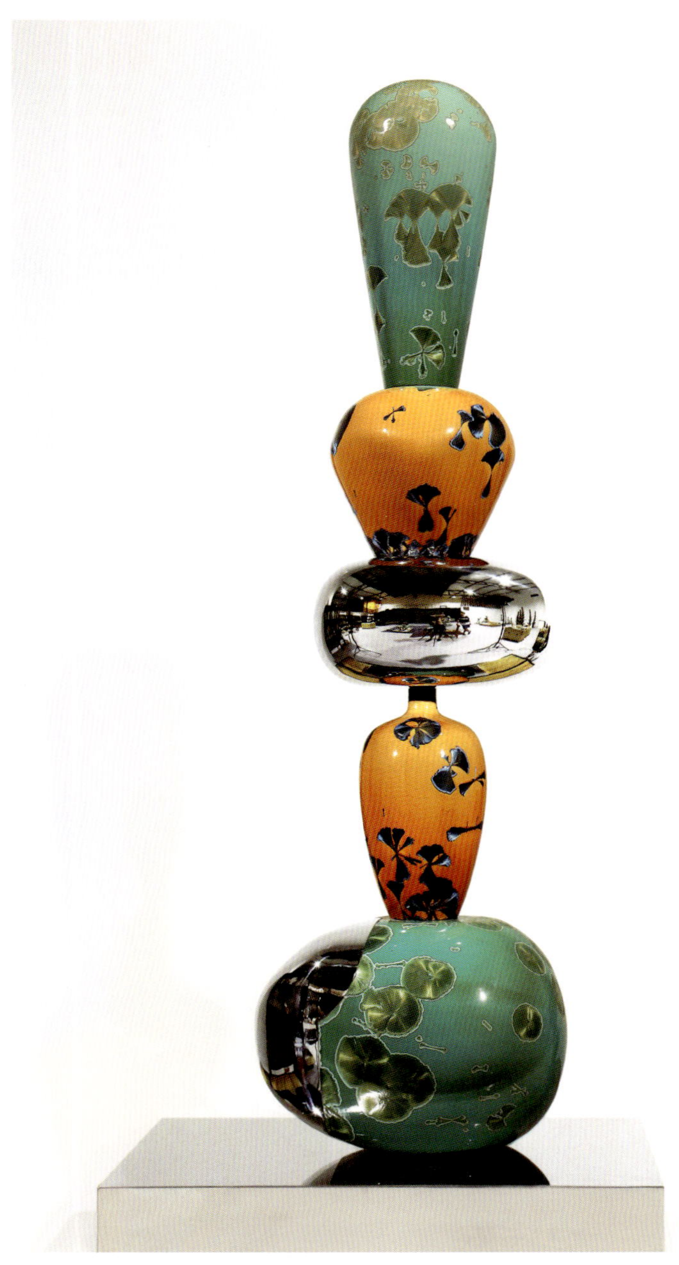

Allegory of Balance #16, 2017. Fired porcelain, stainless steel. 26×18×62 inches. Collection of the artist

Allegory of Balance #16 (detail), 2017. Fired porcelain, stainless steel. 26×18×62 inches. Collection of the artist

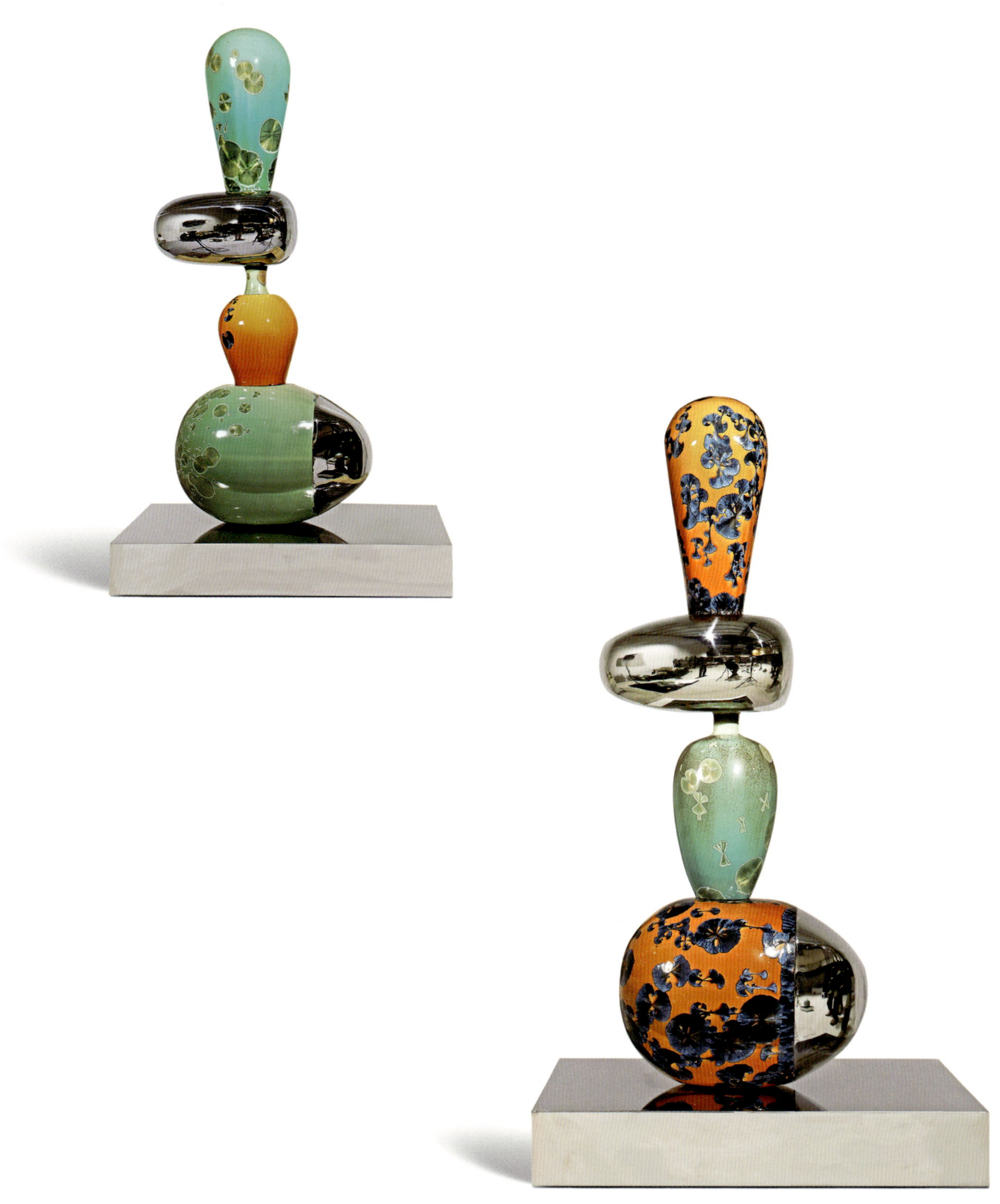

Allegory of Balance #4, 2016. Fired porcelain, stainless steel 26×18×51 inches. Collection of the artist

Allegory of Balance #9, 2016. Fired porcelain, stainless steel. 26×18×47 inches. Collection: Media Group, Guangzhou, China

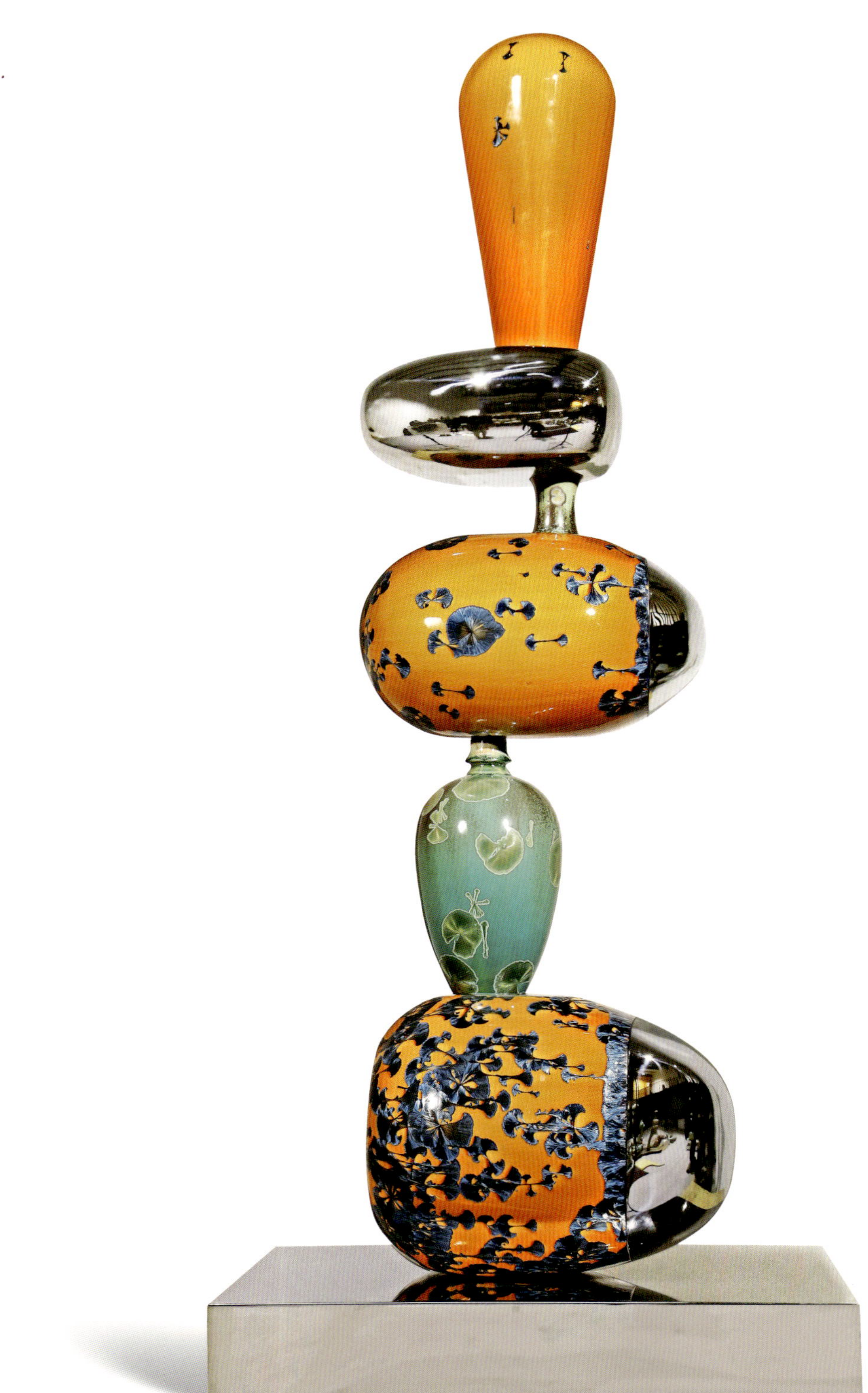

Allegory of Balance #10, 2015. Fired porcelain, stainless steel. 26×18×62 inches. Collection of the artist

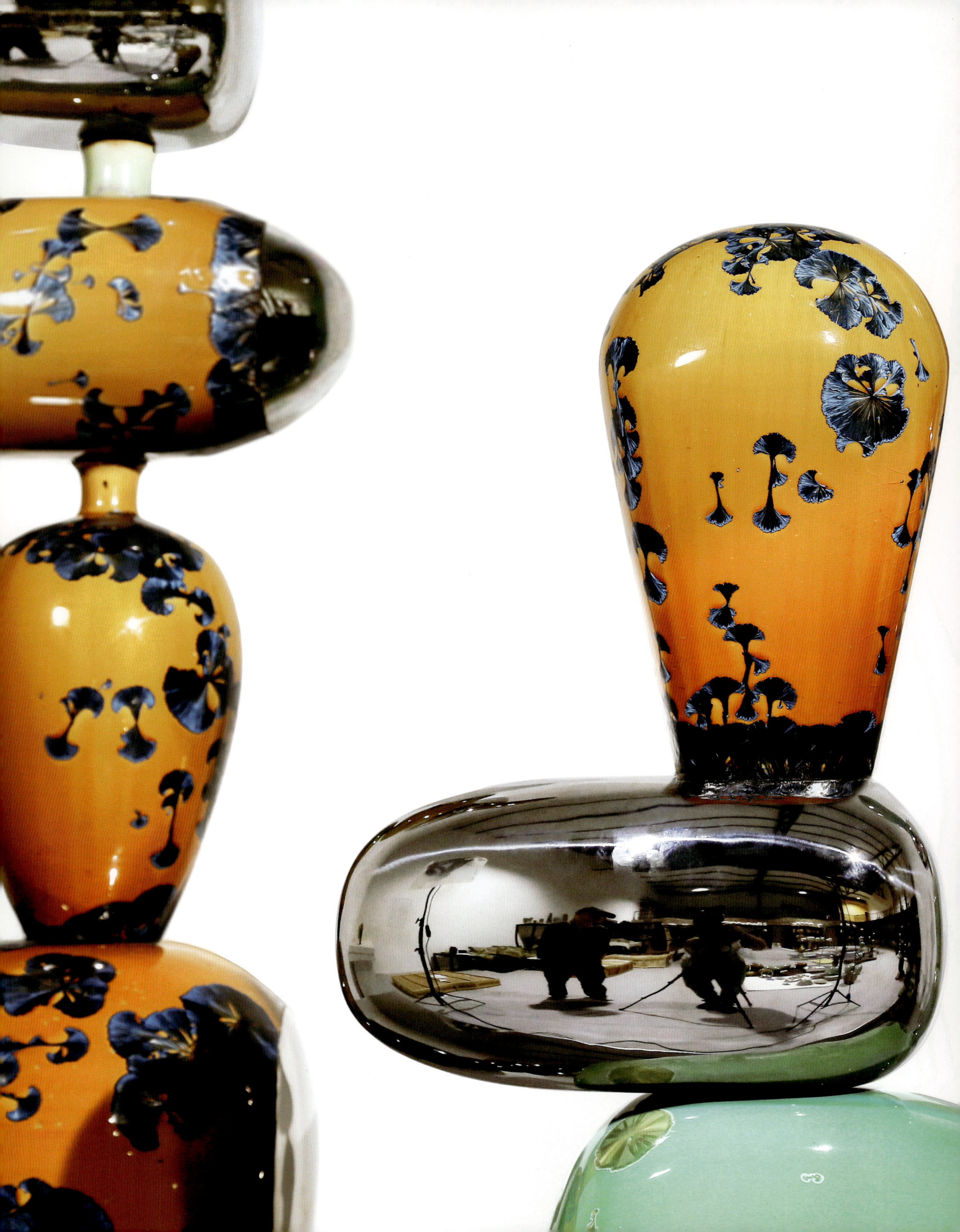

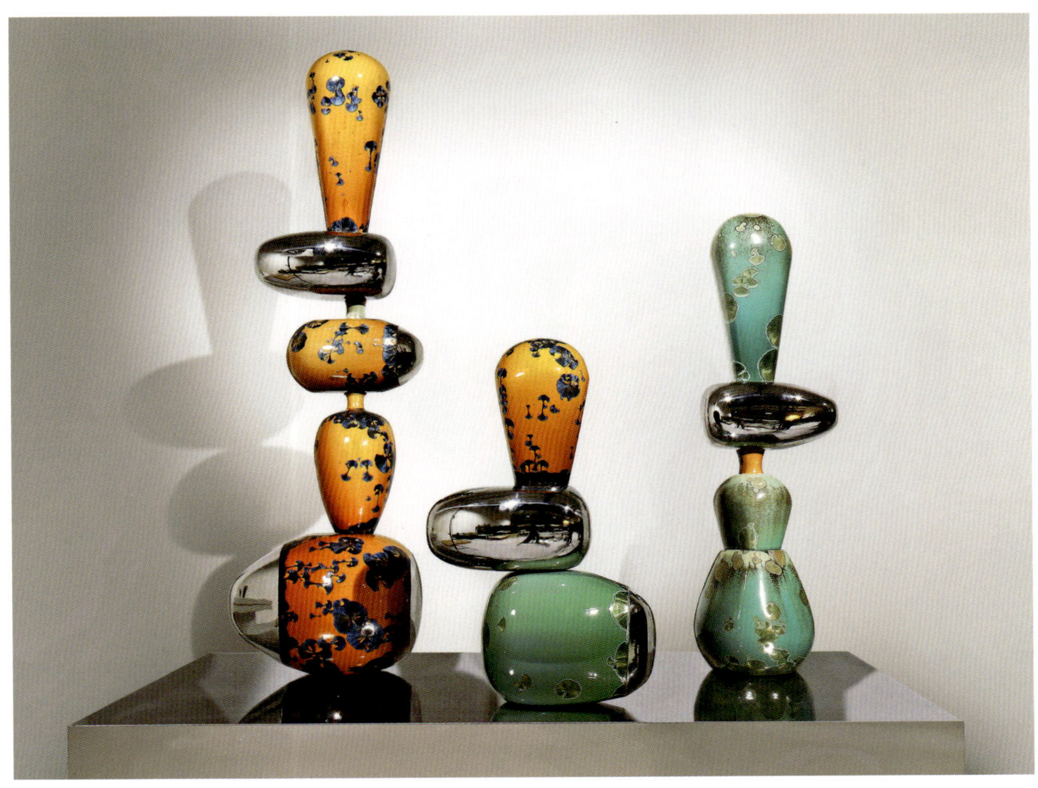

Allegory of Balance #12, 2016. Fired porcelain, stainless steel. 59×35.5×58 inches. Collection of the artist
Allegory of Balance #12 (detail), 2016. Fired porcelain, stainless steel. 59×35.5×58 inches. Collection of the artist

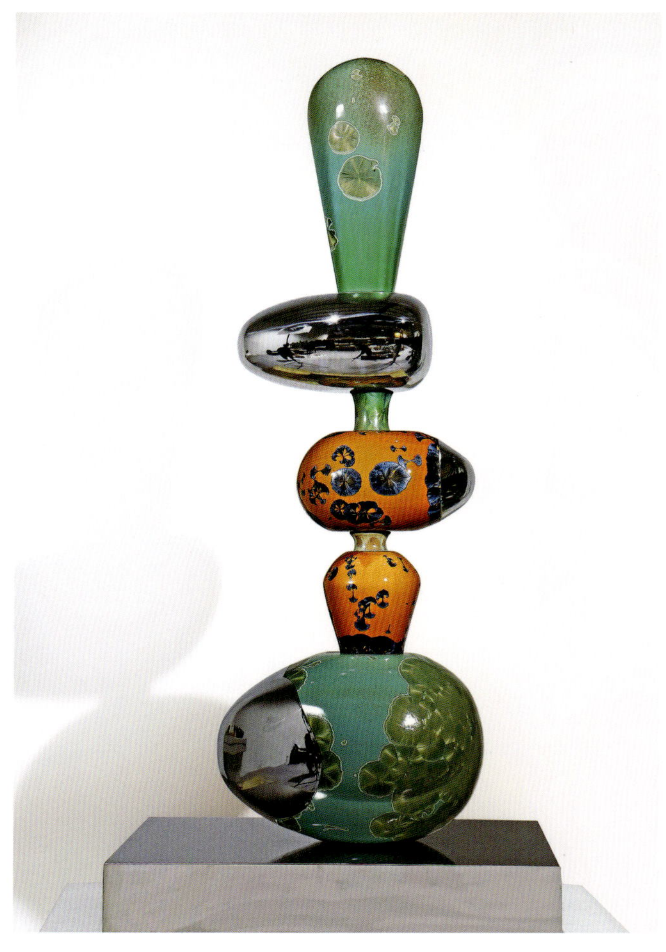

Allegory of Balance #5, 2016. Fired porcelain, stainless steel. 26×18×55 inches. Private collection

Allegory of Balance #20, 2017. Fired porcelain, stainless steel. 26×18×65 inches. Collection of the artist

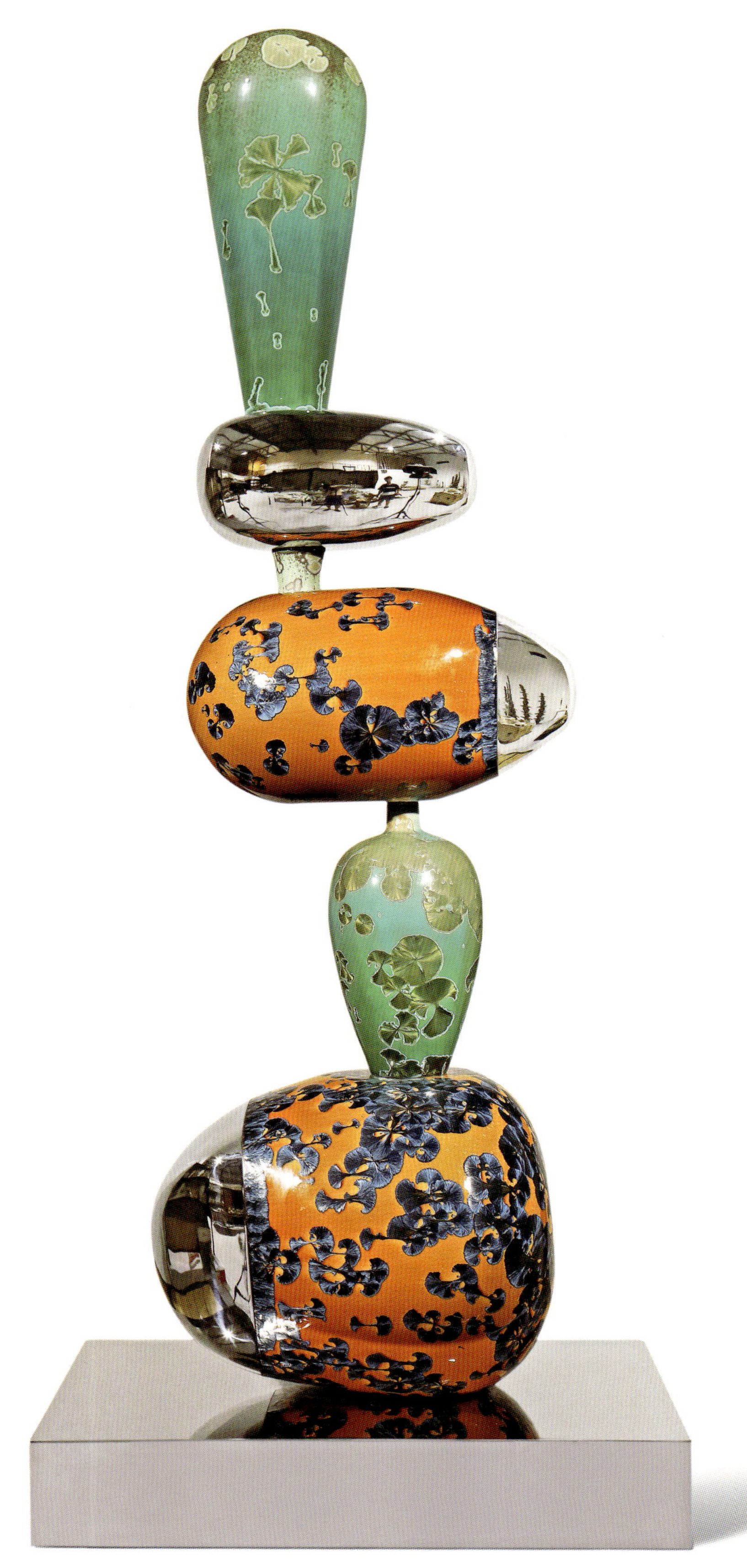

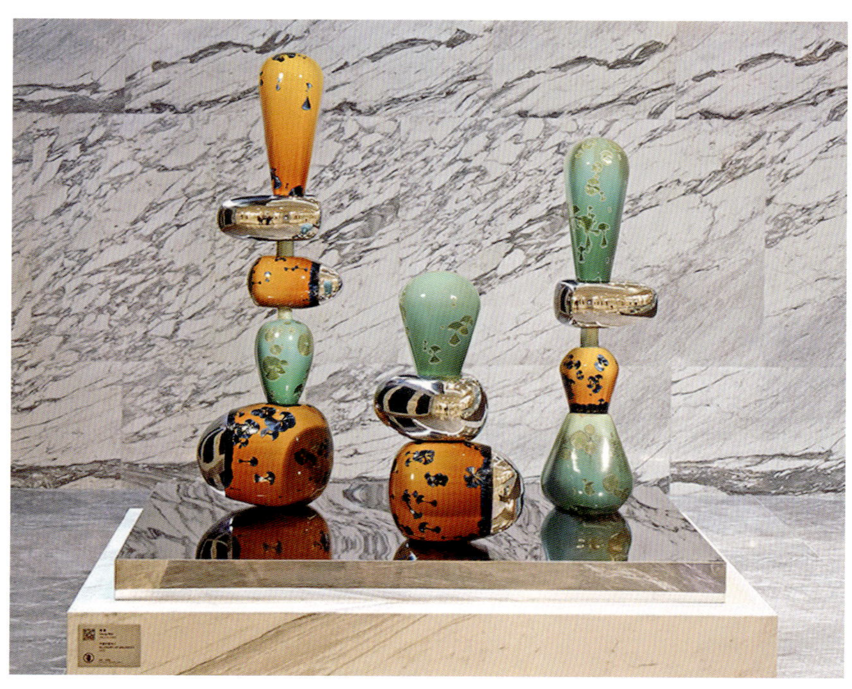

Allegory of Balance #15, 2017. Fired porcelain, stainless steel. 59×35.5×58 inches. Collection: MGM, Macao

Allegory of Balance #17, 2016. Fired porcelain, stainless steel. 26×18×50 inches. Collection of the artist

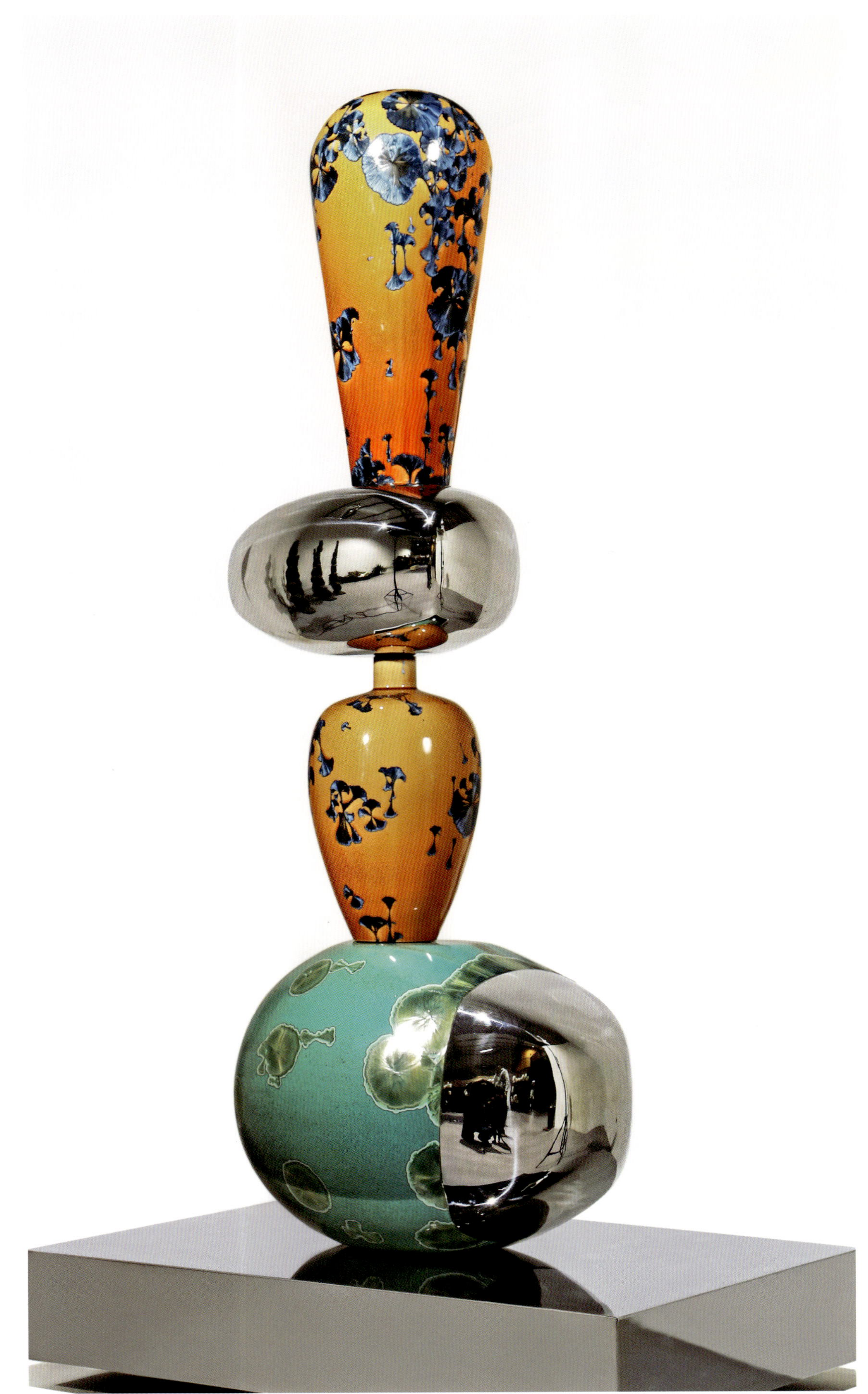

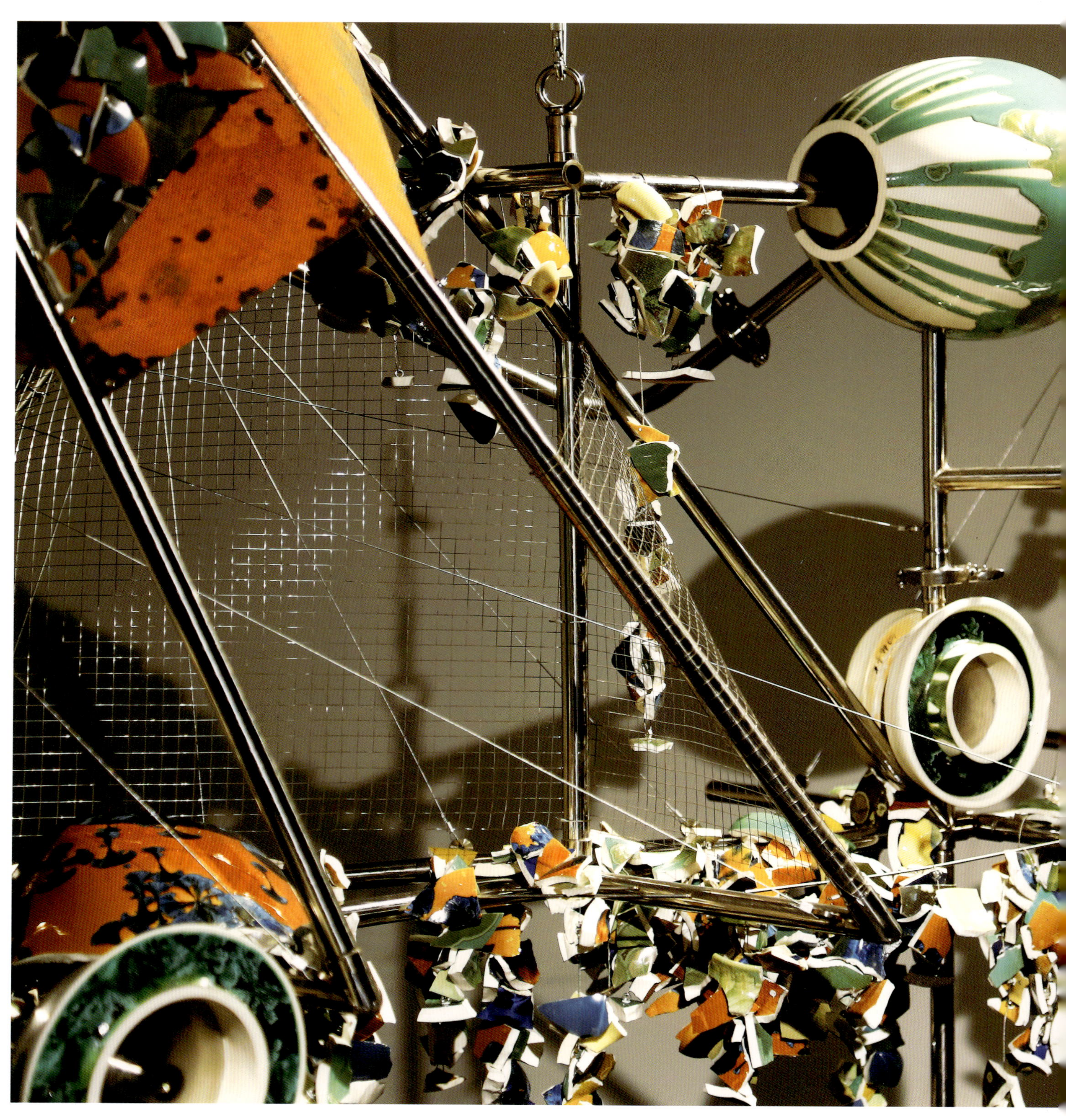

Rebirth in Breakage (detail 1), 2015. Fired porcelain, stainless steel, iron. 108×34×79 inches. Collection of the artist

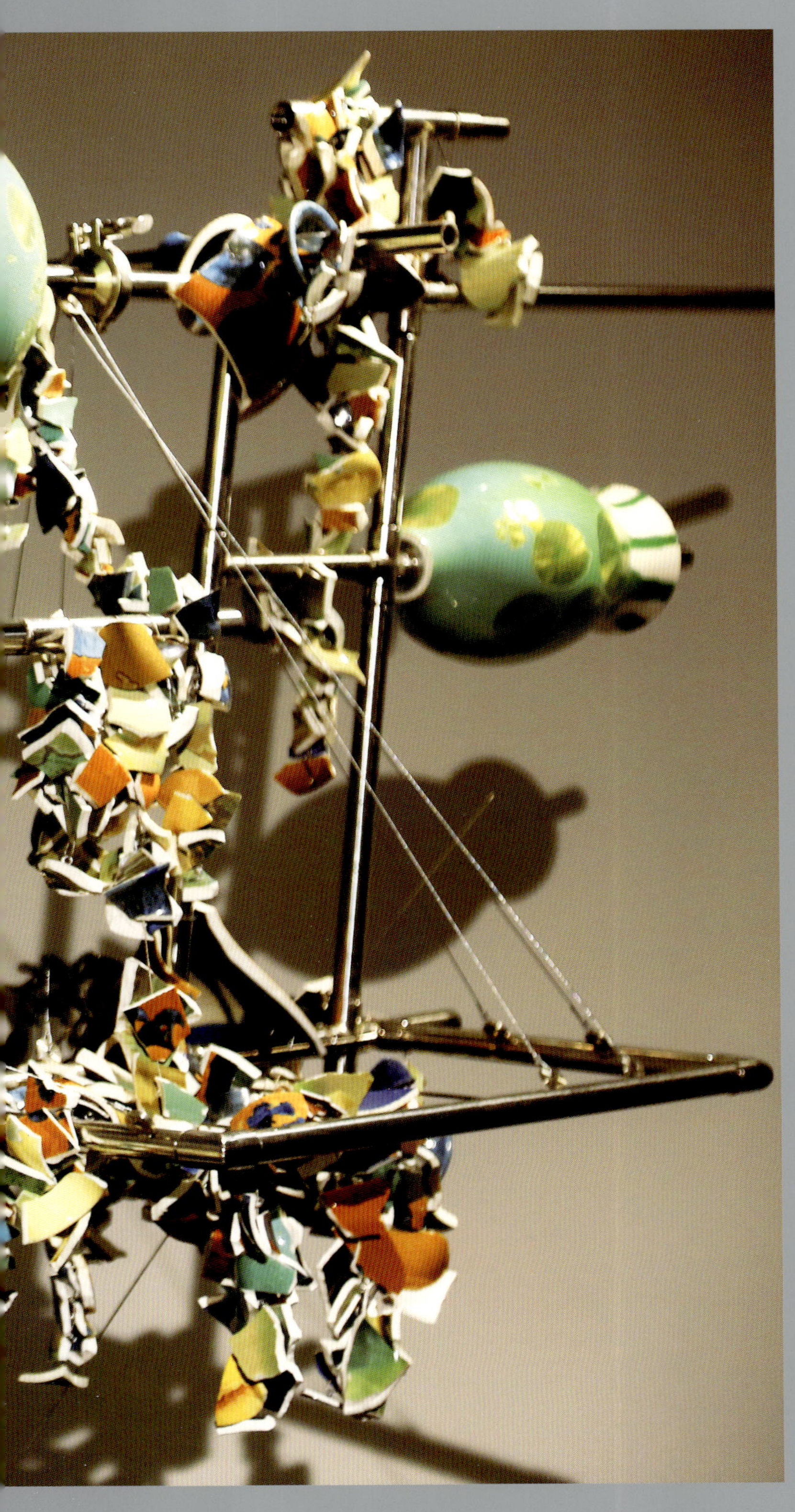

REBIRTH IN BREAKAGE

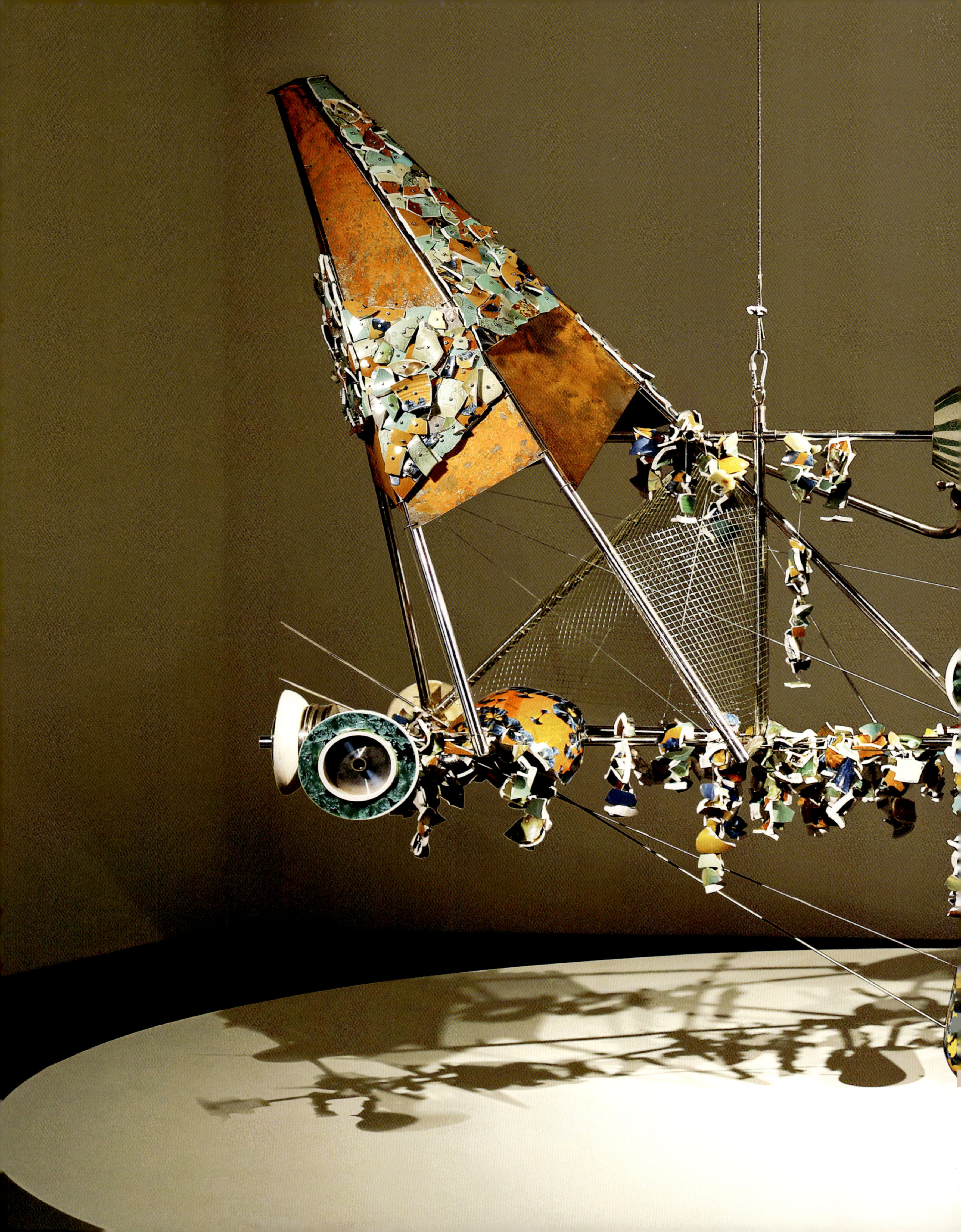

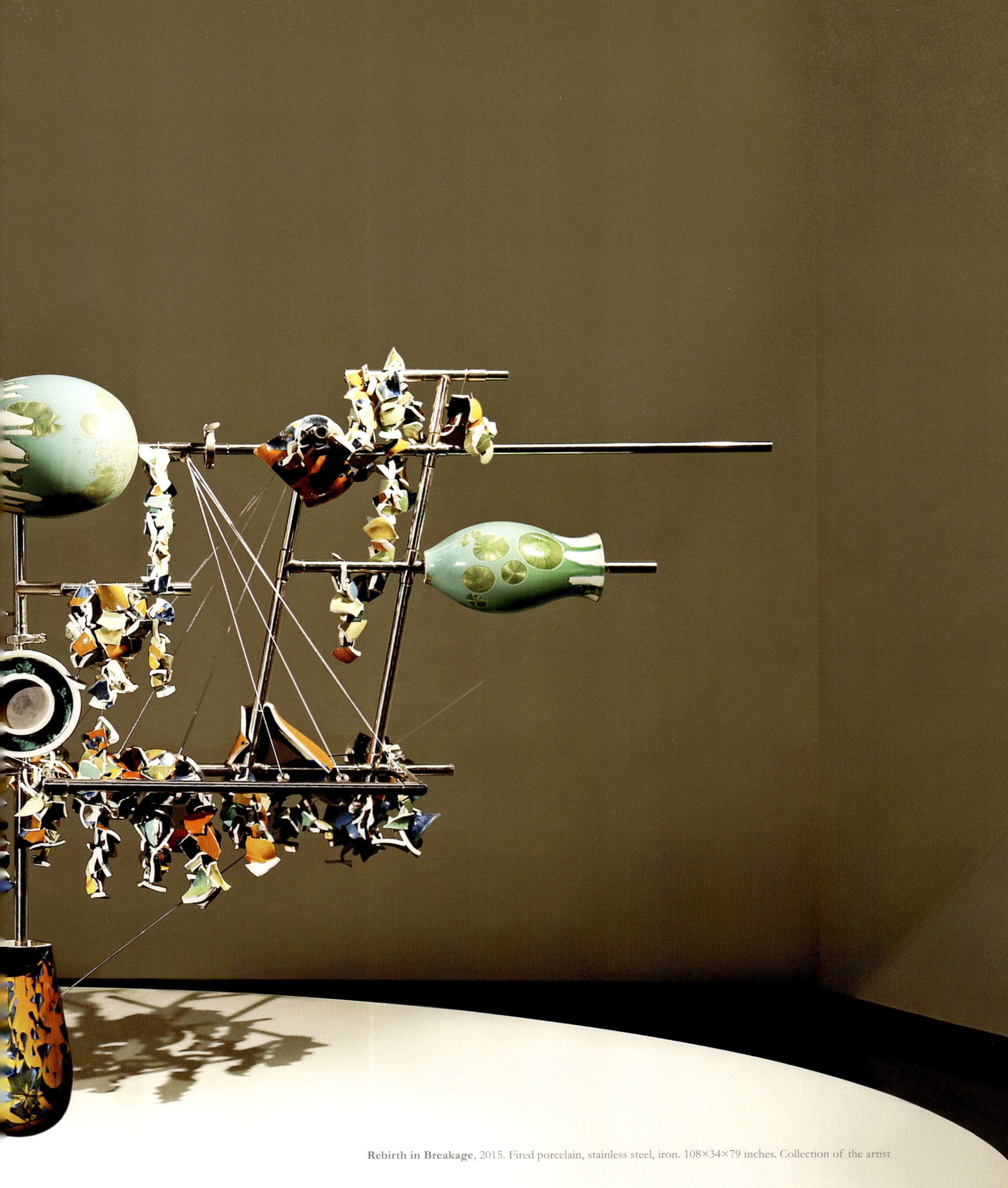

Rebirth in Breakage, 2015. Fired porcelain, stainless steel, iron. 108×34×79 inches. Collection of the artist

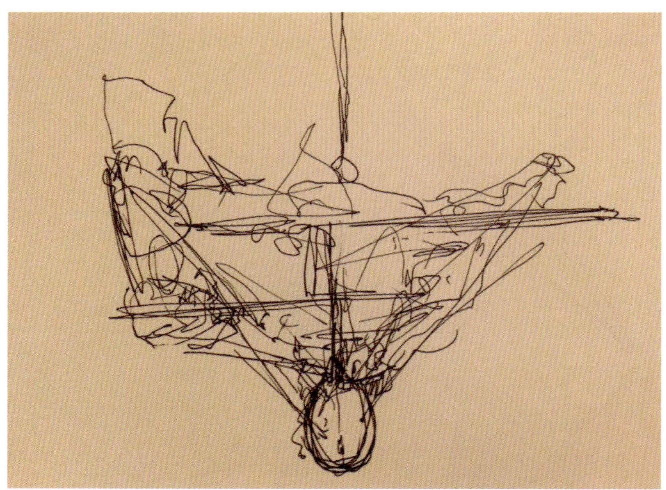

Drawing Study of Rebirth in Breakage, 2015. Ink on paper. 5×6.5 inches.
Collection of the artist

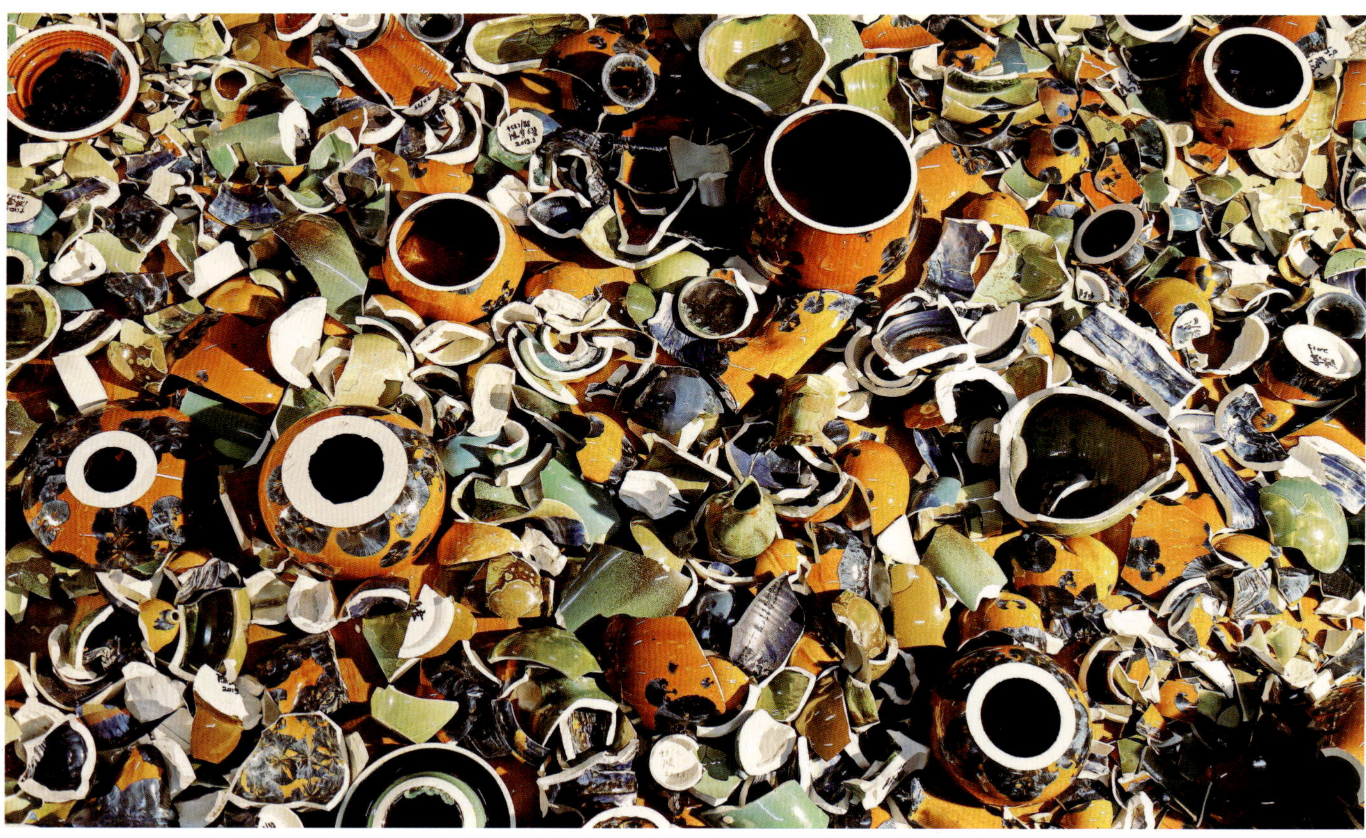

Working Process of Rebirth in Breakage, 2015. Fired porcelain

Rebirth in Breakage (detail 2), 2015. Fired porcelain, stainless steel, iron. 108×34×79 inches. Collection of the artist

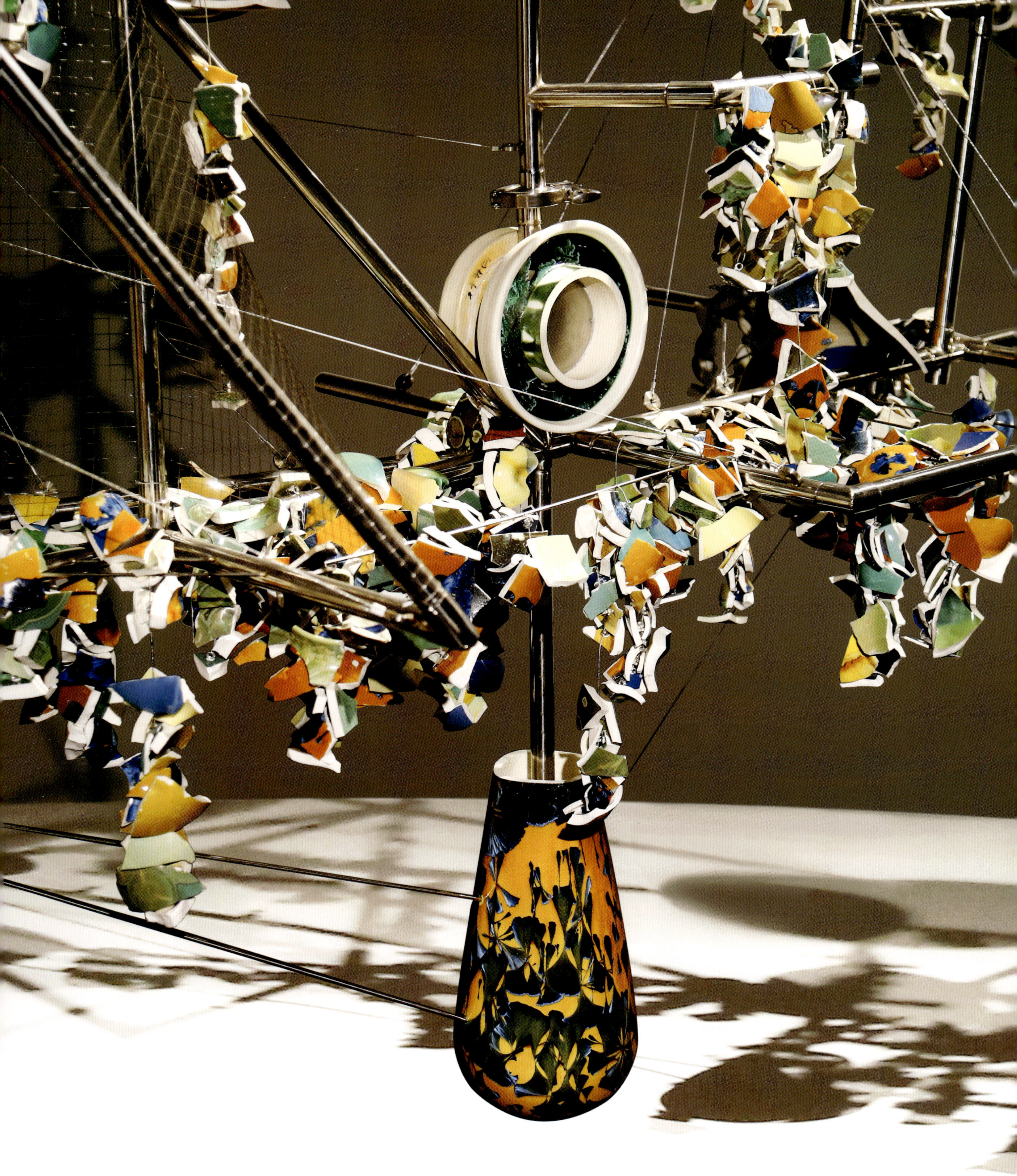

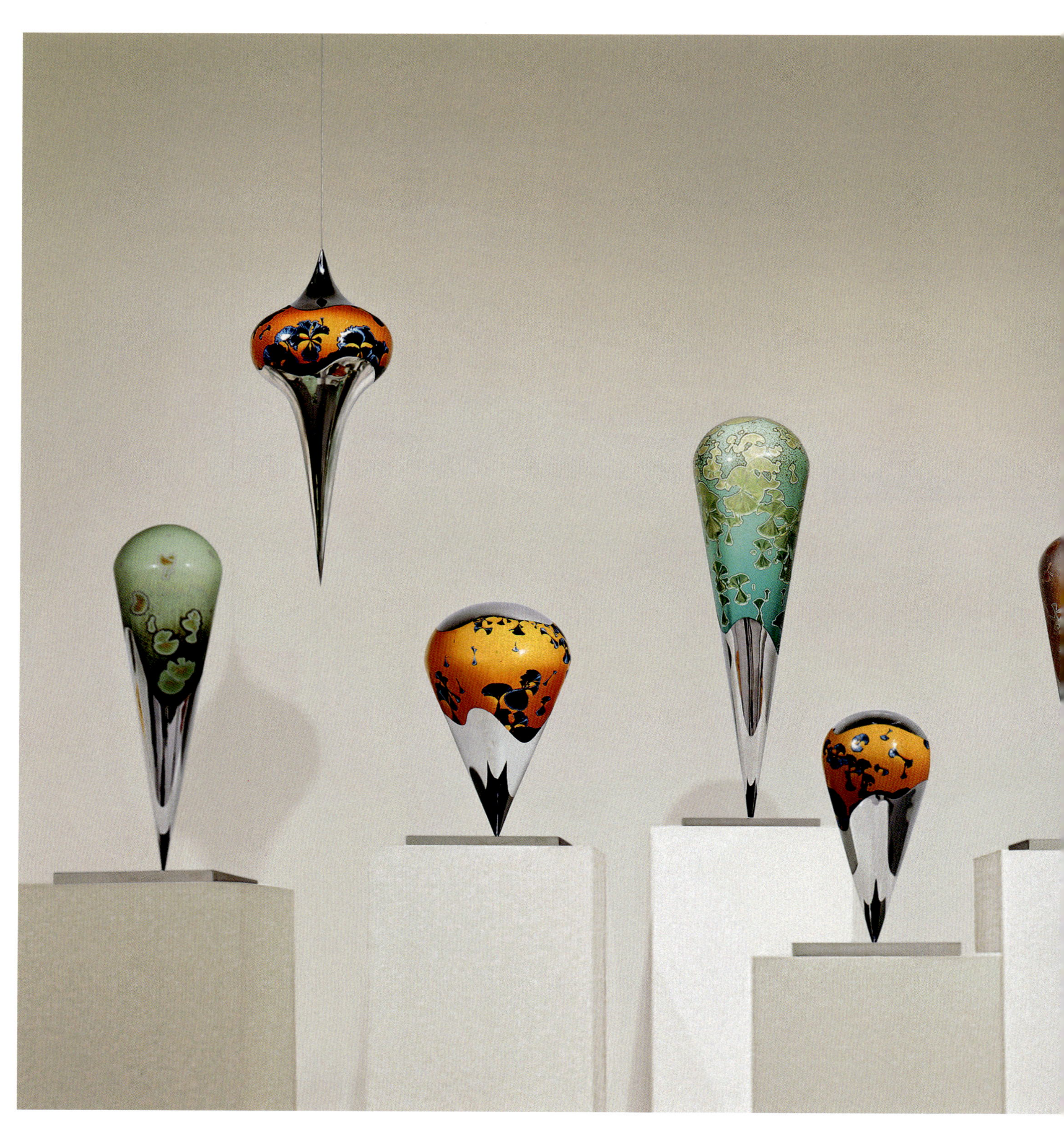

Untitled #1, 2018. Porcelain, stainless steel. Dimensions variable. Private collection

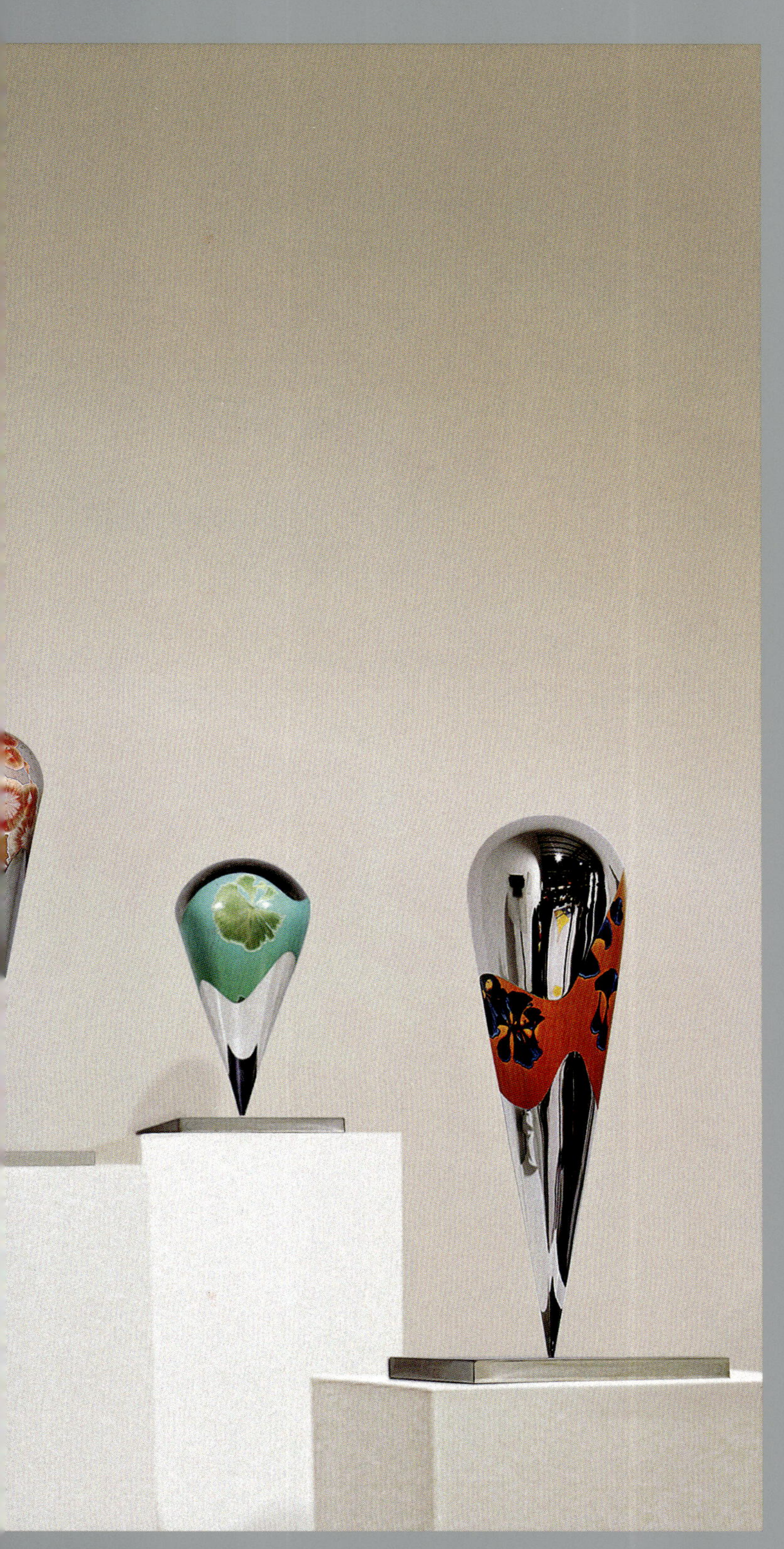

UPWELLING OF GRAVITY

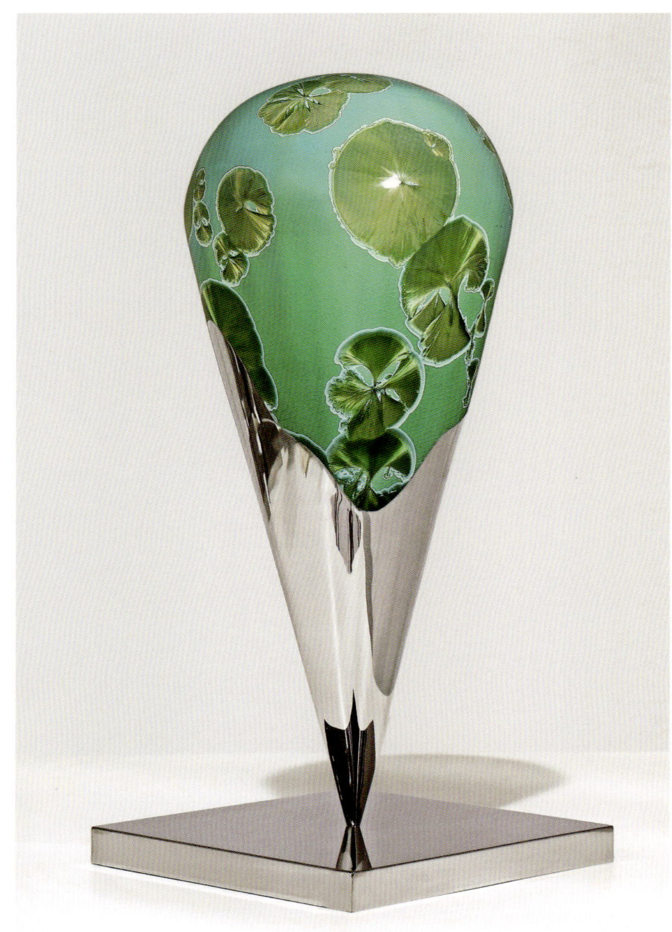

Upwelling of Gravity #21, 2018. Fired porcelain, stainless steel. 11.8×11.8×26 inches. Collection of the artist

Upwelling of Gravity #9, 2017. Fired porcelain, stainless steel. 9.75×9.75×21 inches. Collection: Philadelphia Museum of Art, Philadelphia, PA

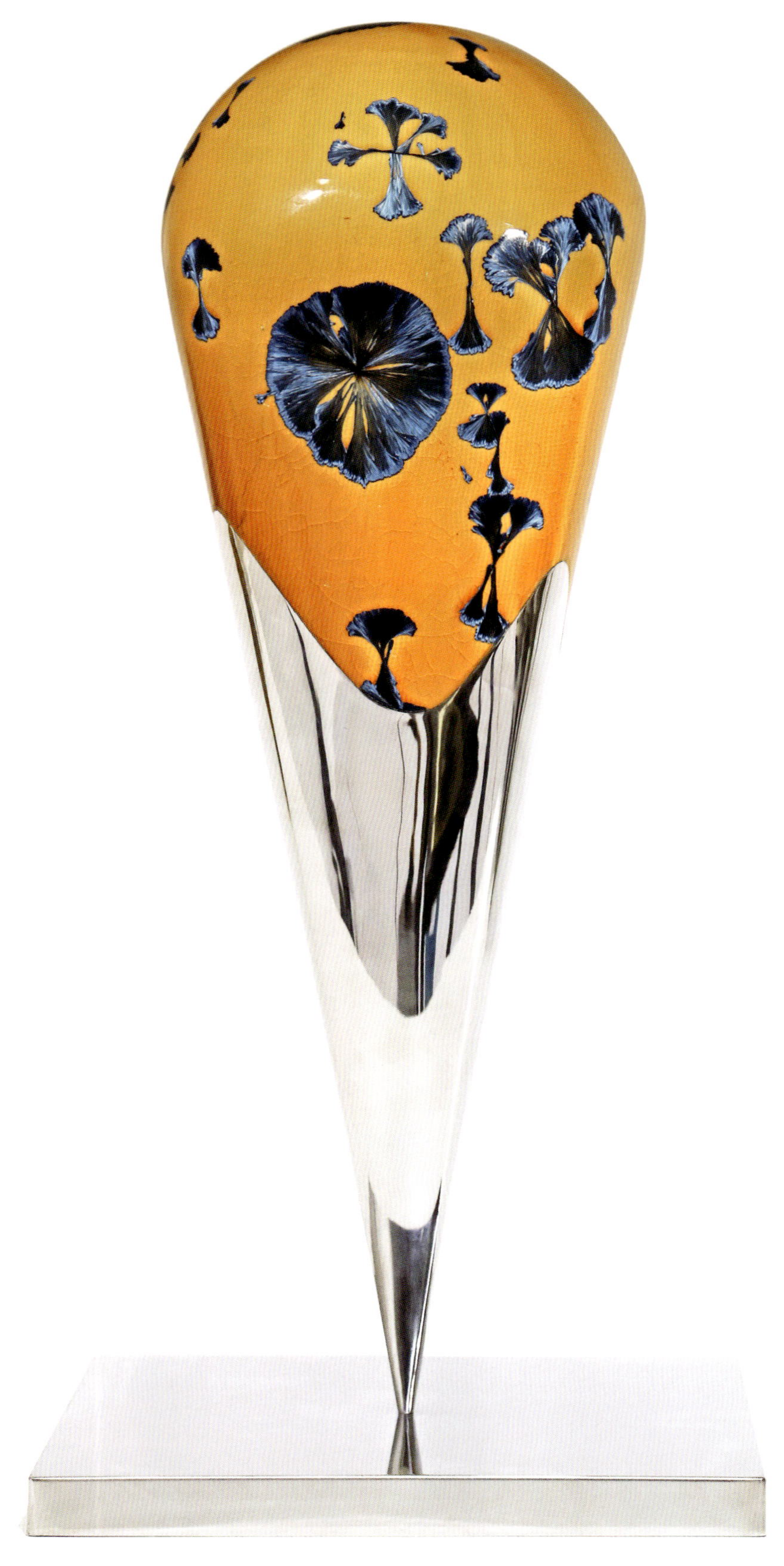

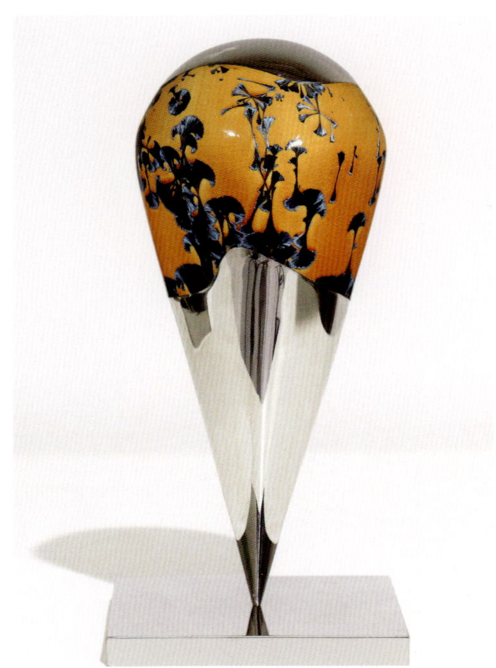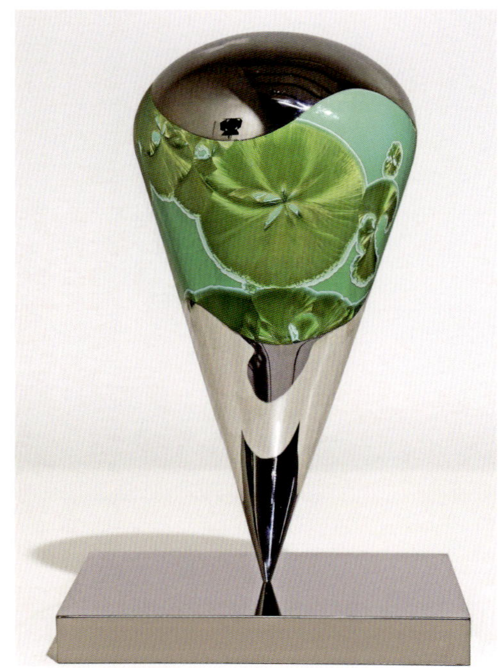

Upwelling of Gravity #4, 2017. Fired porcelain, stainless steel. 8×8×16.5 inches. Private collection

Upwelling of Gravity #5, 2017. Fired porcelain, stainless steel. 10×10×16 inches. Collection of the artist

Upwelling of Gravity #16, 2017. Fired porcelain, stainless steel. 11.8×11.8×26 inches. Private collection

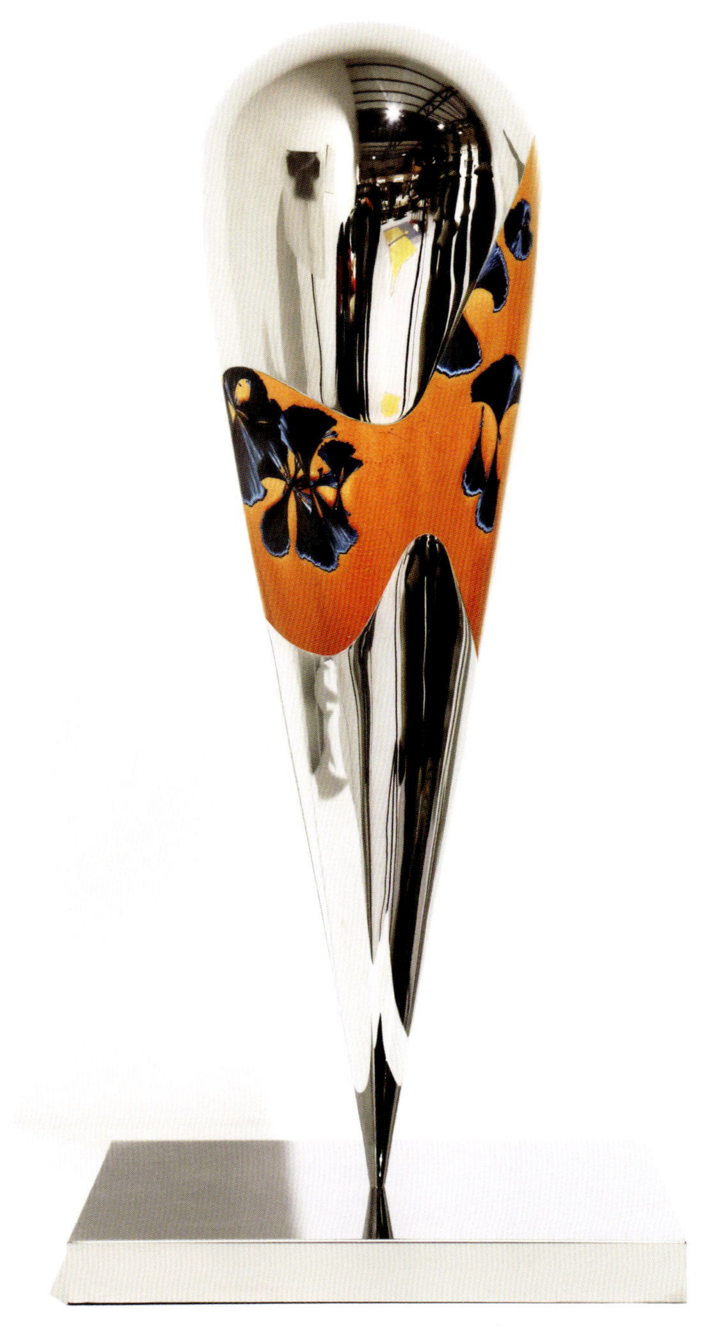

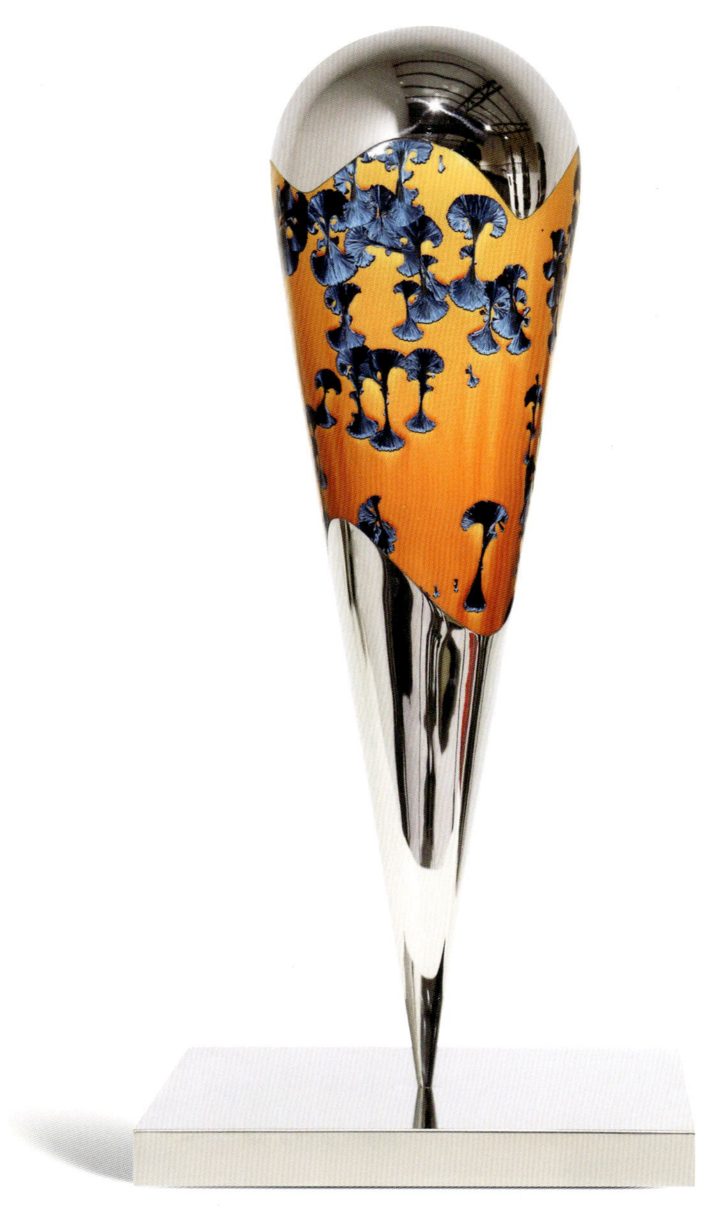

Upwelling of Gravity #6, 2017. Fired porcelain, stainless steel. 9.75×9.75×26 inches. Collection of the artist

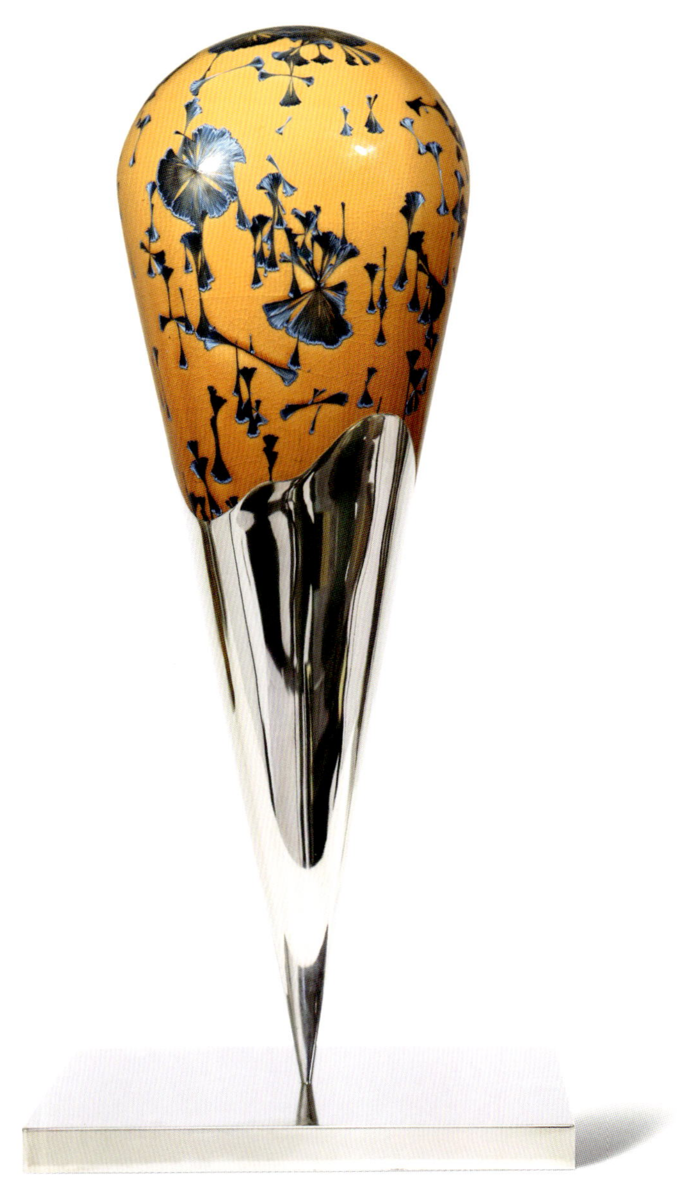

Upwelling of Gravity #11, 2017. Fired porcelain, stainless steel. 10×10×21 inches. Collection of the artist

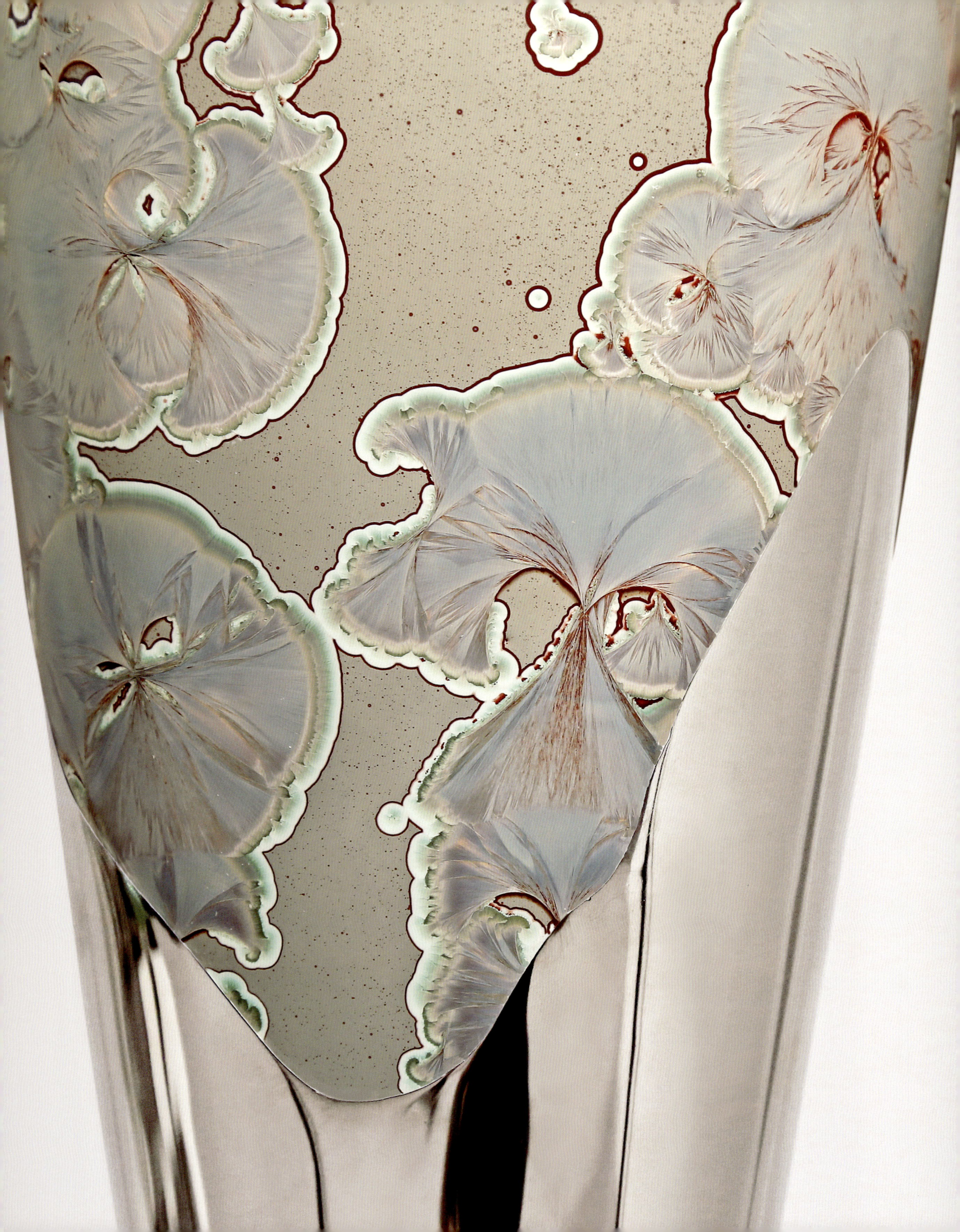

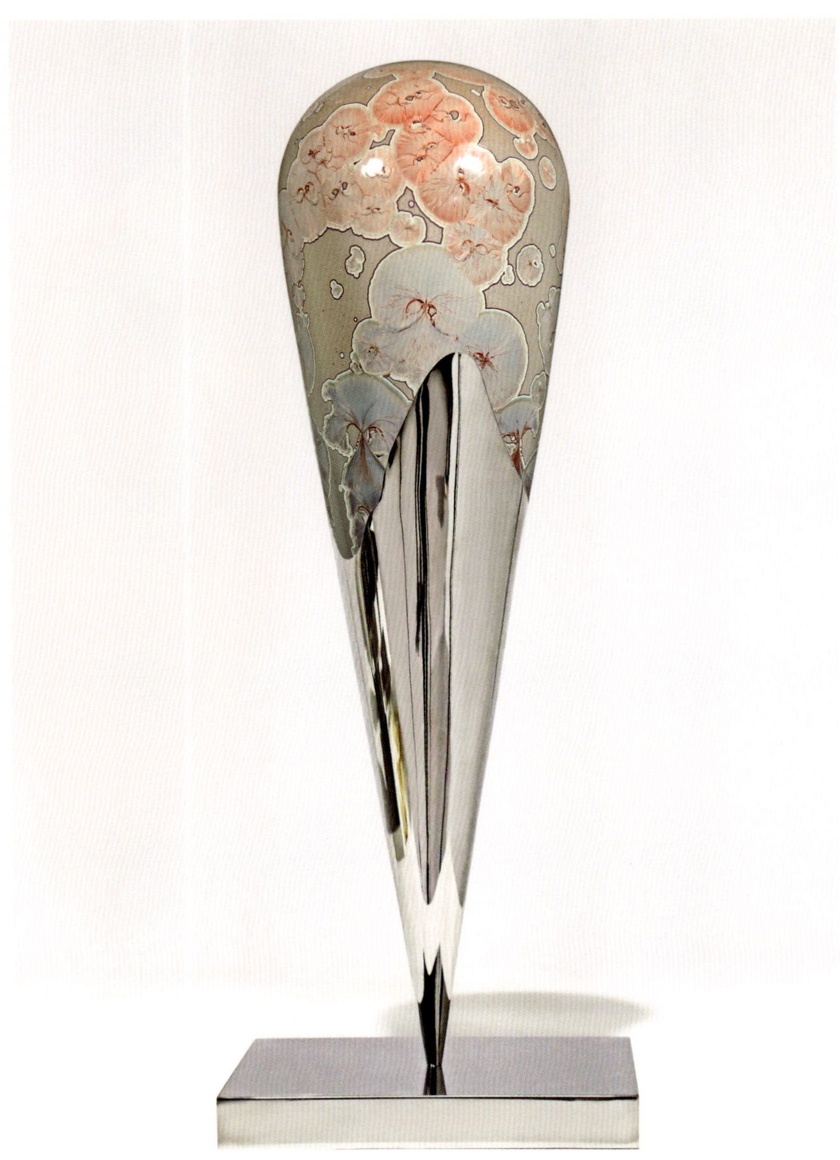

Upwelling of Gravity #20, 2018. Fired porcelain, stainless steel. 9.75×9.75×27 inches. Collection: Alfred University Ceramic Art Museum, Alfred, NY

Upwelling of Gravity #20 (detail), 2018. Fired porcelain, stainless steel. 9.75×9.75×27 inches. Collection: Alfred University Ceramic Art Museum, Alfred, NY

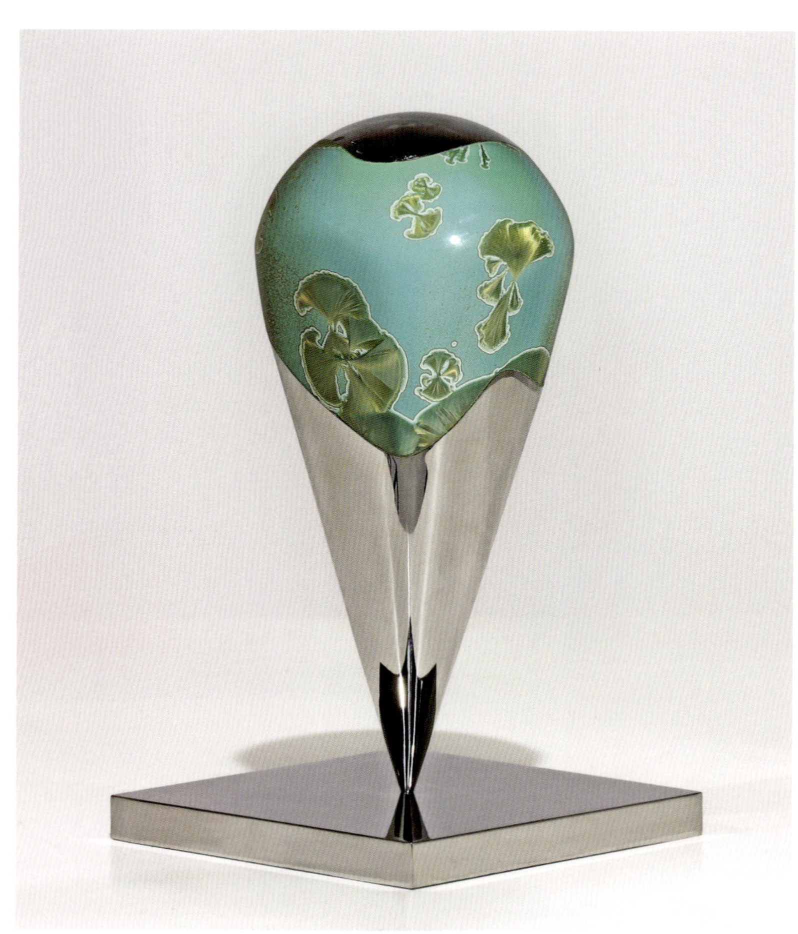

Upwelling of Gravity #34, 2018. Fired porcelain, stainless steel. 8×8×15 inches
Loan to the US Embassy in Bishkek, Kyrgyzstan. Exhibition from March 2019 to September 2021

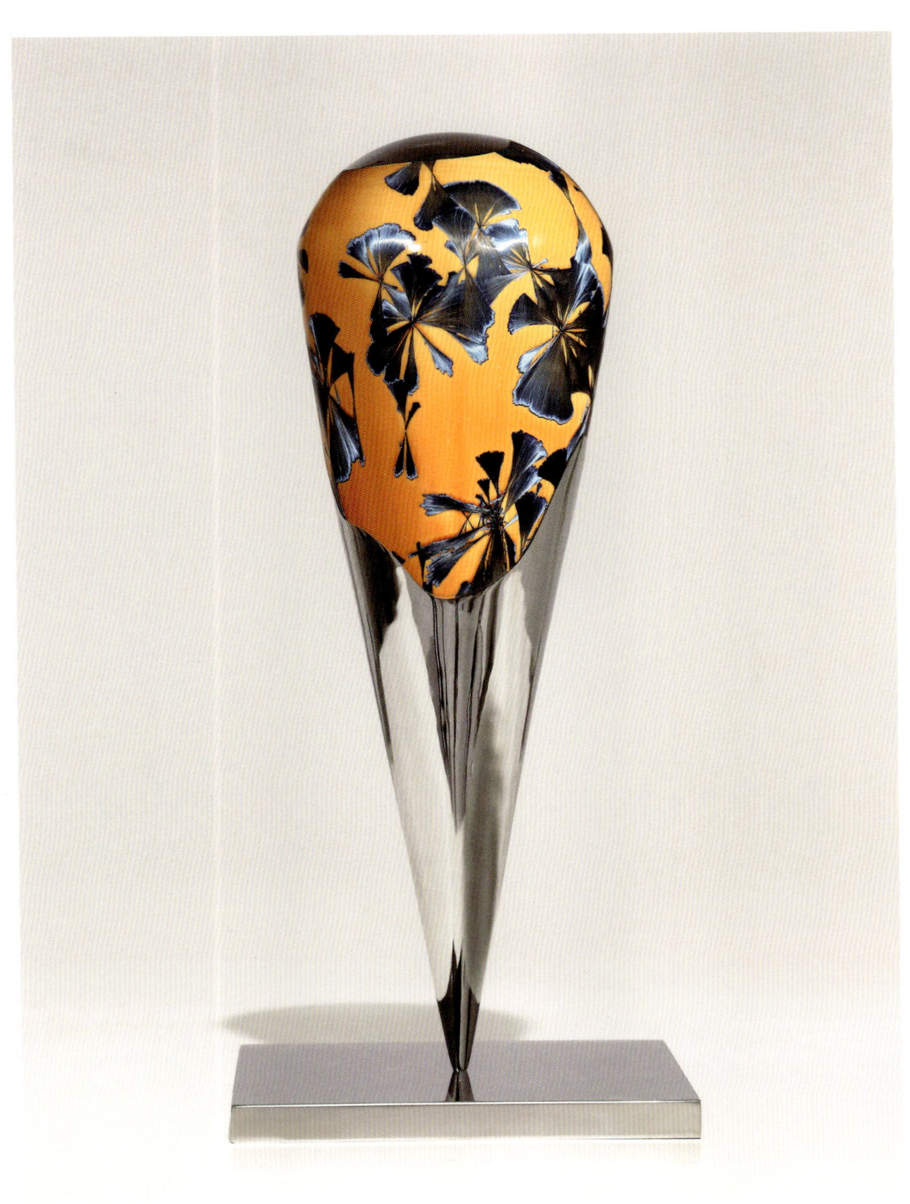

Upwelling of Gravity #42, 2018. Fired porcelain, stainless steel. 10×10×26 inches
Loan to the US Embassy in Bishkek, Kyrgyzstan. Exhibition from March 2019 to September 2021

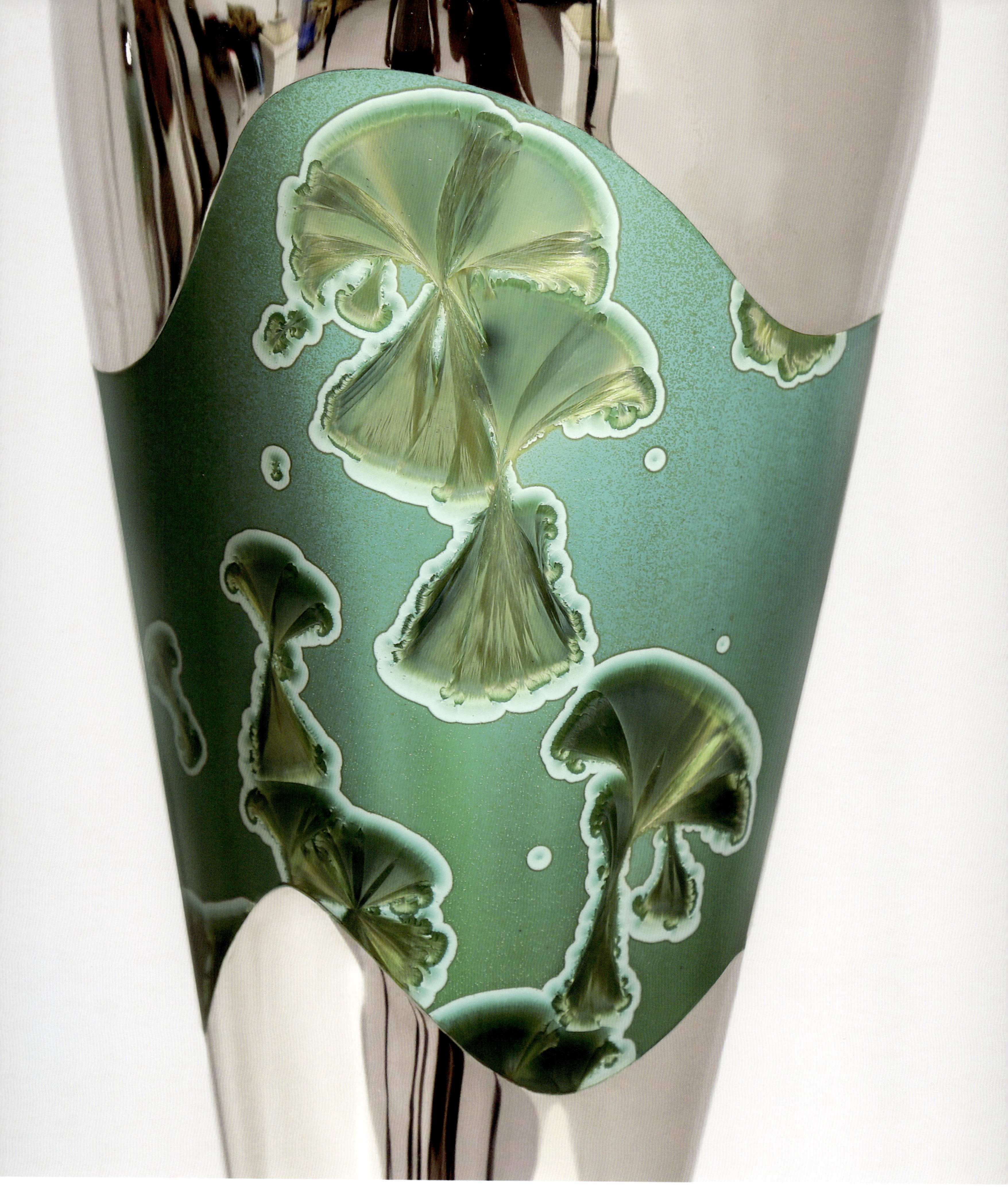

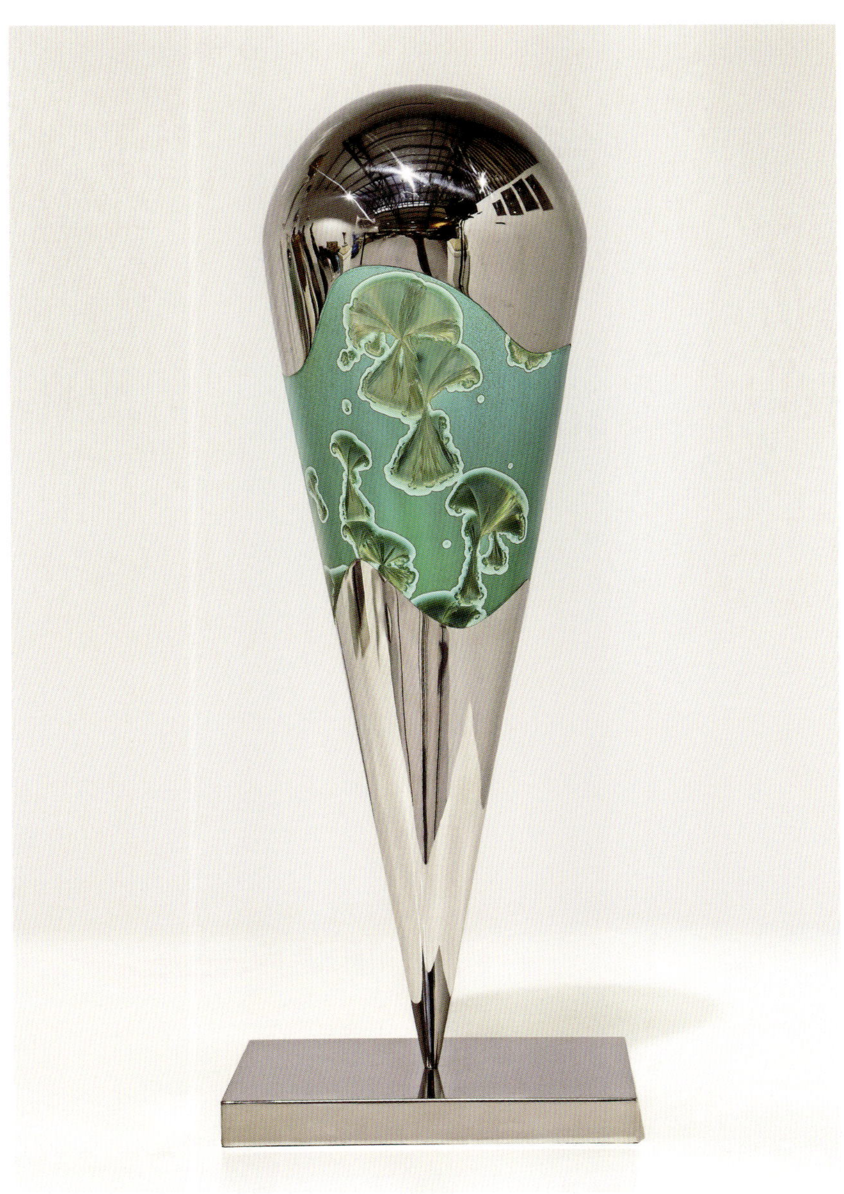

Upwelling of Gravity #29, 2018. Fired porcelain, stainless steel. 8×8×22 inches. Collection of the artist

Upwelling of Gravity #29 (detail), 2018. Fired porcelain, stainless steel. 8×8×22 inches. Collection of the artist

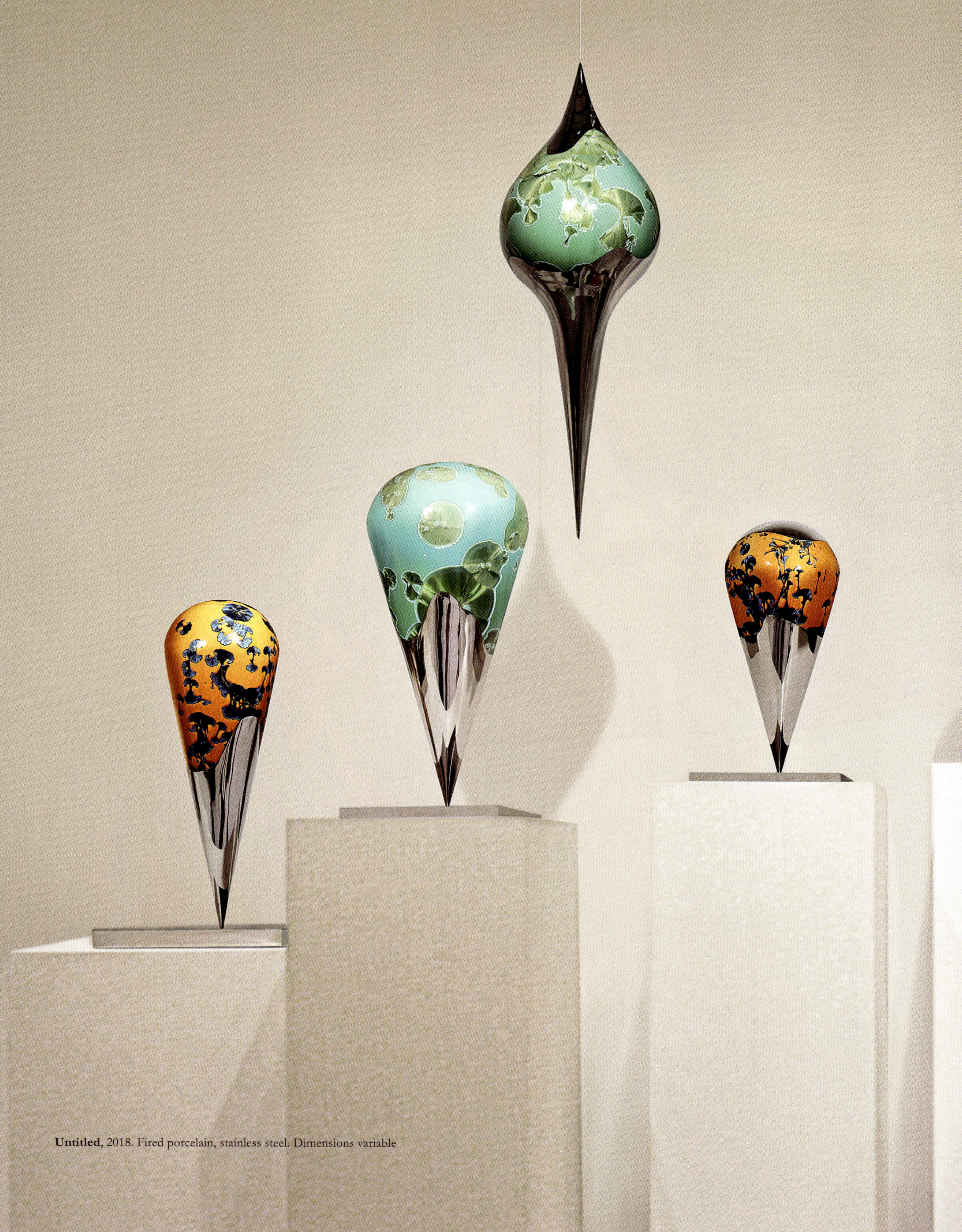

Untitled, 2018. Fired porcelain, stainless steel. Dimensions variable

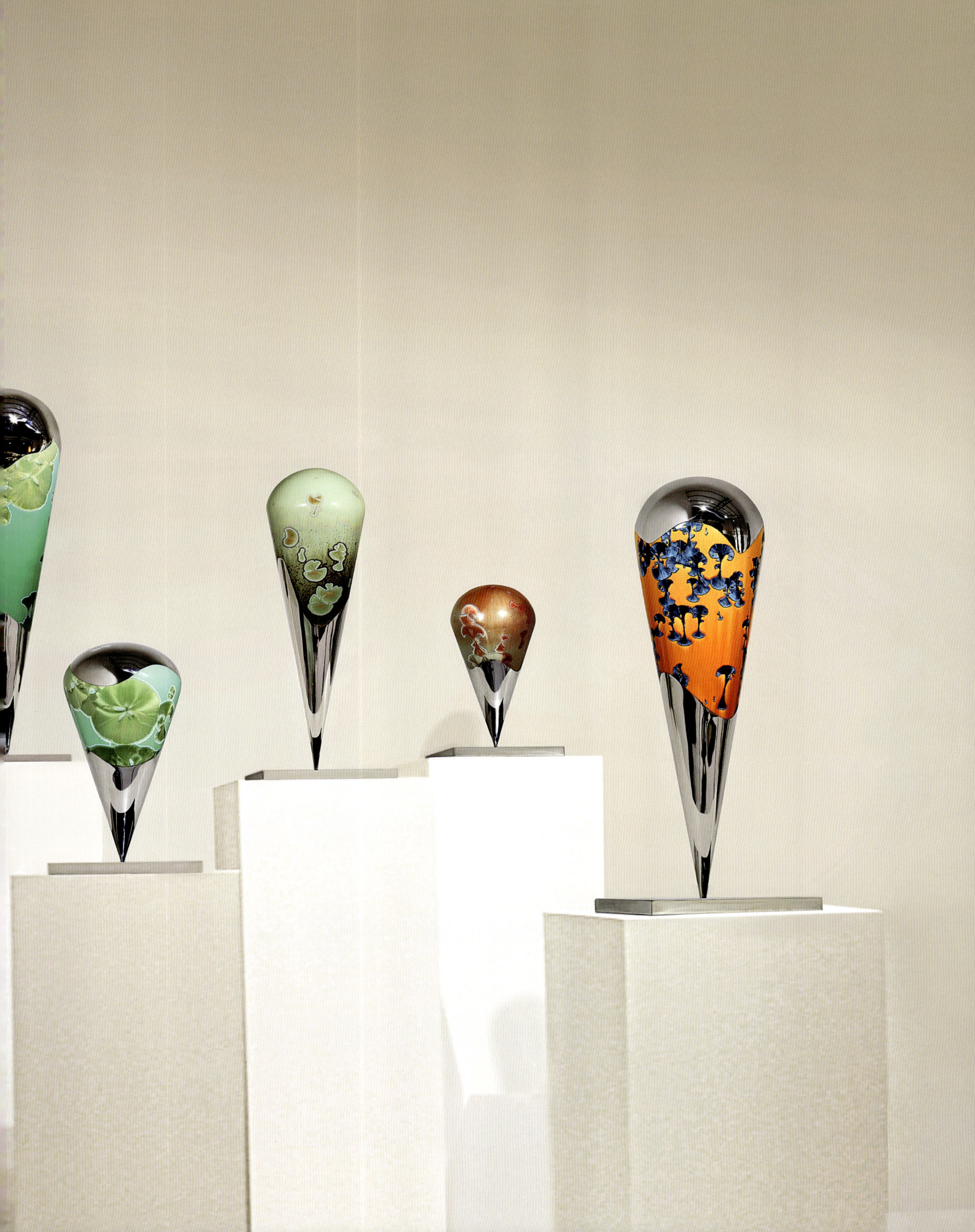

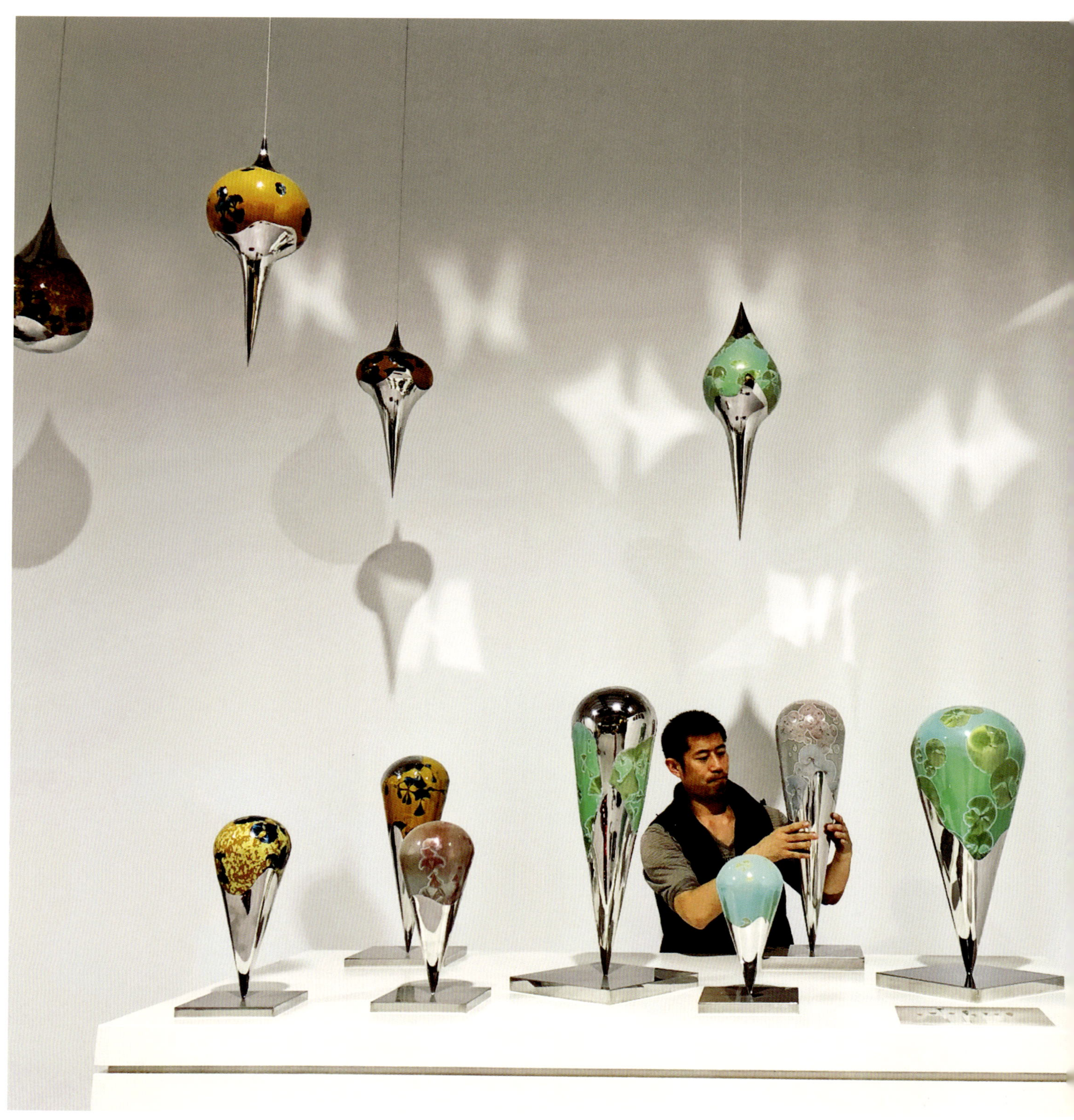

Working in the studio, Beijing, 2018

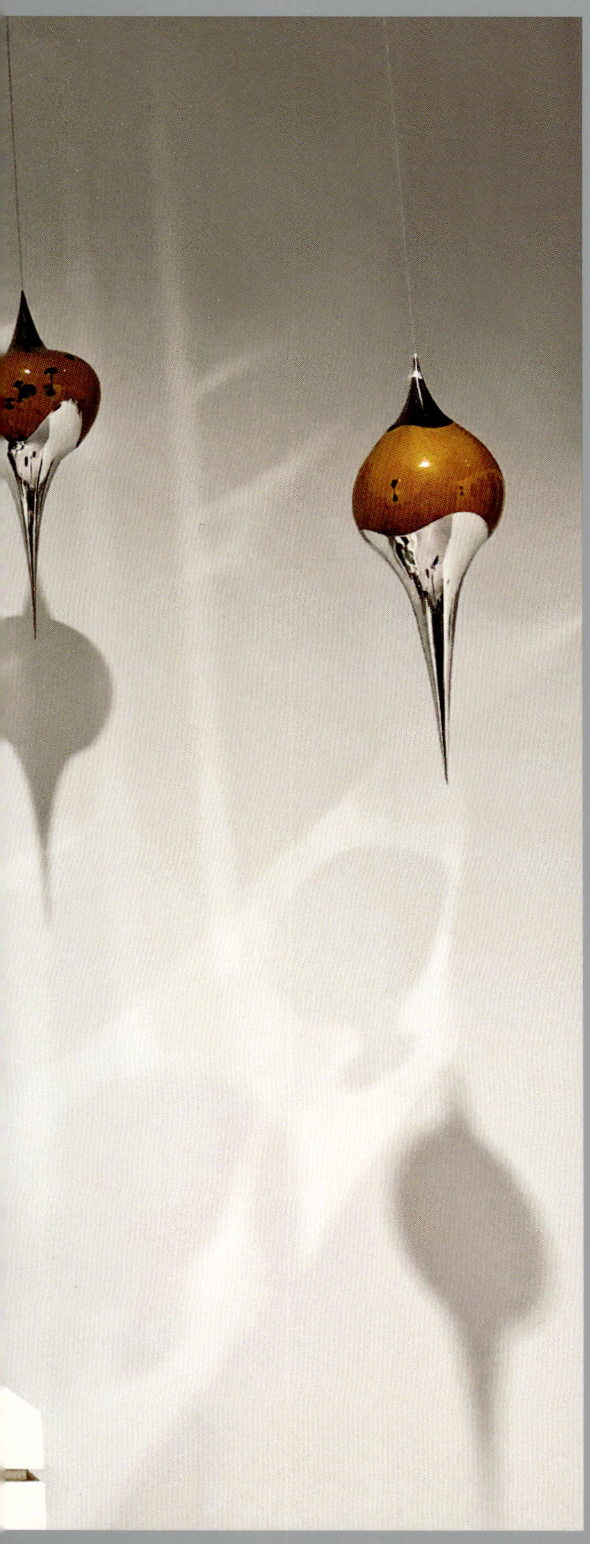

XUAN

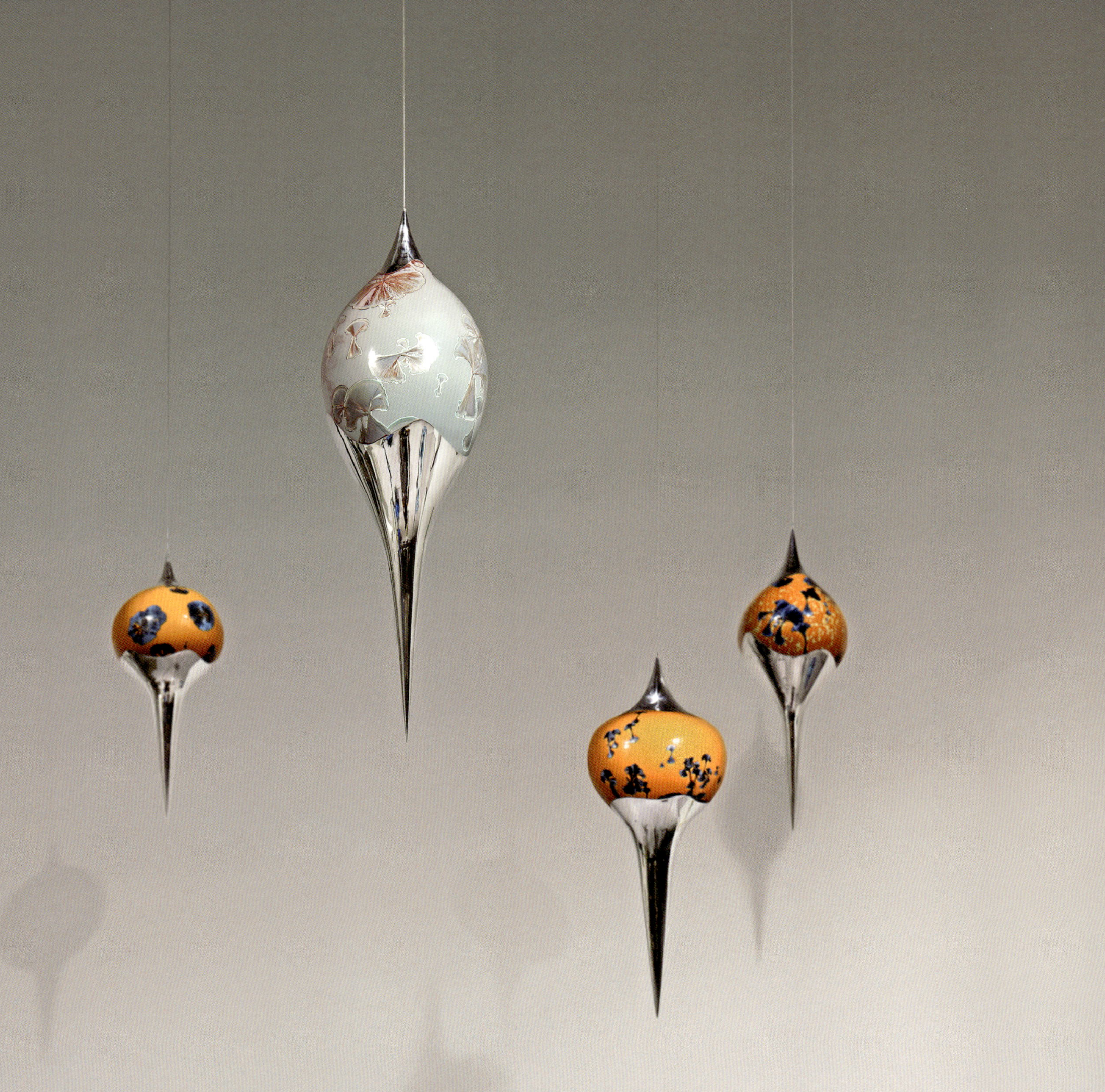

Xuan, 2018. Fired porcelain, stainless steel. Dimensions variable. Collection of the artist
On view in The Art Institute of Chicago from March 2019 to March 2021

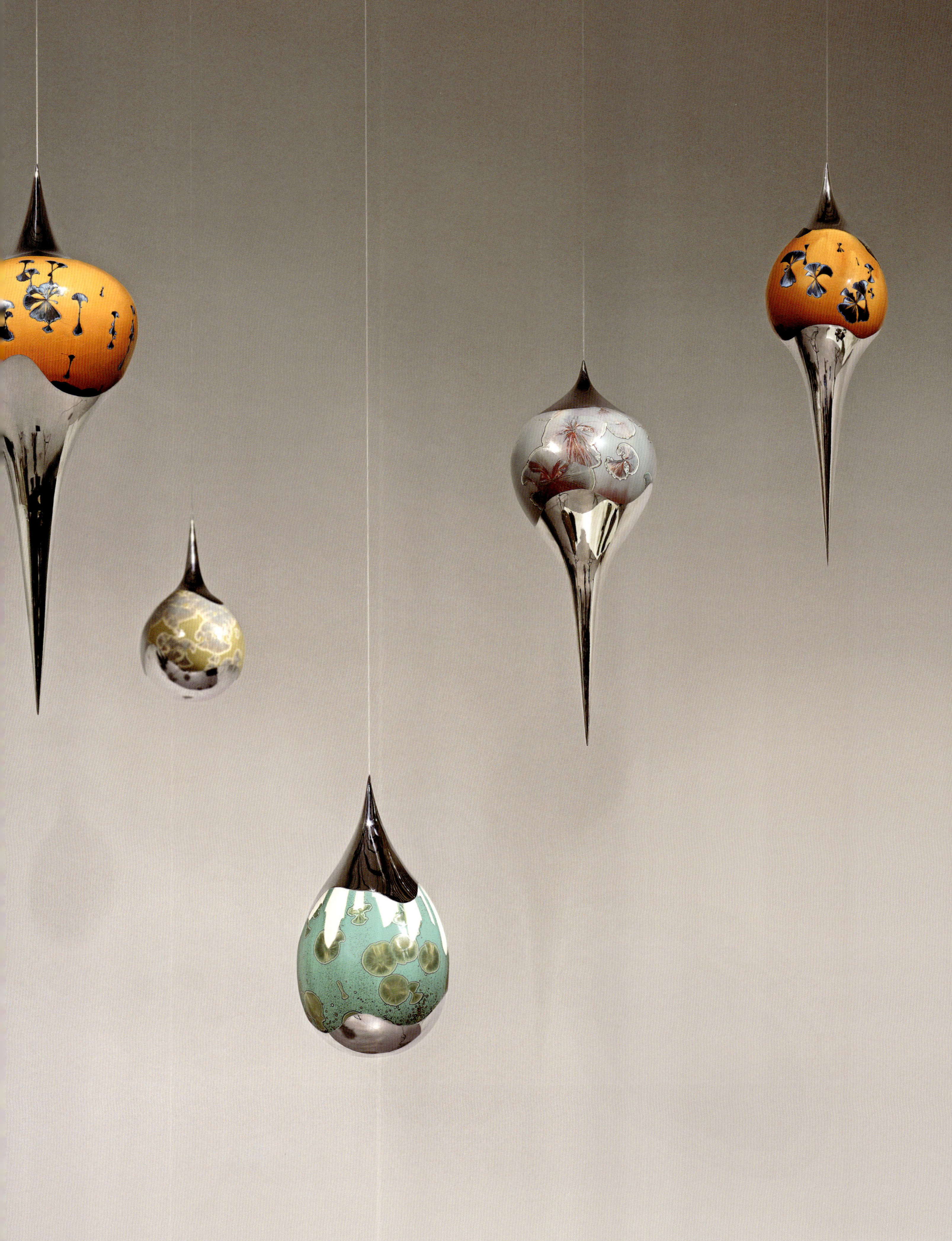

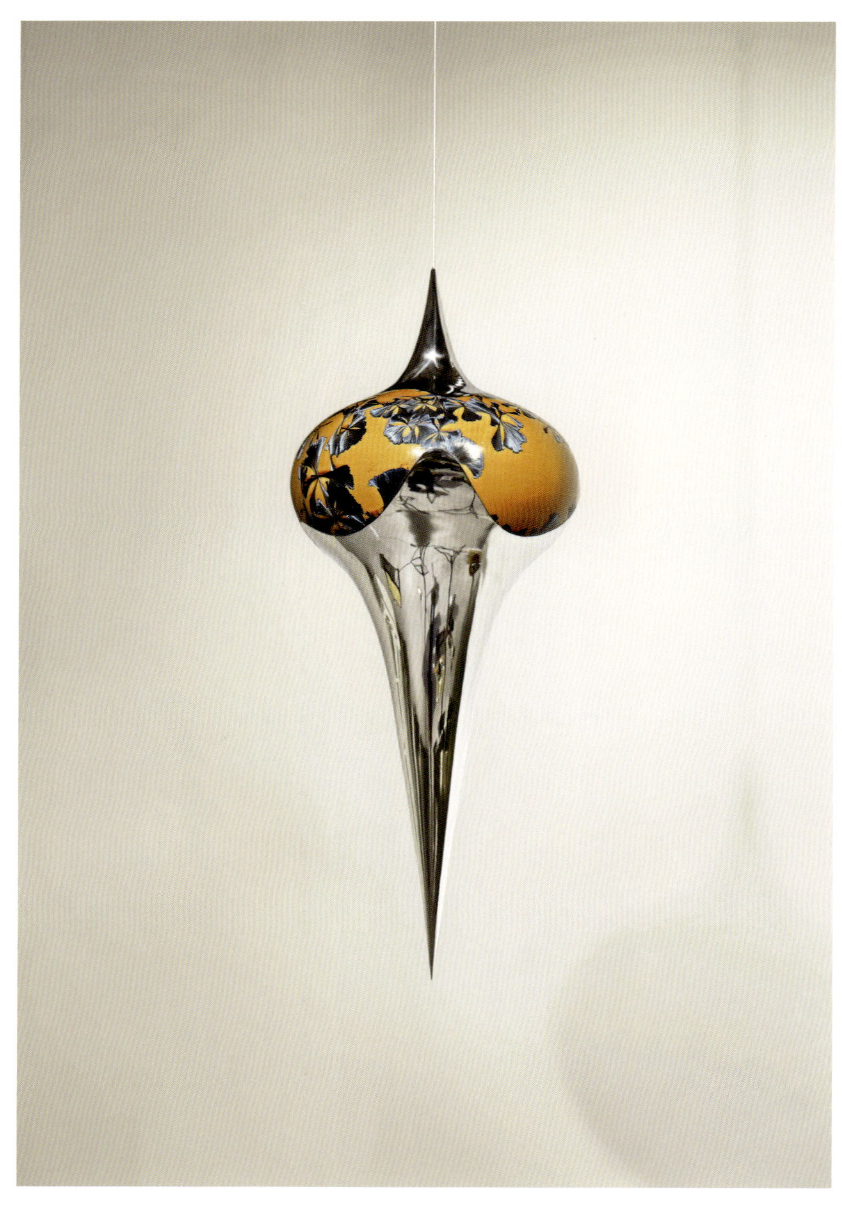

Xuan #3, 2017. Fired porcelain, stainless steel. 8.6×8.6×21.5 inches. Collection of the artist

Xuan #3 (detail), 2017. Fired porcelain, stainless steel. 8.6×8.6×21.5 inches. Collection of the artist

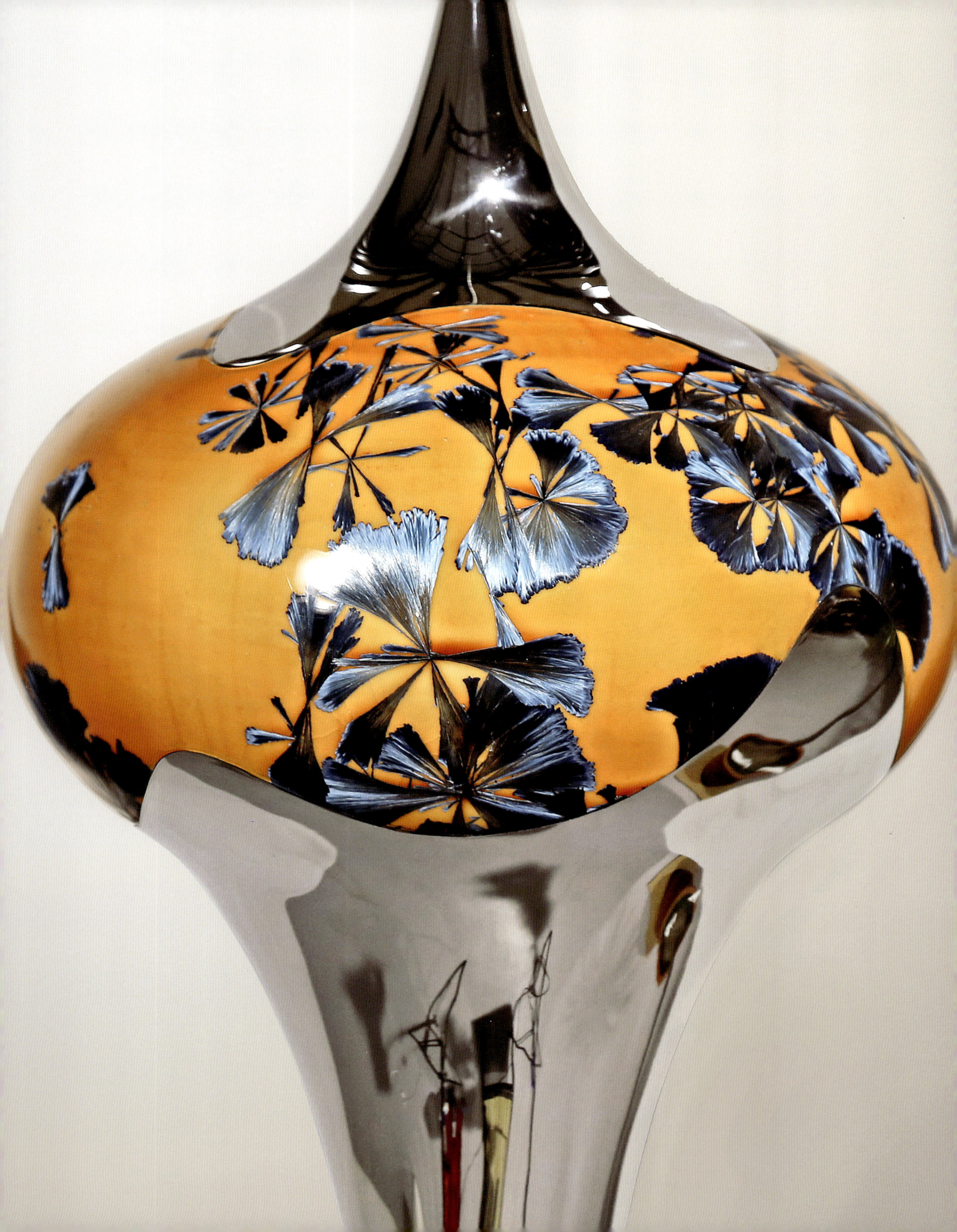

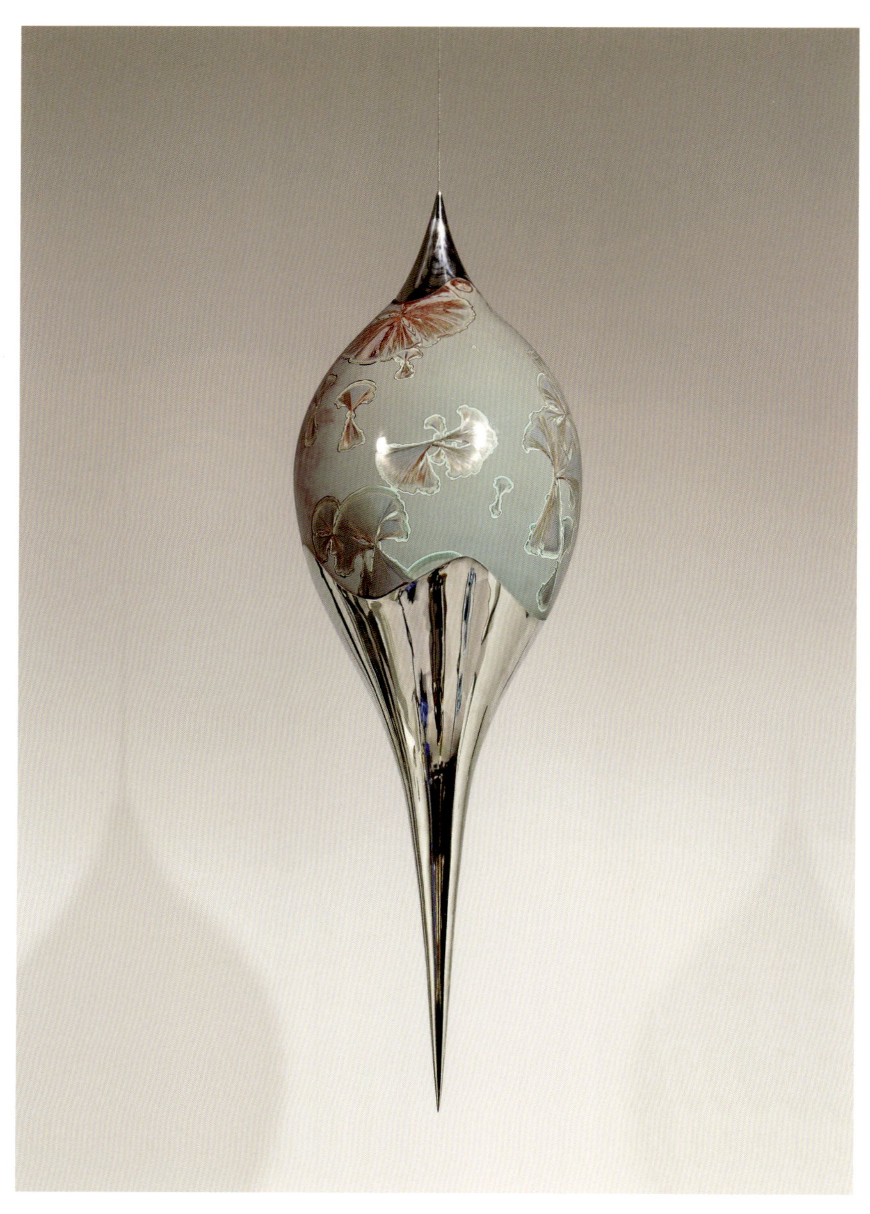

Xuan #13, 2018. Fired porcelain, stainless steel. 8.5×8.5×29 inches. Collection of the artist

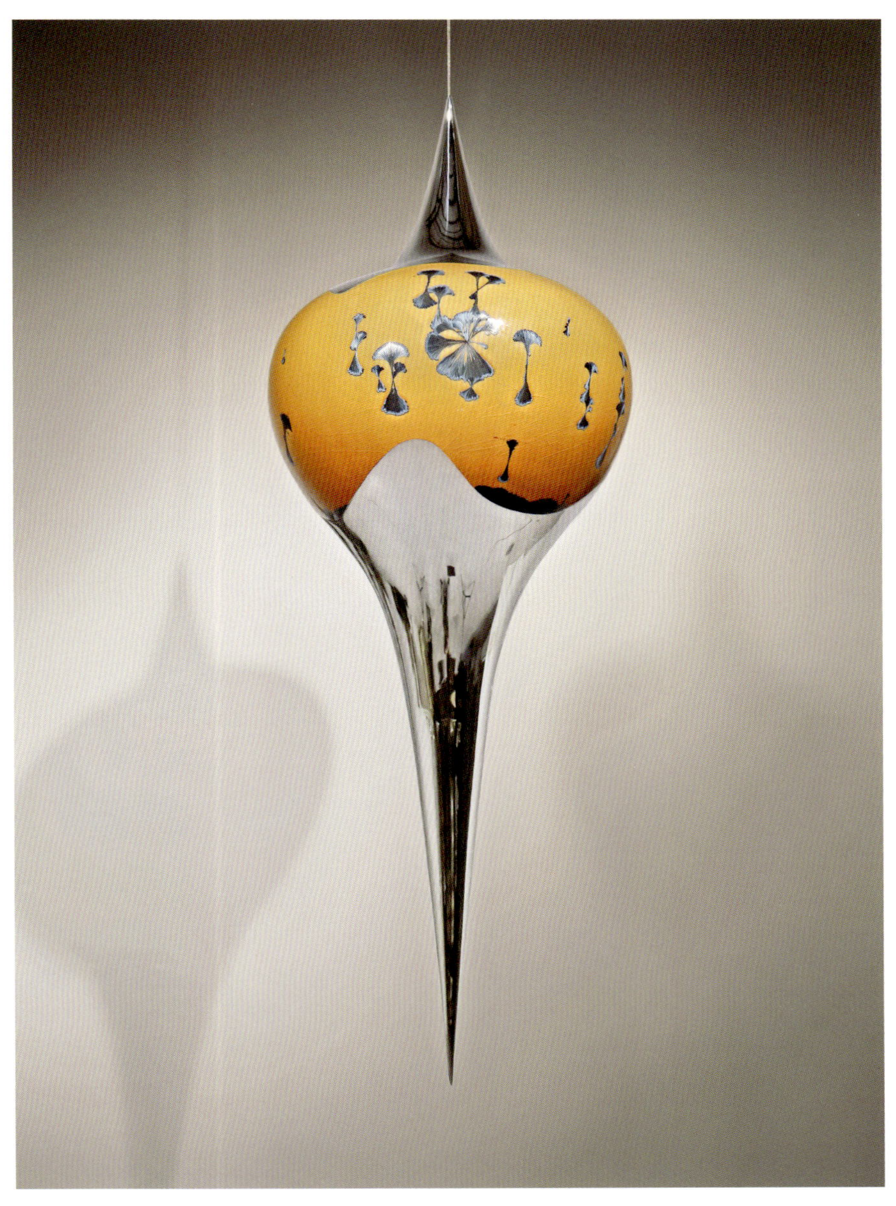

Xuan #4, 2018. Fired porcelain, stainless steel. 11×11×31 inches. Collection of the artist

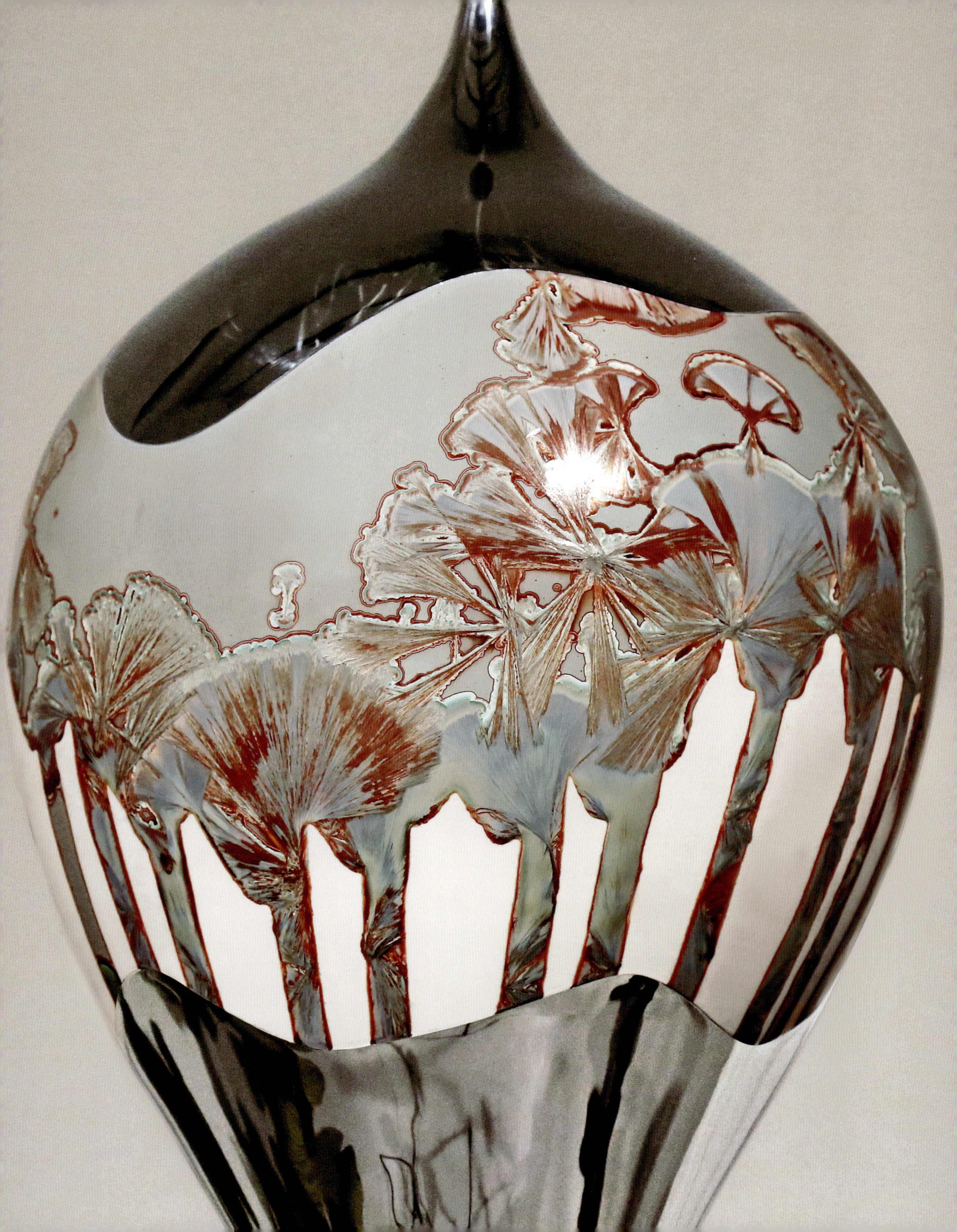

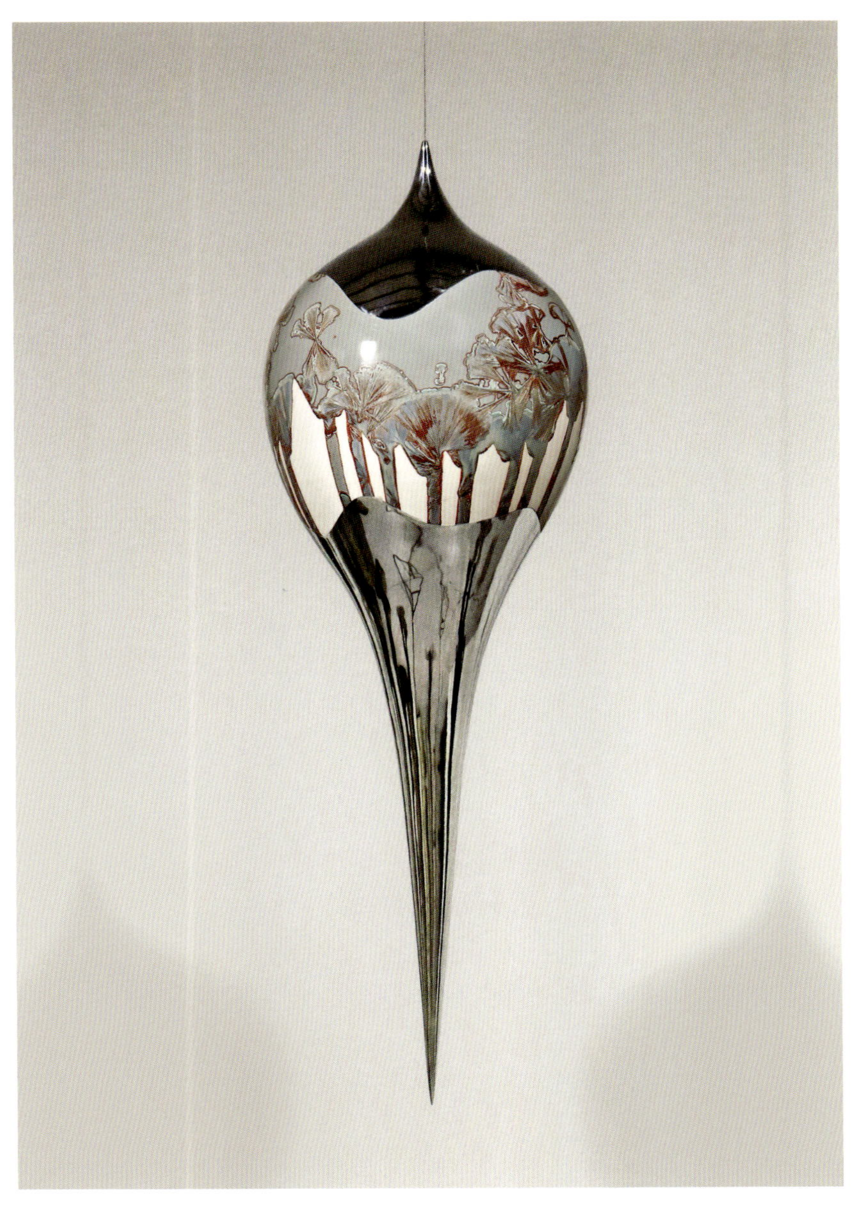

Xuan #20, 2018. Fired porcelain, stainless steel. 10.6×10.6×31 inches. Collection of the artist

Xuan #20 (detail), 2018. Fired porcelain, stainless steel. 10.6×10.6×31 inches. Collection of the artist

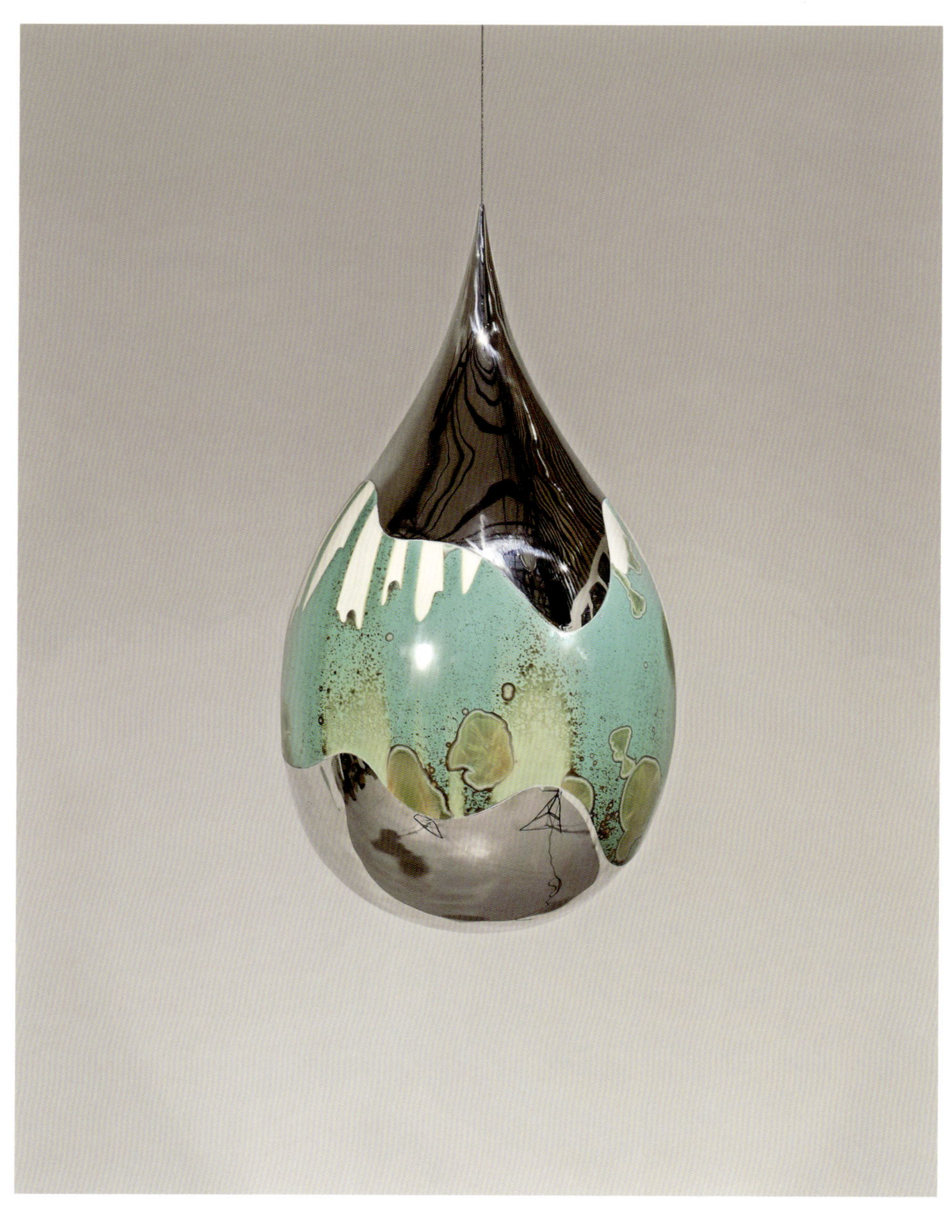

Xuan #8, 2018. Fired porcelain, stainless steel. 10×10×18.7 inches. Collection of the artist

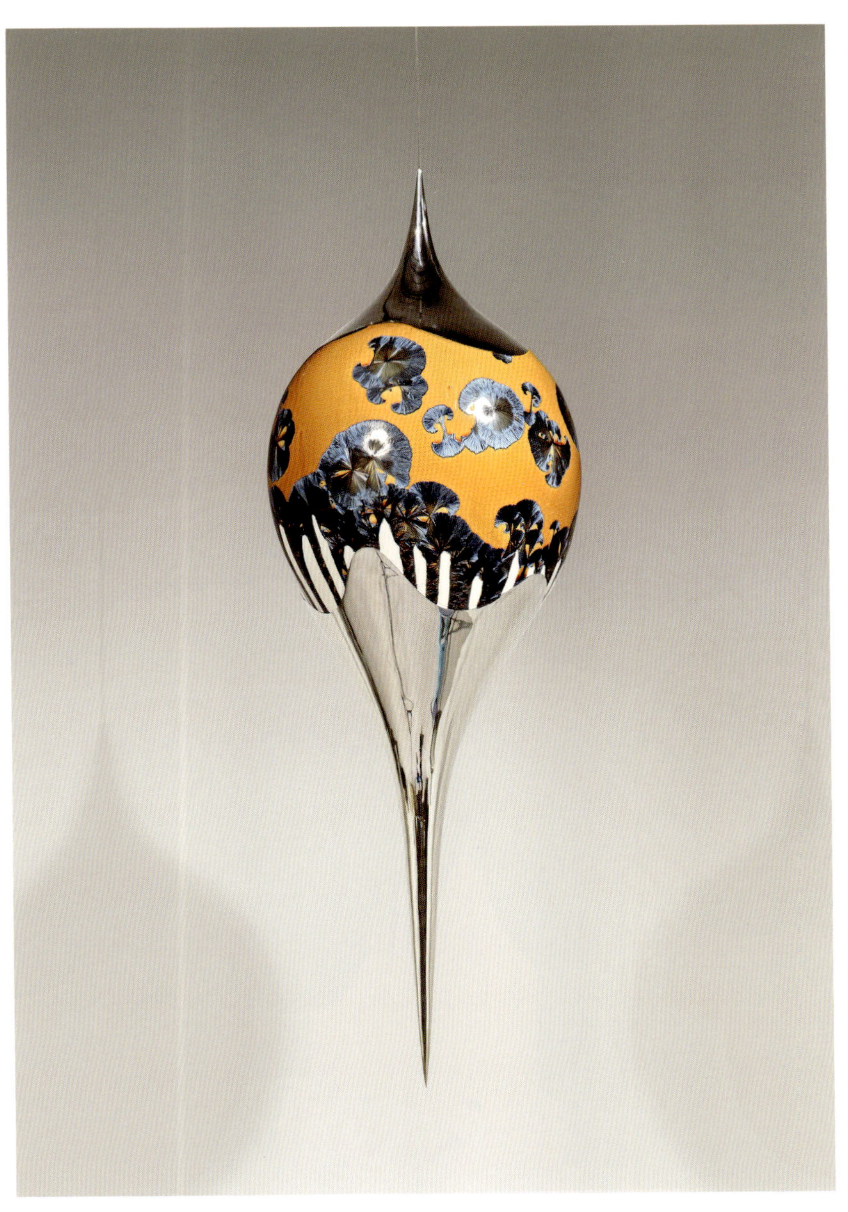

Xuan #9, 2018. Fired porcelain, stainless steel. 10×10×32 inches. Collection of the artist

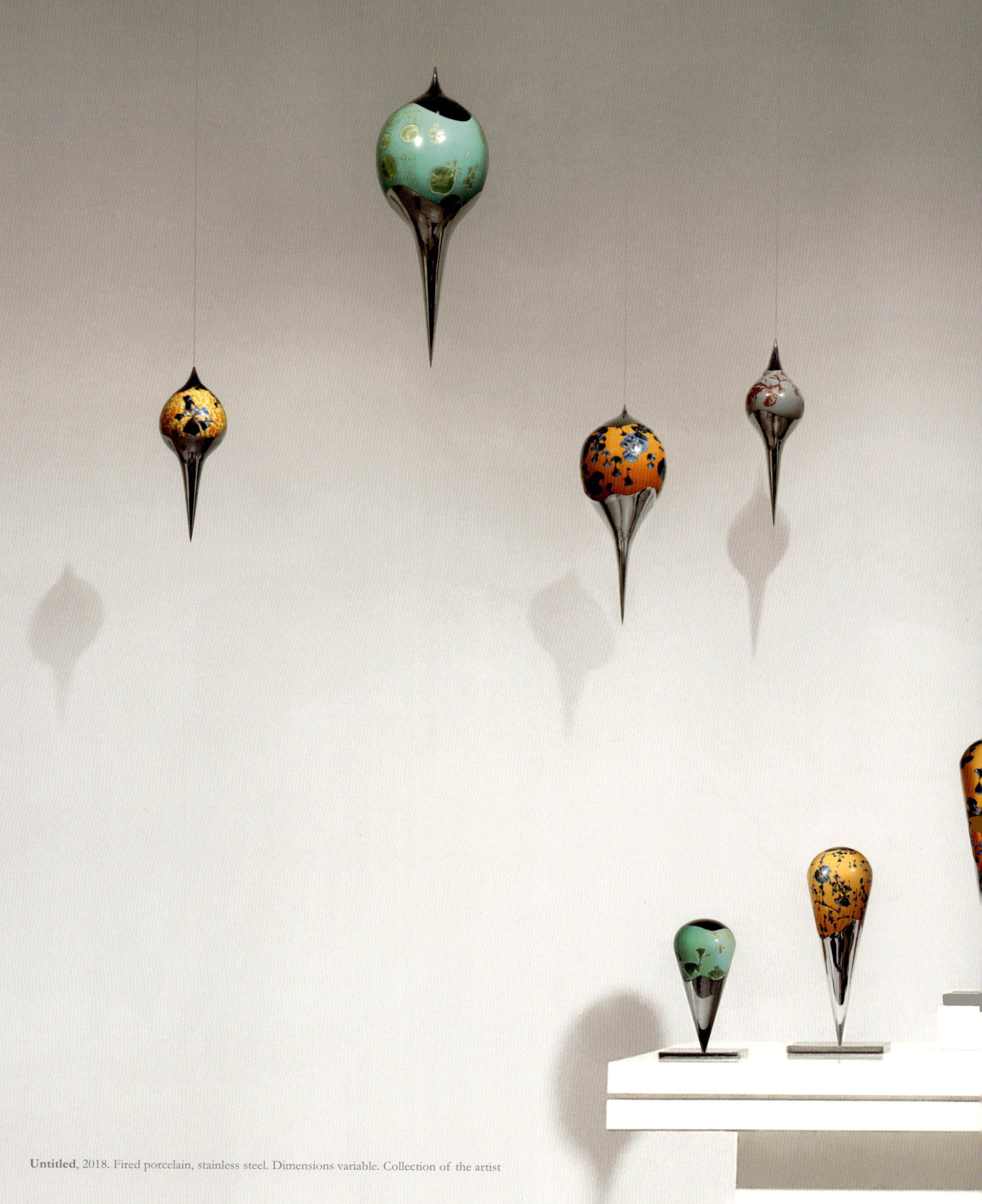

Untitled, 2018. Fired porcelain, stainless steel. Dimensions variable. Collection of the artist

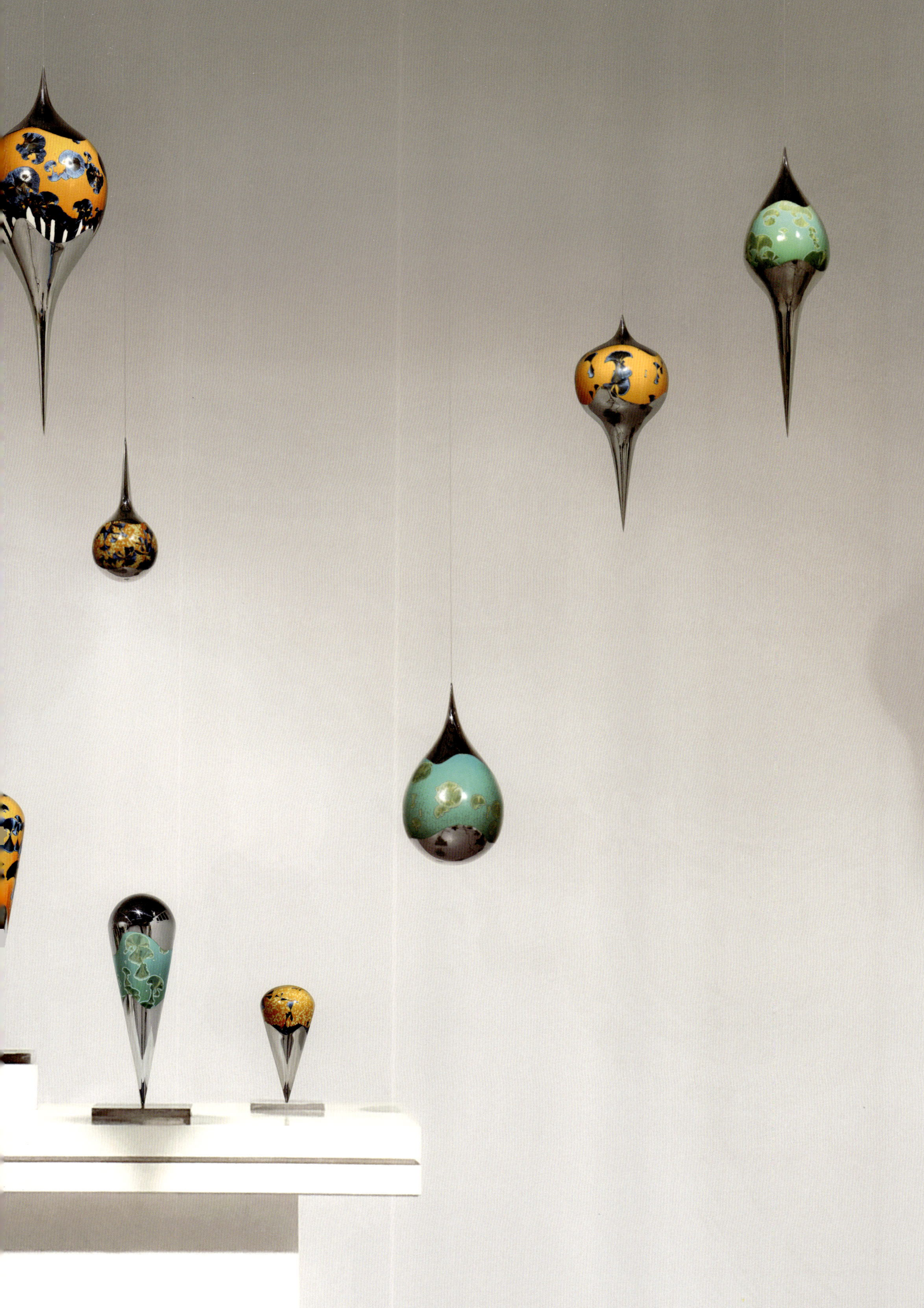

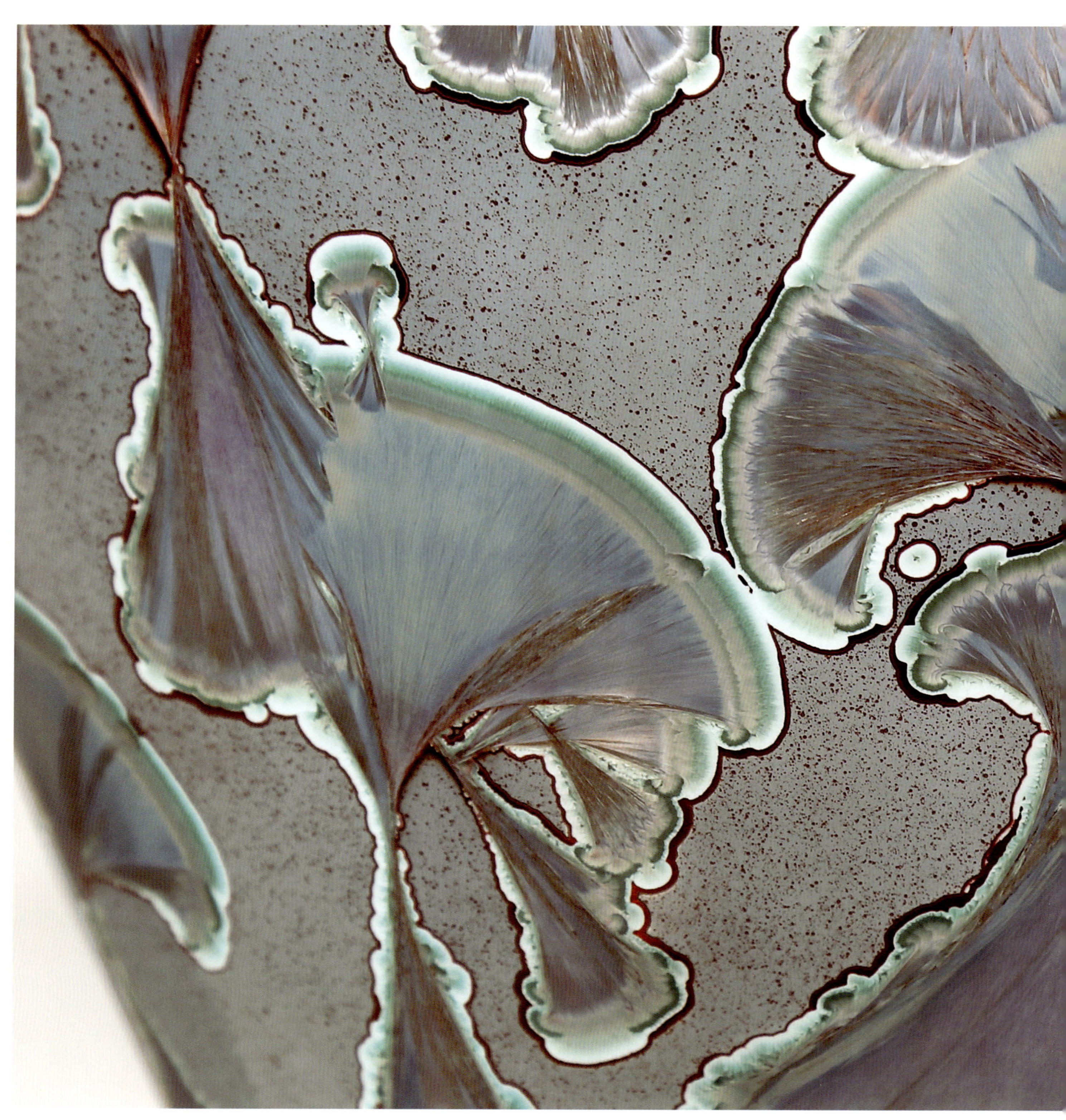

Olive Vase (detail), 2017. Reduction fired porcelain. 8×8×17 inches. Collection of the artist

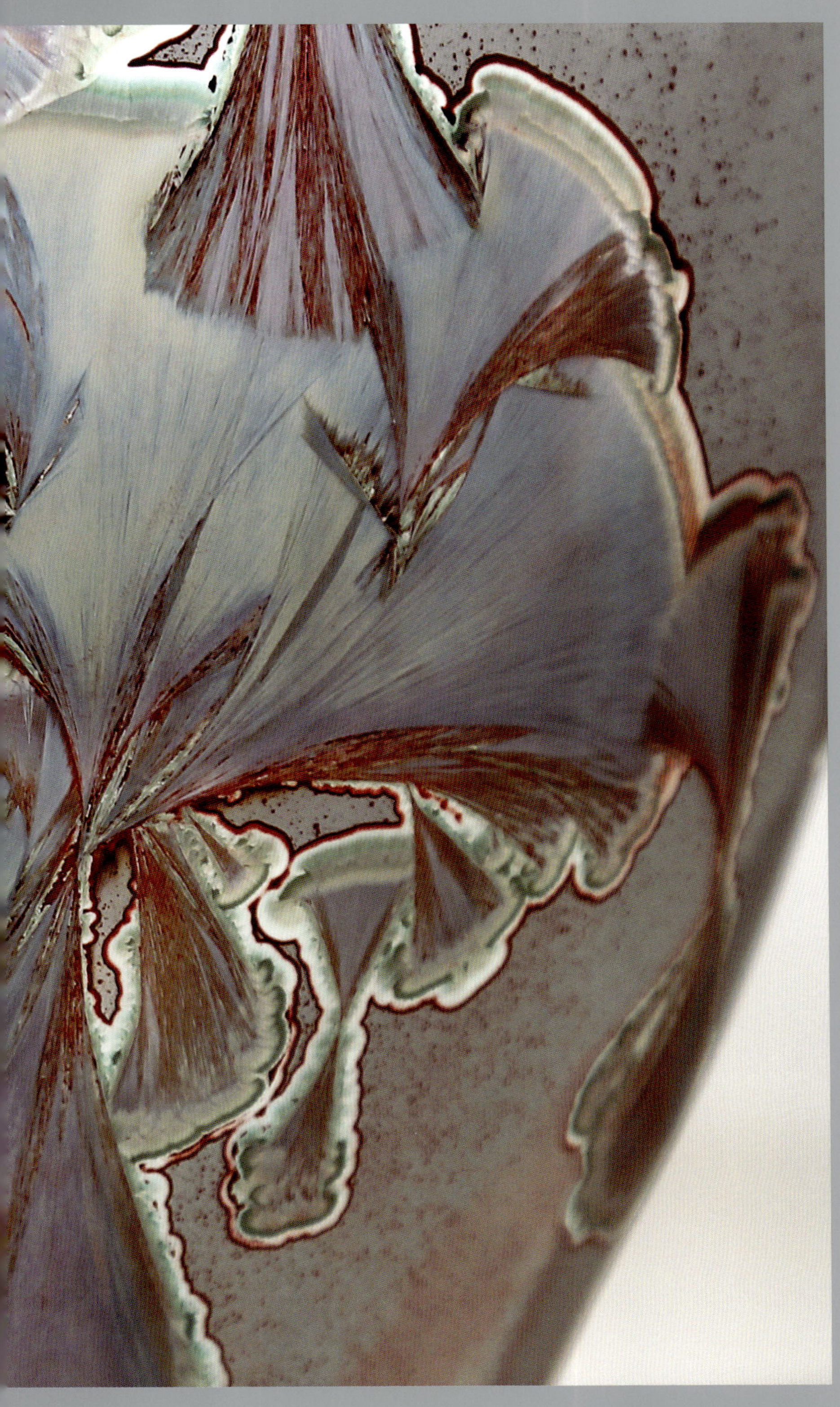

VASE

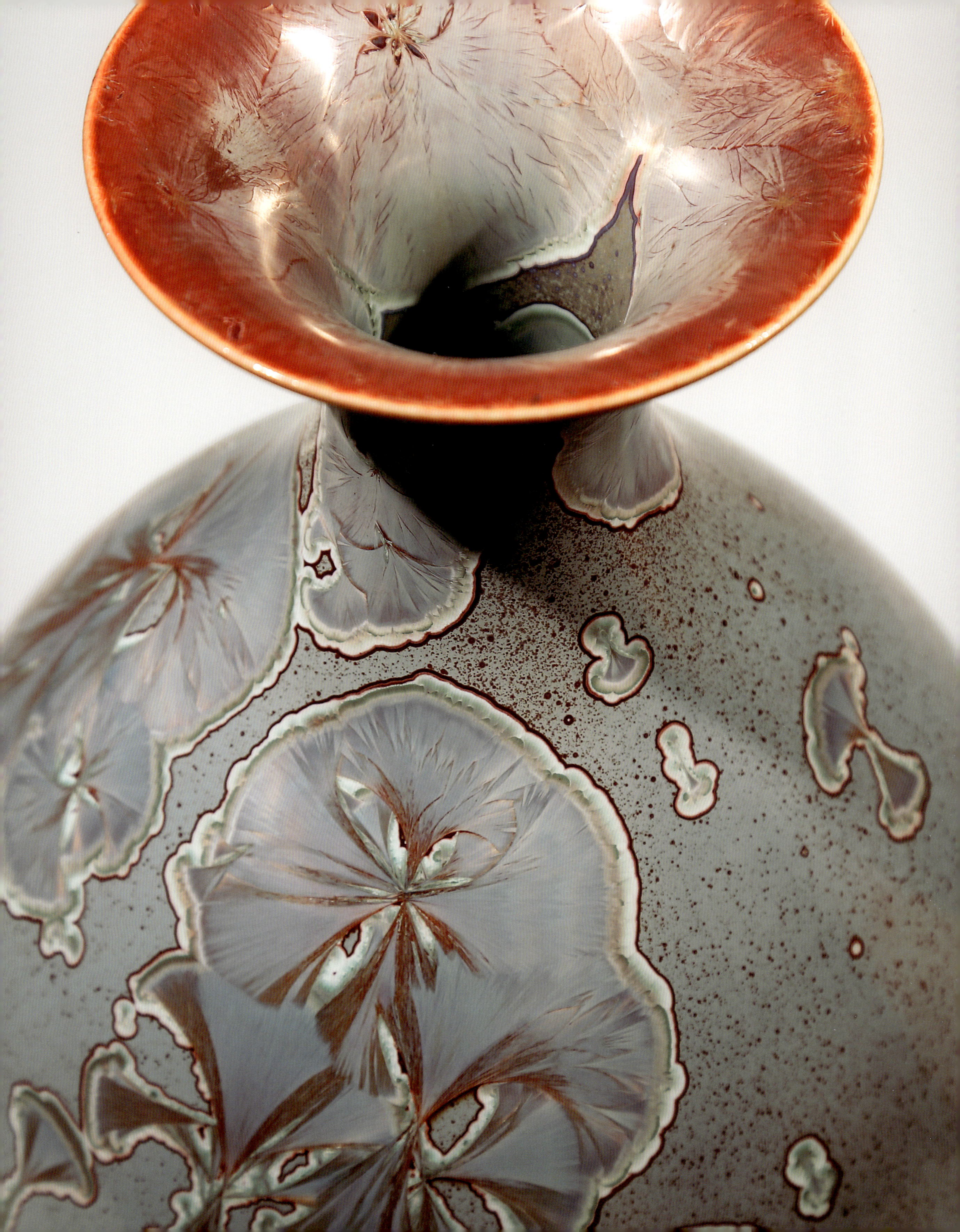

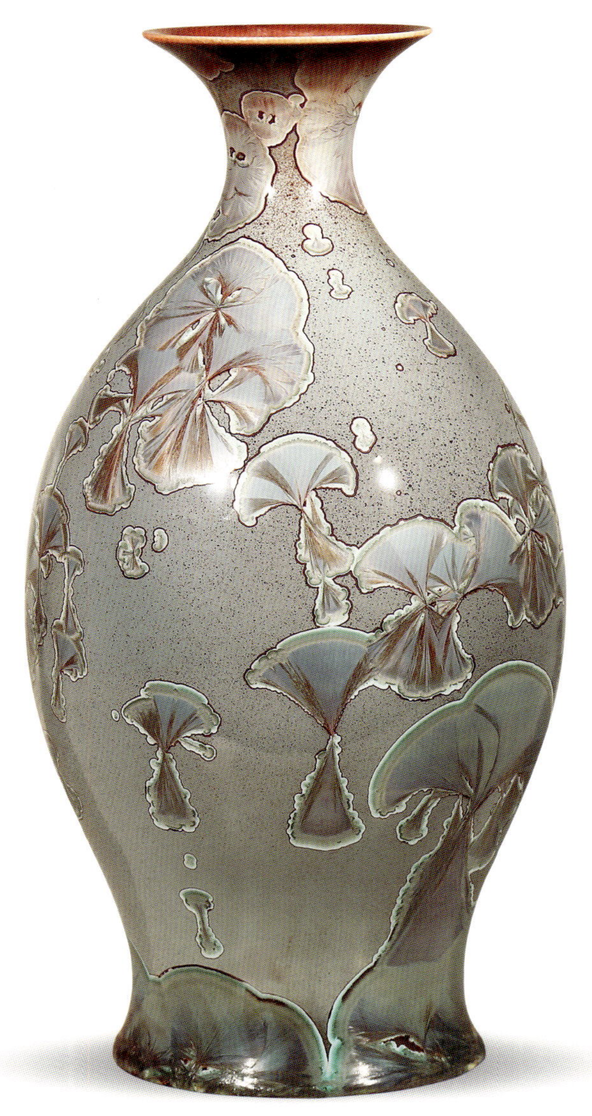

Olive Vase, 2017. Reduction fired porcelain. 8×8×17 inches. Collection of the artist

Olive Vase (detail), 2017. Reduction fired porcelain. 8×8×17 inches. Collection of the artist

Vault of Heaven Vase, 2015. Fired porcelain. 9.5×9.5×15 inches. Collection: The British Museum, London, UK

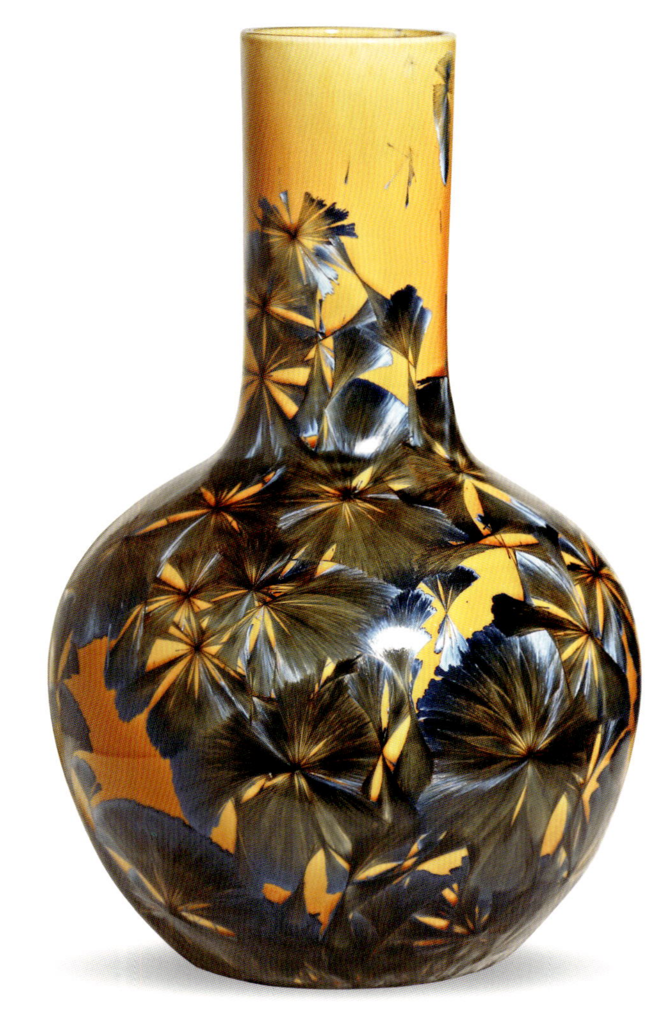

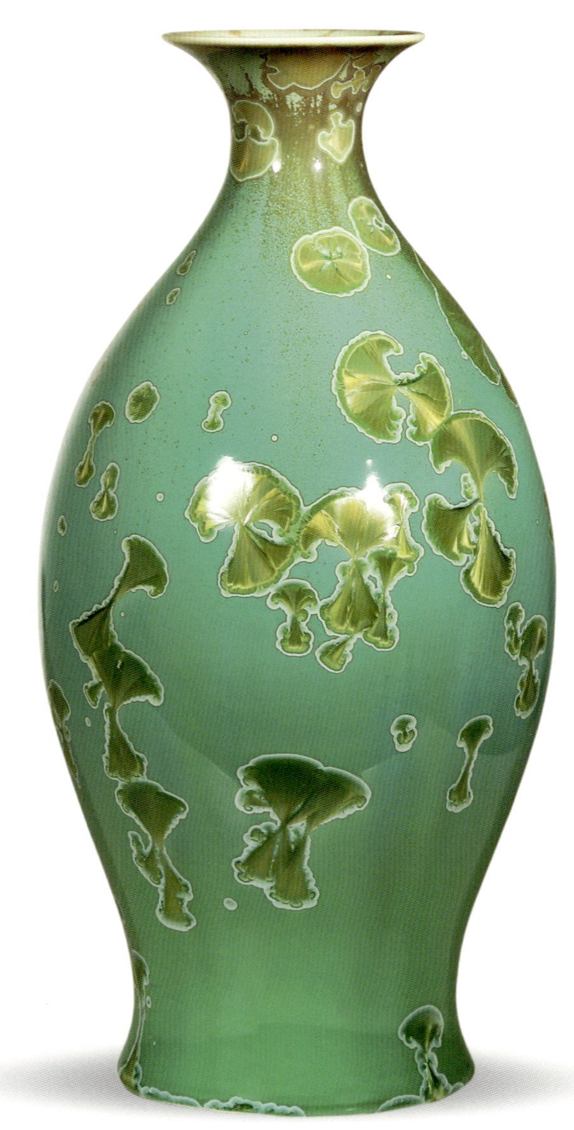

Olive Vase, 2017. Reduction fired porcelain. 7×7×16.25 inches. Private collection

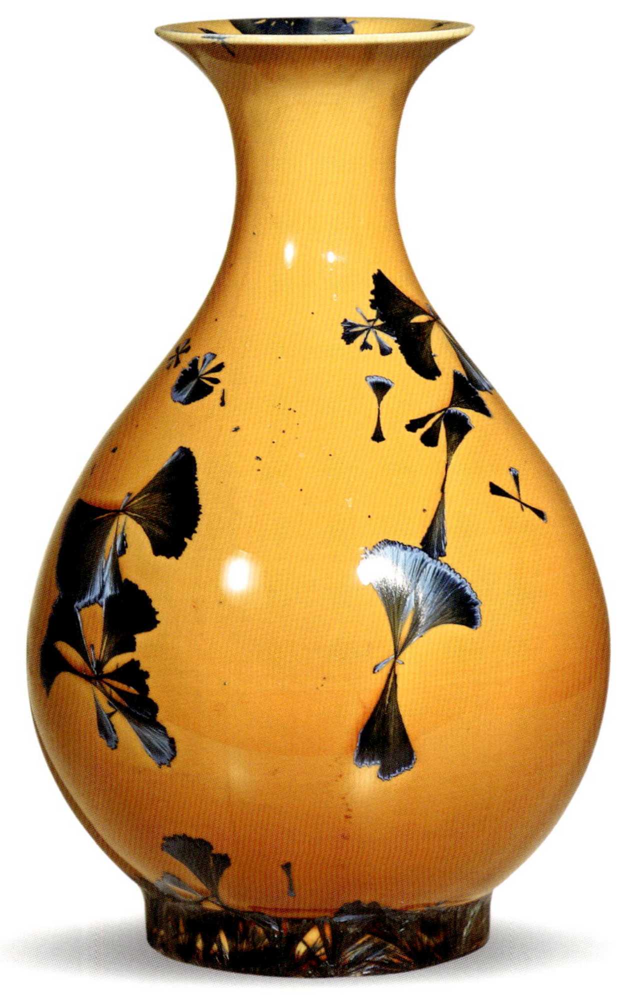

Pear Shaped Vase with a Flared Lip, 2016. Fired porcelain. 6.5×6.5×11.25 inches. Collection: The Israel Museum, Jerusalem, Israel

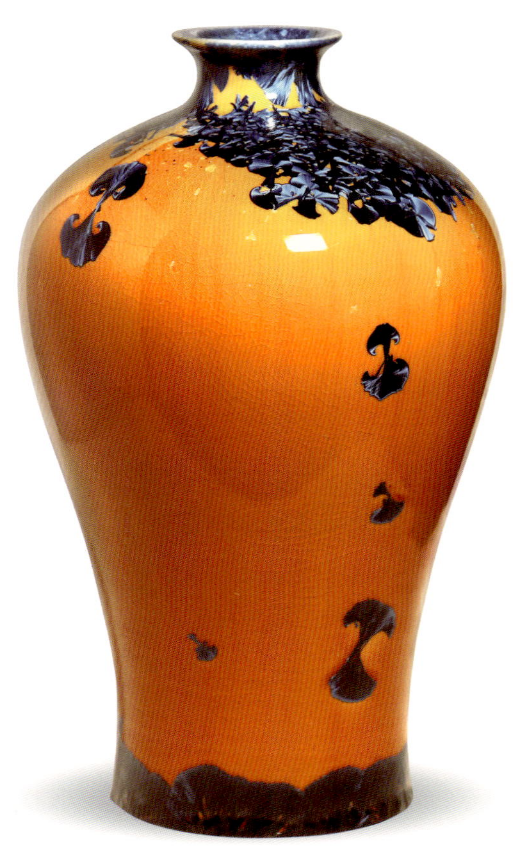

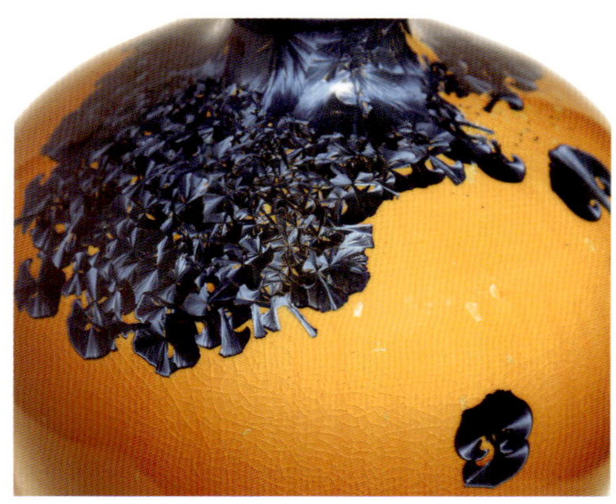

Mei-ping Vase, 2013. Fired porcelain. 6×6×11 inches. Collection of the artist

Mei-ping Vase (detail), 2013. Fired porcelain. 6×6×11 inches. Collection of the artist

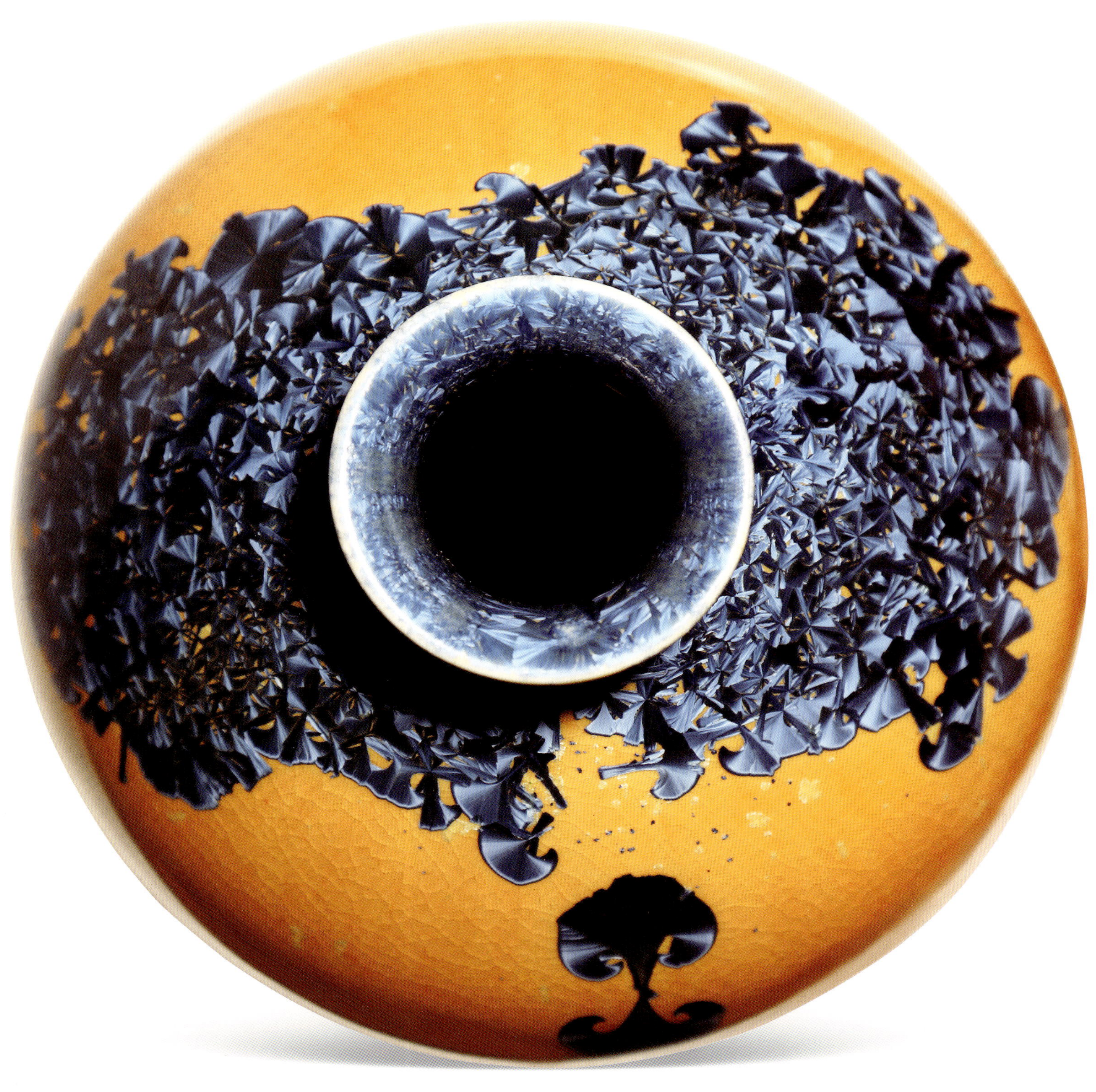

Mei-ping Vase (bird's eye view), 2013. Fired porcelain. 6×6×11 inches. Collection of the artist

Drum Vase, 2015. Fired porcelain. 7.5×7.5×15. Collection: Harvard Art Museums, Cambridge, MA

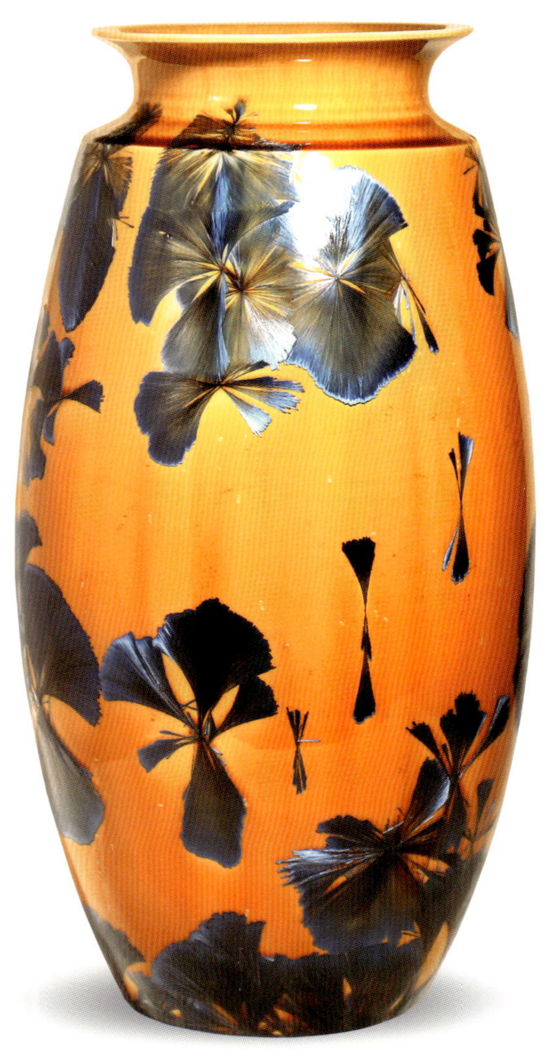

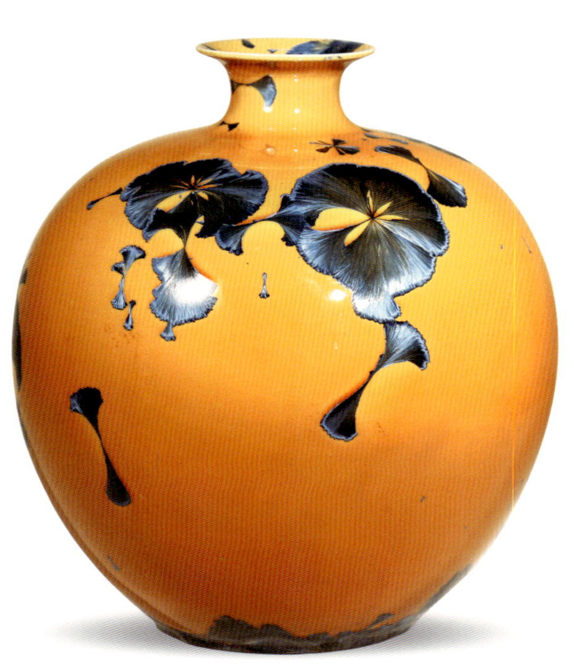

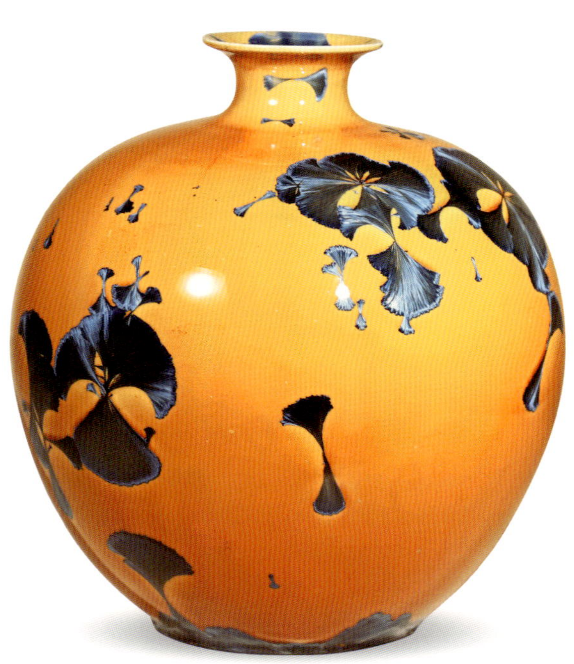

Pomegranate Vase, 2016. Fired porcelain. 10.6×10.6×11.8 inches. Collection of the artist
Pomegranate Vase (side view), 2016. Fired porcelain. 10.6×10.6×11.8 inches. Collection of the artist

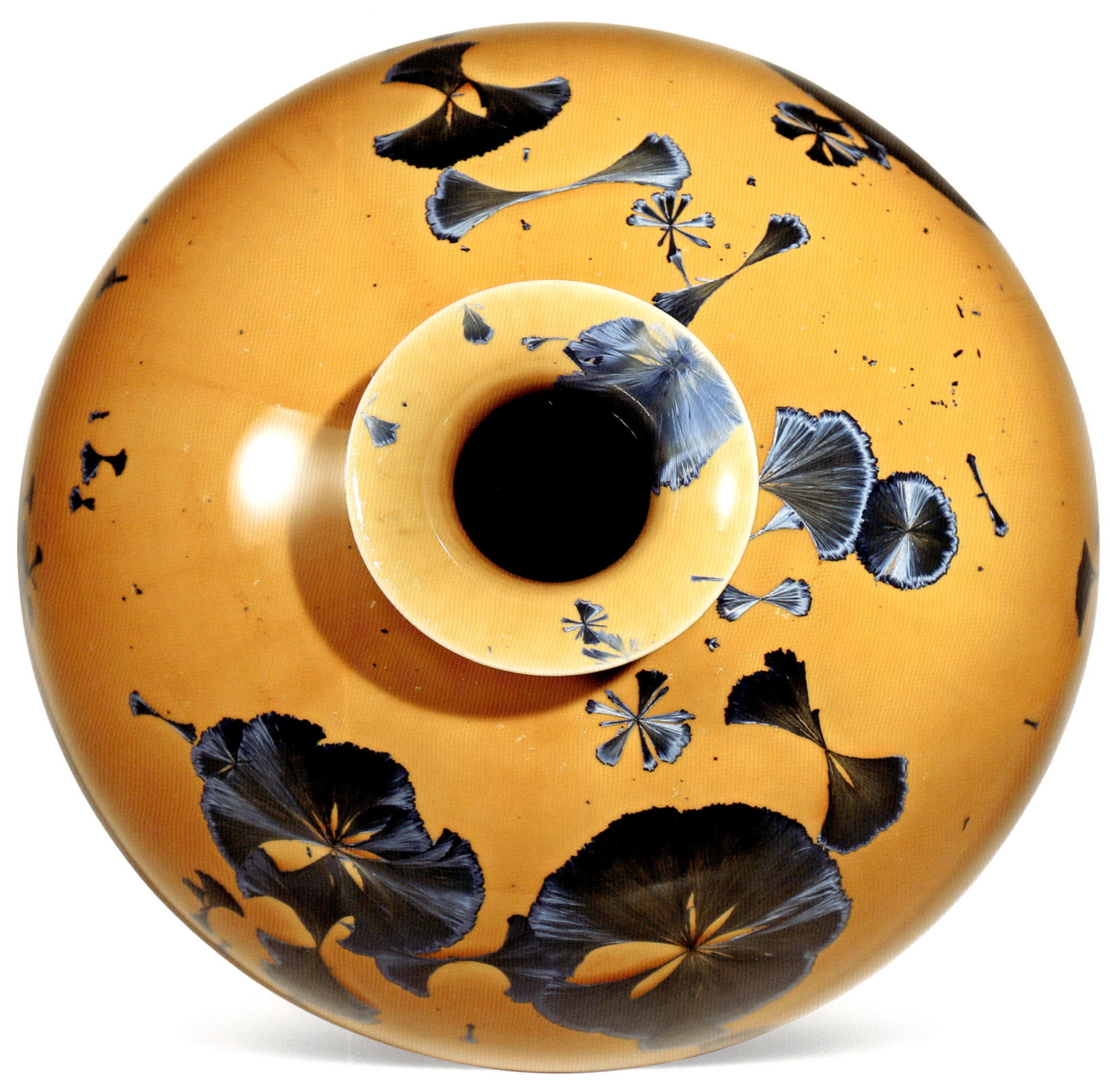

Pomegranate Vase (bird's eye view), 2016. Fired porcelain. 10.6×10.6×11.8 inches. Collection of the artist

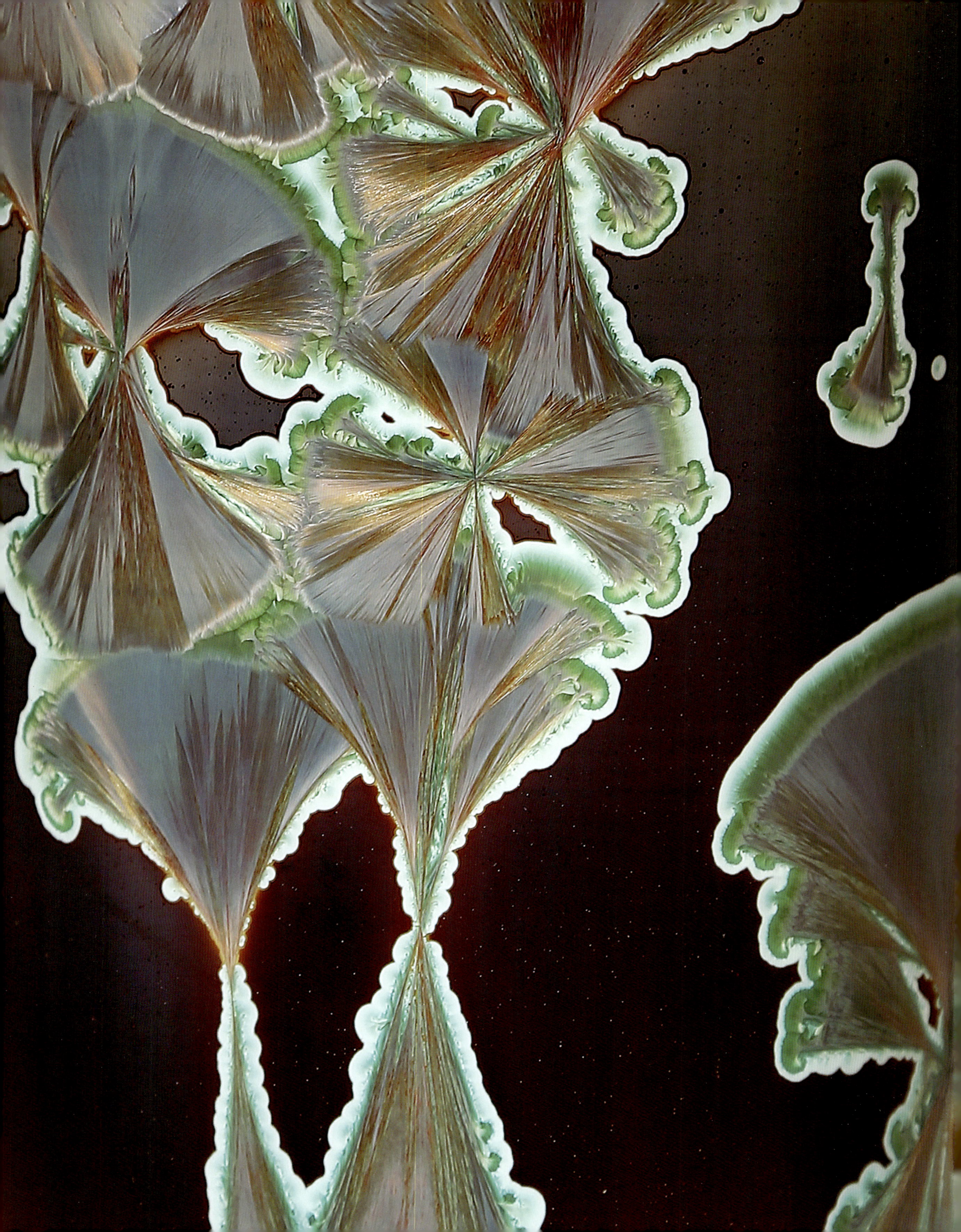

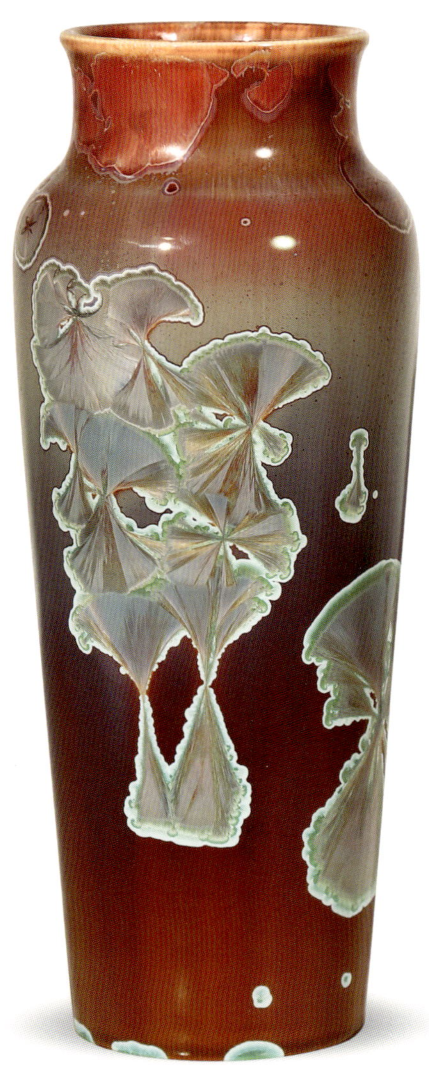

Pilgerflasche, 2017. Reduction fired porcelain. 4.5×4.5×12.2 inches. Collection of the artist

Pilgerflasche (detail), 2017. Reduction fired porcelain. 4.5×4.5×12.2 inches. Collection of the artist

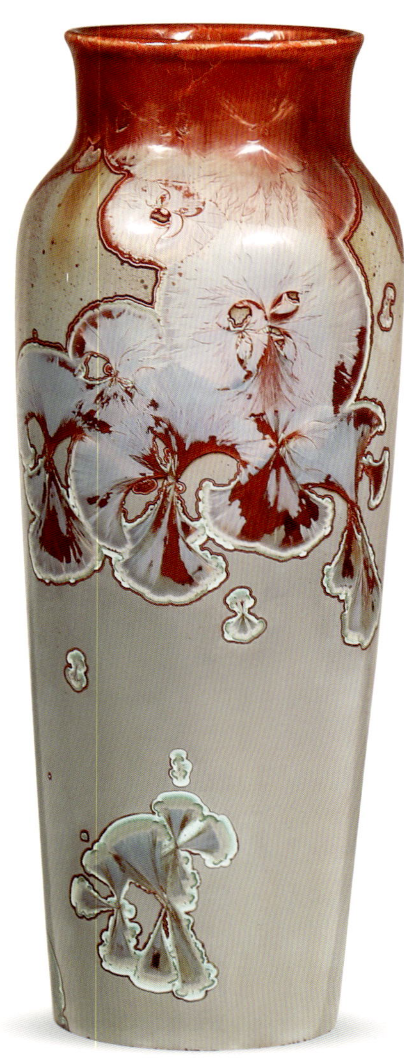

Pilgerflasche, 2017. Reduction fired porcelain. 5×5×12.5 inches. Collection: Vassar College Art Museum, Poughkeepsie, NY

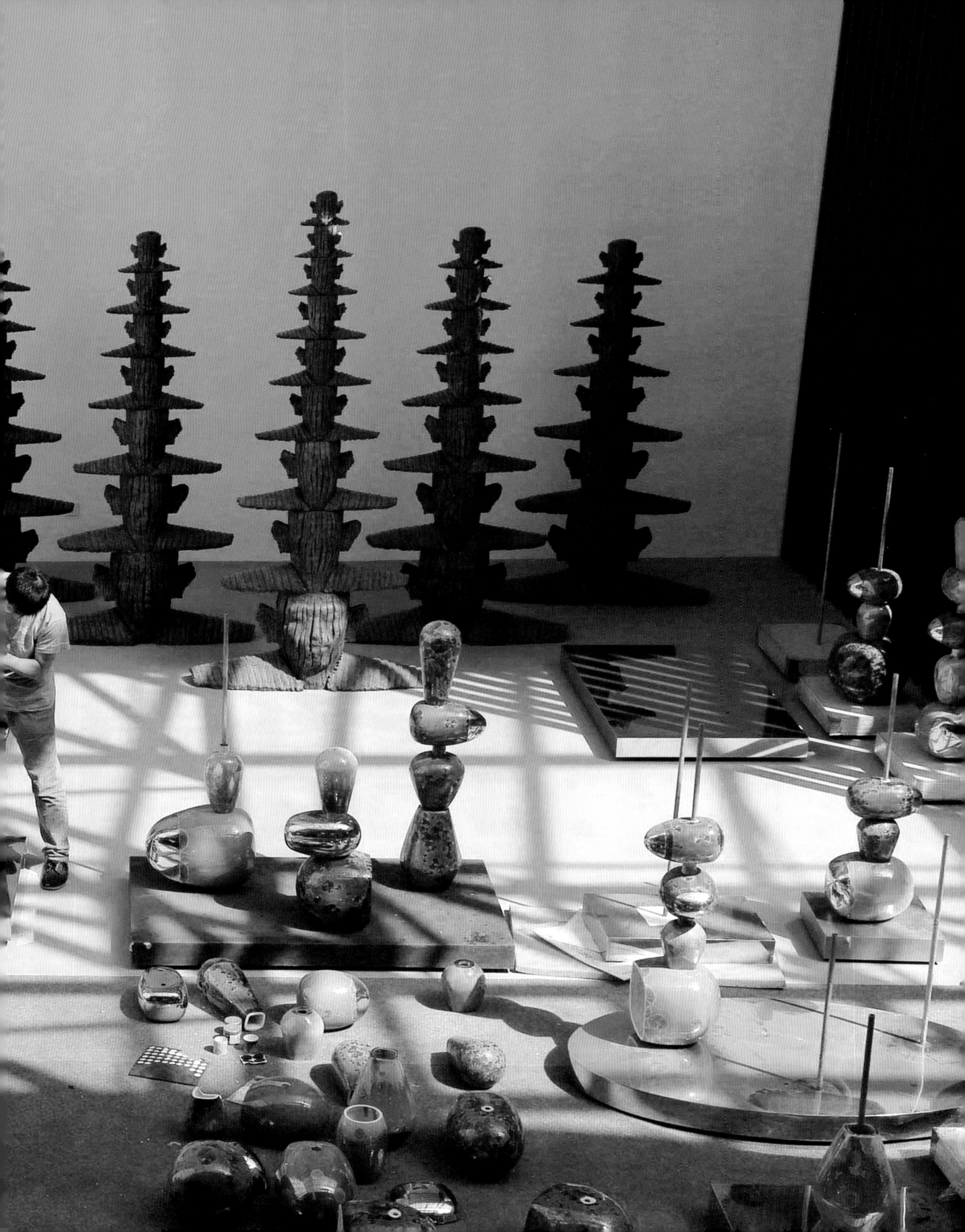

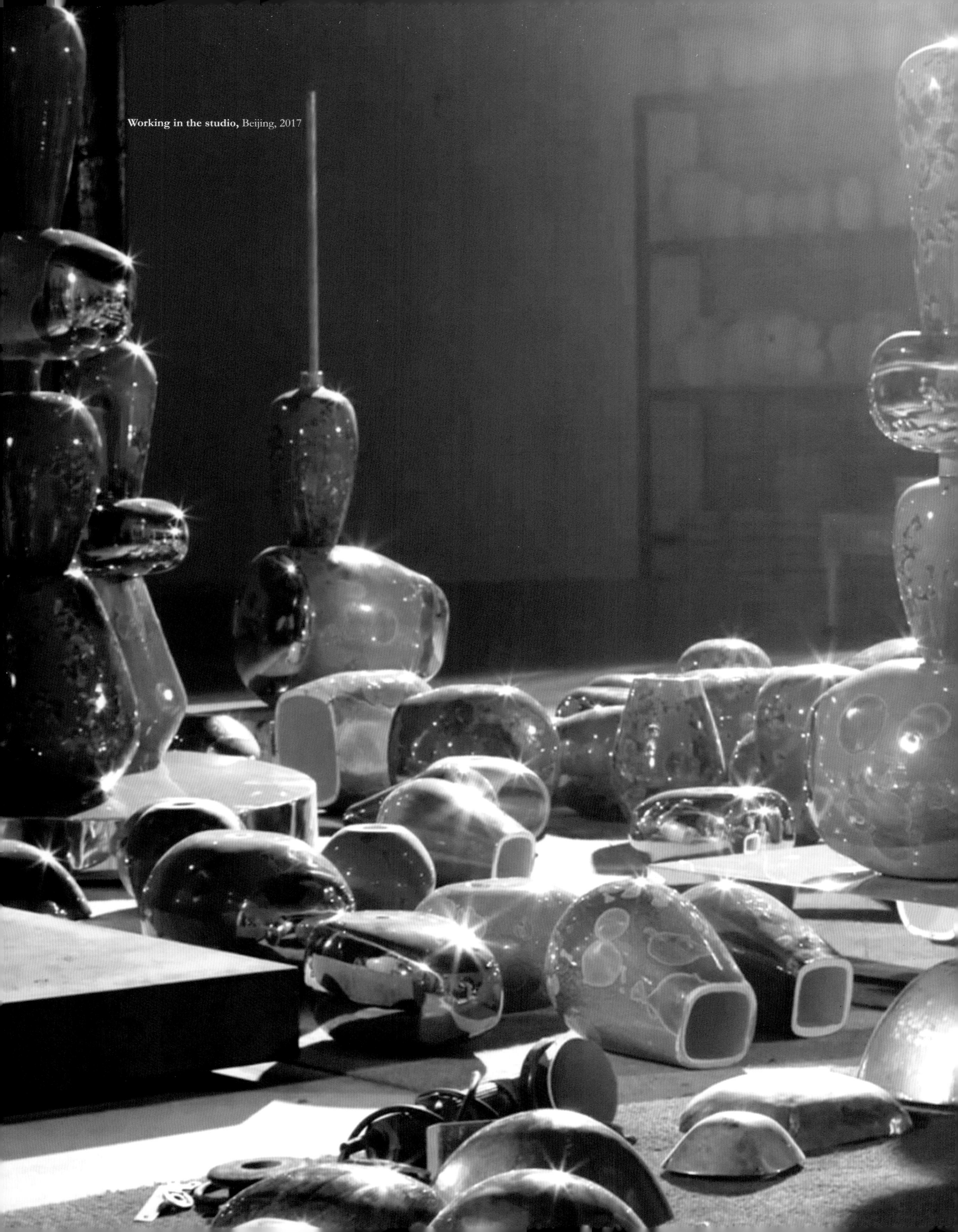

Working in the studio, Beijing, 2017

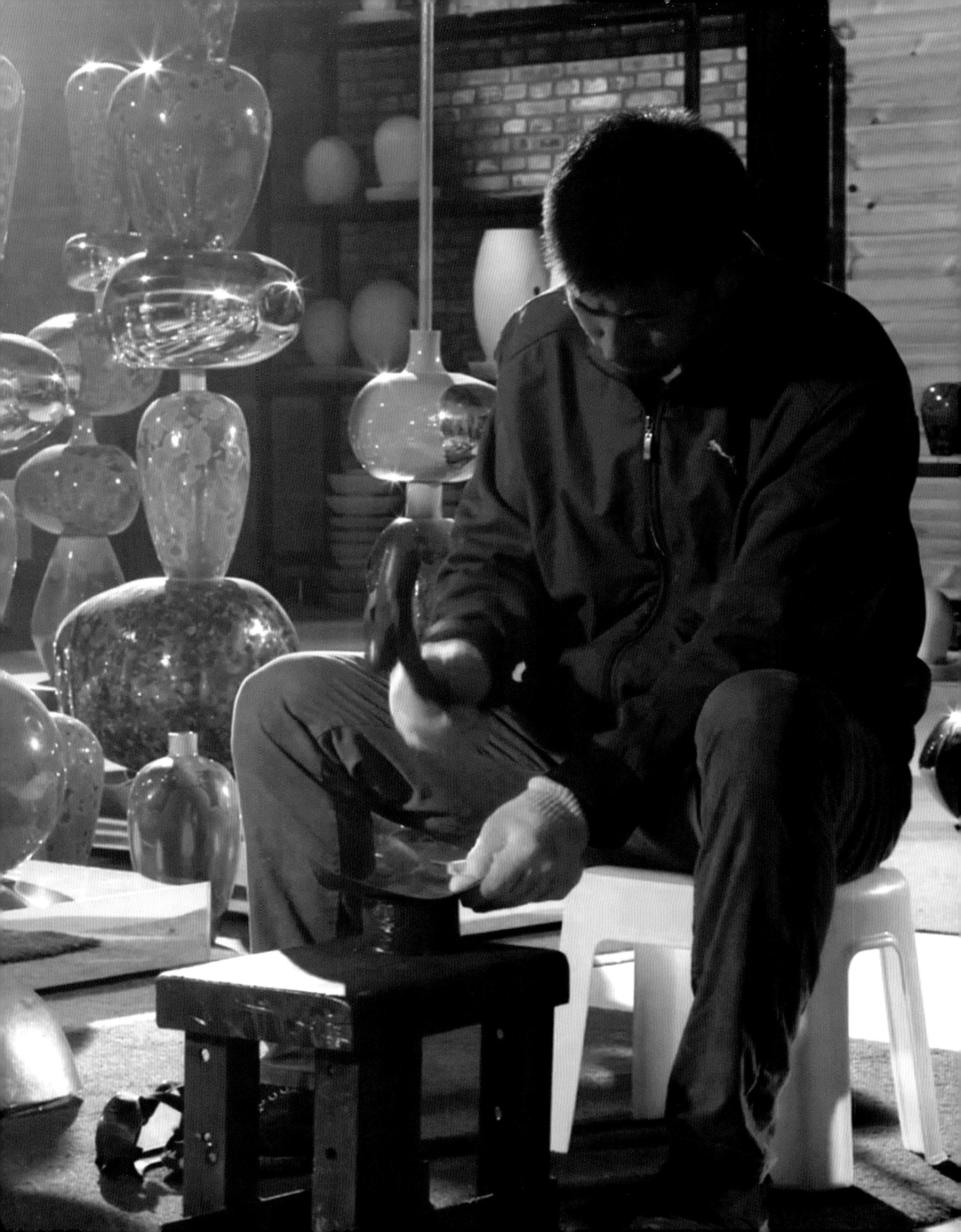

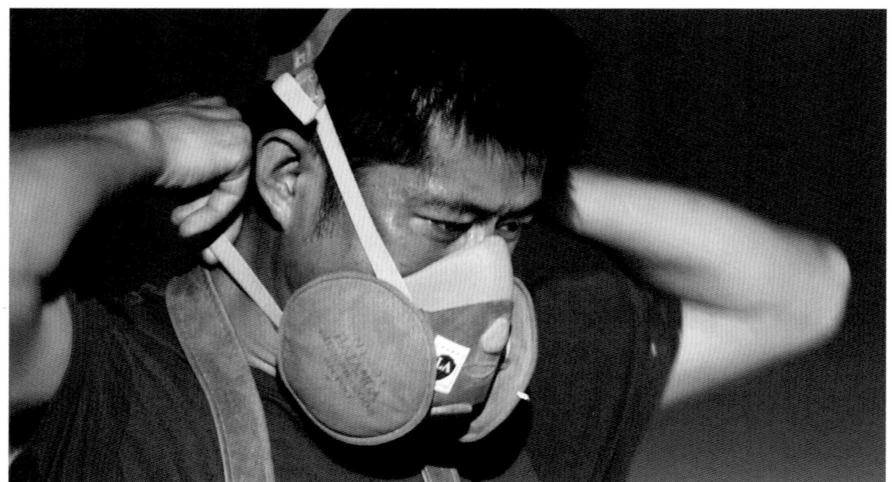

Working in the studio, Beijing, 2016

Selected Resume

Born 1980, Tangshan, P. R. China

Education
2007 MFA in Ceramic Art, New York State College of Ceramics at Alfred University, Alfred, NY
2005 BFA in Sculpture, Central Academy of Fine Arts, Beijing, P. R. China

Selected Awards and Honors
2018   Visiting Artist of University of Kentucky, Lexington, KY
2015   Talents Project of the "Youth Plus" Young Artist Project, China National Arts Fund, Beijing, China
2015   Visiting Artist of Harvard University, Boston, MA
2014   Beijing Outstanding Young Talent Award, Beijing
2013   Taylor Prize, France International Salon of the Louvre, Paris
2013   Award for Excellence, 1895 Chinese Contemporary Ceramic Art Exhibition, Nantong, Jiangsu, China

Selected Group Exhibitions
2019   Collection on view, Philadelphia Museum of Art, Philadelphia, PA
2019   The Art Institute of Chicago, Chicago, IL
2019   US Embassy in Bishkek, Kyrgyzstan
2018   Exhibition of International Contemporary Ceramic works, Tsinghua University Art Museum, Beijing
2018   Datong International Sculpture Biennale, Datong Museum of Fine Arts, China
2016   Core Sample, Collection Exhibition, Alfred University Ceramic Art Museum, Alfred, NY
2016   The Second National Exhibition of Contemporary Chinese Ceramic Art, National Art Museum of China, Beijing
2016   China – Ecuador Sculpture Exhibition, Quito, Ecuador
2015   Century Youth, 2015 China Russia International Fine Art Exhibition, Museum of The Imperial College, Beijing
2014   China The 12th National Fine Arts Exhibition, Taiyuan Museum of Fine Arts, Taiyuan, China
2014   Member Exhibition of International Academy of Ceramics, Dublin Castle, Dublin, Ireland
2013   2013 Louvre Museum International Salon, Paris, France
2012   Member Exhibition of International Academy of Ceramics, New Mexico Museum of Art, Santa Fe, NM
2010   2010 Scripps College 66th Ceramic Annual, Ruth Chandler Williamson Gallery, Claremont, CA
2008   Origins, Fox Art Gallery, University of Pennsylvania, Philadelphia, PA

Selected Public Collections
Alfred University Ceramic Art Museum, Alfred, NY
The Art Institute of Chicago, Chicago, IL
The British Museum, London, UK
China APEC International Conference Center, Beijing
Harvard Art Museums, Cambridge, MA
Herrick Memorial Library, Alfred University, Alfred, NY
The Israel Museum, Jerusalem, Israel
Media Group, Guangzhou, China
MGM, Macao, China
Museum of Fine Arts, Boston, MA
Philadelphia Museum of Art, Philadelphia, PA
San Angelo Museum of Fine Arts, San Angelo, TX
Vassar College Art Museum, Poughkeepsie, NY
Zhu Zhong Art Museum, Beijing, China

Checklist of Illustrations

Self-Portrait #11
2009
Fired clay
8×12×8 inches
Collection: San Angelo Museum of Fine Arts,
San Angelo, TX
p.37

Eternal Life (detail 1)
2014
Bronze, iron, stainless steel
41×20×17 inches
Collection of the artist
p.38

Eternal Life (detail 2)
2014
Bronze, iron, stainless steel
41×20×17 inches
Collection of the artist
p.40

Eternal Life (detail 3)
2014
Bronze, iron, stainless steel
41×20×17 inches
Collection of the artist
p.43

Eternal Life
2014
Bronze, iron, stainless steel
41×20×17 inches
Collection of the artist
p.44, p.45

Xuan #2
2018
Fired porcelain, stainless steel
25.5×7.75×7.75 inches
Collection of the artist
p.48

Upwelling of Gravity #17
2018
Fired porcelain, stainless steel
8×8×15.5 inches
Private collection
p.50

Cover of Asian Art Council
Newsletter of AIC Fall 2016
First acquisition of contemporary
Chinese ceramics and contemporary
Chinese sculpture of AIC
p.51

Allegory of Balance #1
2014
Fired porcelain, stainless steel
59×35.5×53 inches
Private collection
p.52

Xuan #1
2018
Fired porcelain, stainless steel
9.5×9.5×19 inches
Collection of the artist
p.53

Illusion #4 (detail 1)
2017
Fired porcelain, stainless steel
25.6×17.7×9 inches
Collection of the artist
p.58

Illusion #1
2017
Fired porcelain, stainless steel
19.7×15.7×5.1 inches
Collection of the artist
p.61

Illusion #4
2017
Fired porcelain, stainless steel
25.6×17.7×9 inches
Collection of the artist
p.61

Illusion #4 (detail 2)
2017
Fired porcelain, stainless steel
25.6×17.7×9 inches
Collection of the artist
p.64

Illusion #3
2017
Fired porcelain, stainless steel
25.6×17.7×9.6 inches
Collection of the artist
p.66

Illusion #6
2018
Fired porcelain, stainless steel
19.7×15.7×5.5 inches
Private collection
p.67

Illusion #2
2017
Fired porcelain, stainless steel
25.6×17.7×9 inches
Collection of the artist
p.68

Illusion #7
2018
Fired porcelain, stainless steel
25.6×17.7×9.8 inches
Collection of the artist
p.69

Allegory of Balance #18 (detail)
2017
Fired porcelain, stainless steel
28×22×62 inches
Collection of the artist
p.70, p.71

Allegory of Balance #2
2014
Fired porcelain, stainless steel
26×18×43 inches
Collection of the artist
p.72

Allegory of Balance #3
2015
Fired porcelain, stainless steel
26×18×57 inches
Collection: Zhu Zhong Art Museum,
Beijing, China
p.72

Allegory of Balance #18
2017
Fired porcelain, stainless steel
28×22×62 inches
Collection of the artist
p.73

Allegory of Balance #6 (detail)
2016
Fired porcelain, stainless steel
59×35.5×57 inches
Collection: Art Institute of Chicago,
Chicago, IL
p.74

Allegory of Balance #6
2016
Fired porcelain, stainless steel
59×35.5×57 inches
Collection: Art Institute of Chicago,
Chicago, IL
On View in The Art Institute of Chicago
from March 2019 to March 2021
p.75

Allegory of Balance #16 (detail)
2017
Fired porcelain, stainless steel
26×18×62 inches
Collection of the artist
p.76

Allegory of Balance #16
2017
Fired porcelain, stainless steel
26×18×62 inches
Collection of the artist
p.77

Allegory of Balance #4
2016
Fired porcelain, stainless steel
26×18×51 inches
Collection of the artist
p.78

Allegory of Balance #9
2016
Fired porcelain, stainless steel
26×18×47 inches
Collection: Media Group, Guangzhou, China
p.78

Allegory of Balance #10
2015
Fired porcelain, stainless steel
26×18×62 inches
Collection of the artist
p.79

Allegory of Balance #12 (detail)
2016
Fired porcelain, stainless steel
59×35.5×58 inches
Collection of the artist
p.80

Allegory of Balance #12
2016
Fired porcelain, stainless steel
59×35.5×58 inches
Collection of the artist
p.81

Allegory of Balance #5
2016
Fired porcelain, stainless steel
26×18×55 inches
Private collection
p.82

Allegory of Balance #20
2017
Fired porcelain, stainless steel
26×18×65 inches
Collection of the artist
p.83

Allegory of Balance #15
2017
Fired porcelain, stainless steel
59×35.5×58 inches
Collection: MGM, Macao
p.84

Allegory of Balance #17
2016
Fired porcelain, stainless steel
26×18×50 inches
Collection of the artist
p.85

Rebirth in Breakage (detail 1)
2015
Fired porcelain, stainless steel, iron
108×34×79 inches
Collection of the artist
p.86, p.87

Rebirth in Breakage
2015
Fired porcelain, stainless steel, iron
108×34×79 inches
Collection of the artist
p.88, p.89

Xuan #3
2017
Fired porcelain, stainless steel
8.6×8.6×21.5 inches
Collection of the artist
p.112

Xuan #3 (detail)
2017
Fired porcelain, stainless steel
8.6×8.6×21.5 inches
Collection of the artist
p.113

Xuan #13
2018
Fired porcelain, stainless steel
8.5×8.5×29 inches
Collection of the artist
p.114

Xuan #4
2018
Fired porcelain, stainless steel
11×11×31 inches
Collection of the artist
p.115

Xuan #20 (detail)
2018
Fired porcelain, stainless steel
10.6×10.6×31 inches
Collection of the artist
p.116

Xuan #20
2018
Fired porcelain, stainless steel
10.6×10.6×31 inches
Collection of the artist
p.117

Xuan #8
2018
Fired porcelain, stainless steel
10×10×18.7 inches
Collection of the artist
p.118

Xuan #9
2018
Fired porcelain, stainless steel
10×10×32 inches
Collection of the artist
p.119

Untitled
2018
Fired porcelain, stainless steel
Dimensions variable
Collection of the artist
p.120, p.121

Olive Vase (detail)
2017
Reduction fired porcelain
8×8×17 inches
Collection of the artist
p.122, p.123

Olive Vase (detail)
2017
Reduction fired porcelain
8×8×17 inches
Collection of the artist
p.124

Olive Vase
2017
Reduction fired porcelain
8×8×17 inches
Collection of the artist
p.125

Vault of Heaven Vase
2015
Fired porcelain
9.5×9.5×15 inches
Collection: The British Museum, London, UK
p.127

Olive Vase
2017
Reduction fired porcelain
7×7×16.25 inches
Private collection
p.128

Pear Shaped Vase with a Flared Lip
2016
Fired porcelain
6.5×6.5×11.25 inches
Collection: The Israel Museum,
Jerusalem, Israel
p.129

Mei-ping Vase
2013
Fired porcelain
6×6×11 inches
Collection of the artist
p.130

Mei-ping Vase (detail)
2013
Fired porcelain
6×6×11 inches
Collection of the artist
P.130

Mei-ping Vase (bird's eye view)
2013
Fired porcelain
6×6×11 inches
Collection of the artist
p.131

Drum Vase
2015
Fired porcelain
7.5×7.5×15
Collection: Harvard Art Museums,
Cambridge, MA
p.133

Pomegranate Vase
2016
Fired porcelain
10.6×10.6×11.8 inches
Collection of the artist
p.134

Pomegranate Vase (side view)
2016
Fired porcelain
10.6×10.6×11.8 inches
Collection of the artist
p.134

Pomegranate Vase (bird's eye view)
2016
Fired porcelain
10.6×10.6×11.8 inches
Collection of the artist
p.135

Pilgerflasche (detail)
2017
Reduction fired porcelain
4.5×4.5×12.2 inches
Collection of the artist
p.136

Pilgerflasche
2017
Reduction fired porcelain
4.5×4.5×12.2 inches
Collection of the artist
p.137

Pilgerflasche
2017
Reduction fired porcelain
5×5×12.5 inches
Collection: Vassar College Art Museum,
Poughkeepsie, NY
p.138

Making glaze, Alfred, NY, 2005
p.19

Working in the studio, Alfred, NY, 2006
p.20

Working in the studio, Alfred, NY, 2007
p.20

Raku firing, Alfred, NY, 2007
p.21

Raku firing, Alfred, NY, 2012
p.21

Teaching at Alfred University, Alfred, NY, 2016
p.41

Working in the studio, Beijing, 2015
p.54

Working in the studio, Beijing, 2017
p.55

Working in the studio, Beijing, 2018
p.57

Working in the studio, Beijing, 2014
p.60

Working in the studio, Beijing, 2016
p.63

Working in the studio, Beijing, 2018
p.108, p.109

Artist's studio in Beijing, 2016
p.140, p141

Working in the studio, Beijing, 2017
p.142, p.143

Working in the studio, Beijing, 2016
p.144

Cover
Pilgerflasche (detail)
2017
Reduction fired porcelain
4.5×4.5×12.2 inches
Collection of the artist

AUTHORS

Dr. Tao Wang is the Executive Director of Initiatives in Asia, Pritzker Chair of Asian Art and Curator of Chinese Art of the Art Institute of Chicago. Dr. Tao Wang was the former Senior Vice President and Head of Chinese Works at Sotheby's New York.

Wayne Higby is the Director and Chief Curator of Alfred Ceramic Art Museum at Alfred University. He is a professor and the Robert C. Turner Chair of Ceramic Art at the New York State College of Ceramics, School of Art and Design, Alfred University. Higby is a published authority on ceramic art, acknowledged for his articulate lectures, essays and critical evaluations. Higby is a Member of Honor of the United States National Council on Education for the Ceramic Arts (NCECA), Honorary Board Member of the Haystack Mountain School of Crafts, and Vice President of the International Academy of Ceramics, Geneva, Switzerland.

Dr. Mary Drach McInnes is a Professor of Art History at the School of Art and Design at Alfred University. Her research focus is on modern and contemporary sculpture. In addition to academic publications, Dr. McInnes is also a curator and has written several internationally distributed exhibition catalogs.

Michaël Amy is a critic and art historian with a Ph.D. from New York University's Institute of Fine Arts. He is a Professor of the History of Art in the College of Art and Design at the Rochester Institute of Technology, working in Renaissance, Baroque, modern and contemporary art. His articles, interviews with artists, and exhibition reviews have appeared in a wide variety of publications, including *The New York Times, Burlington Magazine, Apollo, Art in America, Sculpture, tema celeste, Viator: Medieval and Renaissance Studies, the Mitteilungen des Kunsthistorischen Institutes in Florenz,* and *CAA Reviews.* Additionally, he has published over fifty essays for books, exhibition catalogues or brochures, on contemporary art. He is the author of *One to One: Conversation avec Tony Oursler* (Brussels, Facteur Humain, 2006), *Michaël Borremans: Whistling a Happy Tune* (Ghent, Ludion, 2008), and *Hiroshi Senju* (with Rachel Baum as co-author, Milan, Skira, 2009), and is a Contributing Editor for the magazine *Sculpture.*

Andrew L. Maske is Associate Professor Art History & Visual Studies, Arts of Asia at the University of Kentucky. He received his doctorate in Japanese Art History from Oxford University. He teaches courses concentrating on the art of East Asia (China, Korea, and Japan). As a curator of Japanese art between 1999 and 2005, he developed the exhibition *Geisha: Beyond the Painted Smile,* and served as editor and primary author of the critically-acclaimed volume by the same name. Dr. Maske also played a major role in the Metropolitan Museum of Art's 2003 catalogue, *Turning Point: Oribe and the Arts of Sixteenth Century Japan,* which examined the revolution in Japanese aesthetics that began in the late sixteenth century. He has published articles and reviews in *Archaeometry, Journal of Japanese Studies, Orientations,* and *Transactions of the Asiatic Society of Japan.* In 2006-2007 he held a Fulbright research fellowship in China to study the development of contemporary ceramic art there.